MLI01487804

Shekinah

by Janice K. Davis

If they just sat there, they would accomplish nothing.
But if they start, the motive of achieving something usually makes
people want to press on! For every step, that's one less step to take
and that much closer to the ultimate goal!
~Charlie, age 11, autistic

While none of the characters in this story are real, I am eternally grateful to several delightful people who have blessed the world in different ways over the years and inspired these characters to come to life. Thank you all for allowing me to take the spark of your own life stories and weave them together into something God has chosen as a beautiful message for others. You know who you are. ☺

A very special thank you to my amazing reviewers!
Sydni and Kerri

So the LORD said to Moses, "I will also do this thing that you have spoken; for you have found grace in My sight, and I know you by name." And he said, "Please, show me Your glory."
Exodus 33:17-18 (NKJV)

Above all, I dedicate this story and all the blessings it may bring to the Glory of God. May Shekinah reign down abundant on you and yours. Soli deo Gloria

PART 1
January – February

Oh yes, you shaped me first inside, then out;
you formed me in my mother's womb.
I thank you, High God—you're breathtaking!
Body and soul, I am marvelously made!
I worship in adoration—what a creation!
You know me inside and out,
you know every bone in my body;
You know exactly how I was made, bit by bit,
how I was sculpted from nothing into something.
Like an open book, you watched me grow from conception to birth;
all the stages of my life were spread out before you,
The days of my life all prepared
before I'd even lived one day.
Psalm 139:13-16 (MSG)

Turmoil to Trains

When he asked her to prom, her heart fluttered in rhythm with the May butterflies just swooning from their cocoons. When he picked her up that night, he could not avert his gaze from the exquisite beauty standing before him with her satiny auburn hair draping effortlessly down her bare shoulders, framing those vibrant hazel eyes as they flashed the perfect mix of sudden awareness of his attention and bashful repose. She felt like a princess wearing make-up for the first time in her 16 years, in the strapless, turquoise gown as it cascaded effortlessly down her slim figure. Her parents snapped photo after photo of the royal couple, delighted in their daughter's first date with Prince Charming. Or so they thought.

They danced as if they were one; she felt perfectly at peace in his arms and melted as he gently kissed her cheek. The most handsome guy in school asked *her* to prom. Life was amazing and perfect, she thought. Her friends whispered in envy; the green in their eyes caused her a moment of guilty joy. As she turned back and looked into his mysteriously-intense emerald eyes, she melted into a fairy-tale world with the "happily ever after" ending. Or so she thought.

When they stopped at his house on the way to the After-Prom-Party, her heart fluttered in compliment that he wanted her to meet his parents. But his parents weren't home; they were out of town. When he pushed her onto the couch and held her down, the flutters turned violently into shudders at the realization of a dream turned instantly into nightmare. From that moment, her life became riddled with an inveterate horror day and night. A month later, the horror collided with turmoil.

It wasn't until seven months later, having left home in shame, she moved to Plant City, Florida and began working at The Whistle Stop. Each day the train whistle announced a new group of excited visitors, filling the empty restaurant with joy and anticipation at what treats and stories they would discover. How she wished her life were like the trains – a sudden whistle would wipe away the void, filling it with delight and hope.

Early January in Plant City, Florida brings with it fairly mild to warm temperatures, some light rain now and then, and thousands of retired people migrating south for the more temperate climate. "Mr. & Mrs. Travis! It's great to see you again," Allison sang out as she dashed across the small span of the 15-table dining room otherwise known as The Whistle Stop. "One fully-leaded dark roast with hazelnut creamer coming right up," she confirmed joyfully embracing her returning friends. Even with her tiny 5-foot, 6-inch, 120-pound body, Allison had a powerful hug; people said her heart was so big that a normal hug just wasn't enough to properly embrace the intensity of her emotions. "And a super strong French Roast – black – for you Mr. Travis." Owen and Louella Travis, a 70+ retired couple, had been Whistle Stop regulars from January through April for five years, ever since they stopped working and joined the migration.

"It's so great to see you too, Allison! We sure have missed this place!" Owen admitted.

"Why do you guys have to stay away so long?" Delia Edmunds, a six-foot, dashing brunette with enormous chocolate brown eyes and Florida-tanned skin popped up from behind the front counter, then hastened to join the reunion. "It's so nice to see both of you again!" Another round of hugging commenced.

Cordelia and Henry Edmunds purposefully chose the abandoned old drug store next to the train stop as the site for their upstart coffee bar, brilliantly foreseeing an opportunity ten years earlier when they first learned of the Silver Star and its scenic tours. The Edmunds had operated the little café only a year when an elderly couple shuffled from the train and immediately crossed the street to inquire about the "amazing fumes wafting out the front door." That was the day Delia had been experimenting with strawberry-white chocolate-macadamia nut bread – just for fun. Sensing their interest, she had quickly offered it as "Special of the Day." From that point on, The Whistle Stop added Delia's culinary experiments to its menu weekly – sometimes daily. The only menu in the place, a huge chalkboard covering over half of the back wall, was aptly titled "Delia's Delicacies … Updated Frequently."

Owen and Louella settled in their favorite corner booth near the back wall, next to the floor-to-ceiling stone-laden fireplace, where they could chat quietly and observe the life bustling all around the little cafe as well as the train stop just outside the patio windows. Allison returned immediately with two tall cups of the cafe's famous coffee – one of the many treats Owen & Louella had longed for all summer in Illinois. "Maybe we will pack up and come down with some of our other retired friends in early December next year. We make coffee every day, but this stuff is so much better," Owen admitted sipping the drink while purposefully avoiding his wife's glare.

Louella contributed, "I'm pretty sure our kids and grandkids would be upset if we skipped out on them before the holidays. Besides, all of our birthdays fall in December, and … well, while some of us would be fine not admitting to another year, we just can't give up those precious moments with the grandbabies." Then, she subtly nudged Owen's shoulder reminding him that she was, as always, in charge.

Allison always enjoyed chatting with the Travis'. They embodied everything she wanted in a relationship – unconditional love, complete devotion to each other's happiness, and civil humor that often appeared more as a comedy duo than a couple celebrating their 49th wedding anniversary that January. "Well, if you ever change your mind," she joked glancing at Owen, "then you must spend Christmas with all of us! It would be perfect with you two here!" The invitation was absolute. One of Allison's dreams included having a huge family gathering at the holidays. Her parents rejected her a little more than five years earlier, when she was just 17 -- soon after she got pregnant with Landon. Due to the violent circumstances resulting in the pregnancy, her parents could not accept her decision to raise the child instead of abortion. One silent night that December, seven months pregnant, she packed a single bag and left Tampa for Plant City where she struggled over a month, facing an impending life as a single parent.

Owen ordered his favorite -- Delia's Delightful Duo -- a cup of potato soup and half-chicken-salad sandwich on whole-wheat bread (bread choice courtesy of Louella's reminder that he watch his cholesterol), then glanced at the little boy "choo-chooing" with the trains in the front window seat. "So, tell us about you and Landon. How's he doing?"

"I've got so much to tell you. But, I better get Louella's order first, don't you think?" Her eyes glistened as she glanced his way.

Louella grinned back, "Thank you for not forgetting me, even though it appears my husband did. I'll take whatever that fabulous dish is that I smelled when we walked in here."

"That's my new soup experiment," Cordelia announced from behind the front counter where she had returned to greet several new customers. "It's a variation on chowder. Red bean and corn chowder with barbecued chicken." All three of the new customers waved in favor of the special as they hoisted up to the old-fashioned, round, metal stools secured into the floor along the front edge of the bar. Louella agreed it sounded amazing, adding a side of Delia's Famous Coleslaw to her order.

"Hey, change my soup to that one also," Owen jumped in. Allison obediently jotted down the order and flew off to the kitchen.

Cordelia's smile could sell anything in the restaurant, good or bad. She was the Plant City Strawberry Queen when she was 18, and her pearly white, winning smile continued to take her far in life. However, she also had a knack for all things culinary, mostly thanks to a family trait that began with her great-grandmother. Yet, her determination and spirit were the true impetus that helped her succeed in everything she did. It was her spirit and profound faith, in fact, which would help her overcome one of the greatest challenges in her life.

A few moments later, Allison reappeared with a basket of steaming honey-wheat pop-overs and fresh strawberry jam. "Here you are. Bread du jour. And, surprise! We have strawberry jam," she giggled. In addition to its rich history, Plant City is home to hundreds of acres of strawberries, so anything strawberry, anytime, anywhere, is generally the norm. Glancing around the shop, Allison carefully noted Delia happily chatting with the front-counter customers and, according to the little engine chugging around the perimeter of the clock centered above the mirrored bar, the Noon train was still 45 minutes out. Another quick glance to the front corner reassured her that Landon was now happily munching on his PBJ and chips. Only when she confirmed all was calm did she pull up a chair to fill in the Travis' on the summer events.

7

Louella noticed Landon seemed perfectly content hanging out in exactly the same spot of the restaurant he'd been during every one of their visits the previous year. His curly brown locks, as usual, plummeted in front of his light green eyes, but he never seemed to mind. Eye contact wasn't really something he was much concerned with. All the regulars knew Landon could be found in the front-window alcove reading a book, lining up his trucks and trains, transforming any number of robots, or fixated on spinning toys. As an infant, Allison kept him snuggled in a playpen back in the kitchen or behind the front counter. But, as he got older, she wanted him to have some space to play, hoping that if he watched the customers enough, he'd eventually learn to socialize like normal people. But he rarely watched the customers. People weren't his thing either.

"Landon turns five this March. It's so hard to believe, sometimes, you know. He's so smart." No matter what Allison was doing at any given moment, she managed to have one eye fixed on him – out of necessity. "He started writing all of his numbers and letters in June! The doctors said he was on the highly intellectual side of the spectrum, but I guess I didn't believe them." Pride sparkled from her vibrant hazel eyes as a smile spread full across her creamy complexion. She wore very little make-up, just enough to cover the freckles that had plagued her since she the day she was born with the deep auburn-brown bush of hair and pale skin-tone.

"Last month he started reading some of his little books! And not just the ones we've read over and over either. Some he picked up on his own. Oh," she paused for a drink then continued, "and he can go to the campus co-op babysitting group now when I have my night classes. I got a little money from a Pell Grant this year, to supplement my scholarships, so I could also afford for him to start at Shiloh preschool. It's just one day a week, but he's learning so much! They said he's way ahead and ready for Kindergarten in the fall.

"And, Delia and Henry let me work full-time hours around my school schedule so I get my insurance covered!" Allison paused, glanced at her son once more, then finished. "'Course I still have to count on Medicaid for him. But that's going to change soon. I start my clinicals and a couple of on-line classes this summer so I can finish school in December. Then I get my respiratory therapist degree." Finished with the rapid-fire updates, she grinned in joy at all she had to share, and at the hope she saw on the horizon.

Louella paused a moment from her second popover. "I've only read about autism before, but he seems so much smarter than the stories tell. Besides, I'm not surprised he's so smart. Look at his mother. Getting all those scholarships every year!" Owen nodded, unable to voice his agreement due to an overzealous bite of popover piled a bit too high with jam.

"Well, I think maybe I'm just a good test-taker," she admitted humbly. However if not for the academic scholarships, she knew college would have been impossible. While most of her friends in high school had studied and taken classes to raise their ACT scores, Allison managed to pull out a 34 the first time around. Known for their generosity in financial aid and scholarship donations, Hillsborough College was thrilled to offer a full-ride scholarship to an applicant of her potential.

Although Allison shied away from talking too much about her own successes, she doted on sharing stories about her son. "And you know he doesn't like eye contact. Wouldn't even look at me when I called his name for a long time. And the doctors said he probably wouldn't really have normal conversations like other toddlers."

"Toddlers don't have normal conversations," Owen finally jumped in. "That's what makes them so cute."

Allison grinned, "Yea, well my toddler sat at that counter and talked to Henry for five minutes last week! They just went on and on about the trains." She pointed toward the trains choo-chooing along tracks secured to shelves hovering over the counter, antique relics reflecting the rich history of the restaurant's location.

Being by a train stop, Henry felt it was only appropriate that he display part of his collection of model trains, rigged on three oval tracks of varied elevations, circling along in perfect sequence above the 10-stool, old-fashioned ice-cream counter. A fourth train, though, was set up on the opposite wall of the restaurant. It was carefully protected inside a clear display case supported on a table, secured into the bricks on the wall. A locked door on the top allowed access to the train – and Henry possessed the only key to the lock. Powered by a Lionel Prewar #249 Gunmetal Steam Engine, the four-car set chugged along haphazardly with a rhythmic bump each time it passed by the upper right corner. Those unaware of the history of the train set would often wonder why something so rickety would be locked away so securely.

"Henry totally glowed as he told Landon the story about that old train set," Allison continued motioning to *the steam engine that could* as it circled the track inside the case a few feet in front of where they were seated. "And Landon didn't take his eyes off the thing the entire time. It was like I had a perfectly normal little boy for a few minutes." But when she glanced over at her son, Landon was completely oblivious to any of the trains or his toys. Sandwich and chips were crumbled on the floor around a little boy staring blankly through the window, somewhere far beyond the city block outside. The sparkle dimmed in her eyes as she wondered if "normal" would ever be a term used to describe her child on a regular basis.

Looking past Allison toward Landon, Louella intuitively responded, "You know how toddlers are. Their attention goes from one thing to the next shiny thing so quickly. Love one toy one moment and could care less the next."

Suddenly Allison's attention was averted from the window and back to her guests. "Oh! I better go get your lunch. Sorry, almost forgot." With that, she scurried to the kitchen and returned with provisions guaranteed to put a smile on the most damper of moments. Balancing the huge tray on one shoulder, Allison masterfully laid out the lunch orders for her friends then reviewed each item to make sure nothing was missing. "Well, that looks like everything. I'll get you more coffee while you get started."

"Hey Allison, wanna say grace with us?" Owen asked.

A grin quickly spread across her face. "I'd love to," she replied.

Owen finished the prayer as Louella and Allison chimed in on the "amen." Just then a loud clamor rose up as one of the counter guests knocked a glass off the ledge, crashing it onto the floor, sending glass shards, tea, and ice cubes spiraling out in a three-foot radius.

To exacerbate the moment, a sudden wail came from the corner where Landon, startled by the raucous, jumped to his feet and began screaming and banging his hands on his head. Topping off the entire scene, Henry chose that instant to walk in the front door of his restaurant.

"I better go check on Landon and that mess," Allison nervously remarked, confused as to which mess deemed her immediate attention and which could wait a moment longer. Delia retrieved a mop from behind the counter while waving Allison's attention toward her son.

Noticing the chaos but choosing to ignore it completely, Henry walked right past the noise to the back of his restaurant. "Well, look what the cat drug in!" he exclaimed in Owen's direction. "Louella, you are as young and beautiful as ever! But, who's this old man with you? Your dad?"

"Speak for yourself old man," jibed Owen. "At least I still have some hair!" Cordelia and Henry were actually 20-plus years younger than Owen and Louella, but Owen referred to them *old souls in middle-aged bodies*. It was a genuine compliment. To Owen, old souls were the epitome of wisdom. And, Henry and Cordelia exuded wisdom. "Where you been keepin' yourself?" Owen asked as Henry plunked down in Allison's abandoned seat.

"Little here. Little there." He grimaced only a moment as he glanced toward the window, then turned back to his friends. "Just tryin' to keep up with all the stuff needed to keep this place runnin'. Tough business this restaurant thing, you know?"

"No, I wouldn't know. Don't wanna know," Owen remarked. "I just visit a few weeks each year. That way I get the good food without any hassles, well except from you," he responded grinning his signature ear-to-ear smile. "Did enough of that administration stuff during my working years."

"Work? You call what you did work? You told people what to do and they did it. Come to think of it, that's pretty much what you're still doing!" Henry continued the ribbing. "Except for you, Louella. You don't let him boss you around, do ya?"

"He tries, but I just pretend to listen and then I walk away. He forgets in a few minutes anyway," cajoled Louella. With the spill under control, Delia grabbed a pitcher of fresh-brewed iced tea in one hand and a steaming pot of coffee in the other before returning to the table herself.

"Wasn't sure if you two wanted to continue with the coffee, so brought you some fresh-brewed southern iced tea just in case." Setting down both pitchers, she moved to embrace her husband, "Hey Babe. How'd it go at the warehouse?"

"Not bad. Got in a bid on a new dishwasher. Should know tomorrow." Henry finally paused to take in the exterior scene as Allison continued to rock Landon while his wailing began to resolve. "Having a rough day, huh?"

"He's been good as gold until the spill. I think it just set him off is all," Cordelia confirmed. "Hasn't had that happen in over three months," she concluded sadly. In stark contrast to his wife's naturally dark locks and golden complexion, Henry stood an inch shorter with vampire-white skin and an ashen receding hairline. However, in spite of their opposing features, together they were striking. It was hard not to stare at them really. When their eyes locked, pupils dilated immediately, and a glow radiated from their cheeks, giving away an intensity of love most people dream of experiencing someday. Theirs had only intensified over 25 years. That was why when the doctors found the lump in her breast a month earlier, Henry wondered if God had suddenly abandoned them.

Sensing that Allison needed a bit more time to help Landon calm down, Delia spoke up. "Henry, how about let's try you telling the story about your dad's train again? I think that might help."

He was all too happy to oblige; Henry lived for telling stories. Soon after The Whistle Stop opened, he envisioned a place where stories filled the air like fresh oxygen. He would occasionally tell his own tales, but he wanted the customers to feel comfortable sharing their stories even more. "It bonds people together," he explained one day as he taped the sign to their front window that reads: *If you have a reservation, you're at the wrong restaurant. Otherwise, come on in! Tell us your story and get 10% off the bill!* Nearly all customers left The Whistle Stop with new, interesting stories about strangers or a reduction in their own bill.

Henry excused himself from the Travis' table and grabbed the "storyteller chair" near the front window, positioning it just next to Landon and Allison. "Okay, let's see." Henry turned to Landon, touching his shoulder gently. Landon instinctively jerked away from the touch until Allison quietly reminded him that Henry was his friend. "Hey Landon. Remember my story about that train?" he began pointing to the #249 shuffling along the side wall. "Would you help me tell it again? These folks never heard it before, see. And they're *beggin'* me to tell it now." He grinned at the crowd who, on cue, began begging Henry to tell the story.

"Okay," Landon whispered wiping his runny nose on his mother's shirt. Her smile lit up the corner once more, in spite of the fresh soiling from her son. Landon crawled into Henry's lap as they both nestled comfortably into the wooden rocking chair reserved only for those willing to relive a favorite tale with the crowd.

"When I was about your age," Henry began pointing to Landon, "my daddy bought the most amazing train set in the whole wide world! It was a bright silver engine that pulled four other cars. That engine was strong and quiet. And, it would run forward or backward! That was pretty special for a train from the 1930s. On the front were two bright red lights that really worked. And the boiler front – the big piece on the top of the front of the engine – it actually opened so we could see what the inside parts looked like! Sometimes we'd turn off the lights in the room and just leave on the train lights. Then we'd watch that engine go shuffling around the track. *Oooo wee!* That was one awesome bright headlight too! And that engine could pull those other four cars with no trouble at all. It was smooth!

"Then one time my daddy went to a convention for a week and he said I couldn't play with the train until he got home. But I just couldn't wait. That silver train just kept staring at me and I knew it was begging me to turn it on so it could get some exercise around that track. So I got out that old train and announced, 'Full speed ahead!' And that train sure 'nuff went full speed ahead, right off the tracks and into the concrete fireplace hearth." Henry paused a moment and checked in with Landon. "Wanna tell what happened next?" he asked.

"You broked it," Landon offered with no emotion, just recall.

"Yep, that's right. I broked it." He grinned over Landon's shoulder, toward Allison. "Two of the wheels busted off. My momma came running in to see why I was crying and all upset. I said, 'The train just started going and I tried to stop it but it was too fast. I don't know how it happened.'"

"You lied to your momma," Landon interjected, that time without invitation.

"I did indeed. And what do we say about lying?"

"It's not nice to lie. Makes your mouth all dirty." Allison grinned in embarrassment at her son's confusion; idioms were a problem for his literal brain. After a moment though, she moved to sit on an end-stool at the counter, peaceful once more as she watched Henry and Landon reliving the story again. The other guests were riveted in attention from their respective spots around the restaurant.

Henry continued. "So, my momma was pretty smart. 'I think you are lying to me, young man,' she told me. I just started crying right then and there. I felt so bad for breaking the train and then lying. But my momma is a great woman of God. She helped me try to fix Daddy's train, but we knew it would never be the same. Then she said to me, 'Don't you ever lie to me again. God hates lying. It's ugly and very dirty. Anytime you get in trouble, your daddy and I will always help you. But it's really hard to help you if you lie.' I promised I'd never lie again.

"When my daddy got home that weekend, I had to tell him what happened as part of the consequence my mom and I worked out. He was pretty mad when he saw the train's wheels all bent out and clanking against the track. I just cried and cried and said, 'Daddy please don't hate me. I'm so sorry!' But do you know what he said to me?"

"'It's just a toy,'" Landon quoted from memory, no intonation.

"Were you there?" Henry joked, lightly tickling his ribs. Landon jerked away with an irritated grimace.

"I don't like tickling," he stated simply.

"My bad," Henry apologized. "So anyway. You're exactly right! My daddy was pretty upset about that train but he just hugged and hugged me and kept saying, 'That's just a toy. You are my boy and nothing you do could ever make me love you less!'

"Well, a long time later, I came home from college for a weekend and I found that old train carefully boxed up in the attic. I missed how my dad and I used to play together. So while he was still at work, I got out that old train and set it up again. He was so excited when he came home that we ran that rickety ole' thing around and around that track for an hour straight. Then, every time I'd come home from college, he'd have it set up again for us.

"When I graduated from college, he wrapped it up and gave it to me as a gift. 'Take time to play with your own kids, son. The time goes by way too fast. Make every moment count.' I never forgot that advice. As soon as my son, Radmund, was old enough, I got out that train and taught him how to set up the tracks. Whenever my dad would visit, the three of us would sit and play for hours.

"Then one day, when Radmund was 10, my dad passed on to be with God. Rad came in the living room to find me playing with the train, sobbing as I thought about all the times Dad and I sat together with that thing. 'Daddy,' Rad said as he handed me a hankie, 'Daddy, I think Grandpa is having so much fun playing with trains in Heaven. And I bet his Heavenly Father is sitting with him and they are having a great time because it's really cool to play trains with your Dad.'" Henry paused to manage the catch in his throat that came at that same point in the story every time. Then he turned his attention to the little boy. "Landon, why do I make sure that train runs all the time now?"

Landon looked over at the encased train on the side wall as he replied, "You think about your daddy and God playing trains together in Heaven."

"Just like my dad and I did, and just like Rad and I still do whenever he's home." Henry finally looked up at the patrons – not a dry eye in the house, except for Landon of course.

Allison lifted Landon off Henry's lap and resituated him with toys and books by the window. "Momma will be done in a couple more hours and then we'll go to the park for a few minutes before my class, okay?"

"Okay Momma," and immediately Landon's focus turned to a battle between his favorite bright red and neon yellow Battle Striker Turbo Tops.

Henry grabbed a large glass of iced-tea and rejoined the Travis' as they were finishing their meal while blinking away tears. As he sat down, Owen sniffled determined to alter the mood. He couldn't resist. "*Radmund*? You named your kid *Radmund*?"

"That's what you got from the story?!" Henry tried to look seriously offended in spite of his smirk and the twinkle in his eyes. "I tell a beautiful story about my dad and all you do is make fun of my son's name?"

"Owen, leave him alone! You've heard them talk about Radmund and the air force before," Louella remarked, sneaking in a dab at her nose with the napkin. Owen flashed a devilish grin.

"I'll have you know Radmund is a very special family name. I'm deeply hurt you'd make fun of it, and you've never even met the boy." Henry wasn't offended in the least. Owen's humor was one of his most endearing qualities.

"Really?" Louella chimed in before Owen could get another punch. "Was Radmund your dad's name?"

"No. It's special for other reasons," Henry admitted hesitantly.

"His dad's name was Thomas ... Tom!" Cordelia stated glaring at her husband as she delivered two heaping bowls of the best strawberry shortcake in town. "Tell them Henry. Tell them how Radmund became such a *precious* family name." Her voice resonated the same cynicism that began the conversation.

Her husband squirmed a moment then conceded, "Well, when Rad was born he came out with a head full of strawberry red hair. My dad ... Tom ... laughed hysterically telling us that Delia must have eaten too many strawberries while pregnant. Then, later that day he comes back and tells us he found the perfect name for my boy – Radmund. 'Means red-haired defender,' he announced. My mom smiled in agreement but Delia and I thought he was nuts. We'd planned on Henry Thomas, but by that time, Dad had developed some stupid infatuation with the name Radmund. So we made a compromise – Henry Thomas Radmund Edmunds. When the doctors came to ask for the baby's name, Delia was all drugged up from the C-section, and I was hunkered in the corner trying to avoid being sprayed as I changed a diaper for the first time ever. So my dad jotted down my son's name for the doctor. He *said* he forgot his glasses, which was why he mixed up the lines. It wasn't until we left the hospital three days later when we looked at the certificate and realized Dad wrote "Radmund Henry Thomas" instead. Seeing it in print seemed so different than just hearing it, so Delia and I decided it wasn't that bad after all. Now whenever I see him, he just looks like a Radmund."

"I love it," Louella concluded. "When do we get to meet this boy of yours anyway?"

Delia perked up instantly, "He's supposed to be home by Valentine's Day, which just happens to also be my birthday! Best gift I could ever get! His rotation in Iraq ends then and he's decided to switch to the Guard and stay closer to home now, what with my upcoming surgery and all. He's been so disillusioned by the war lately. Felt like a traitor to his country sometimes for wanting to quit, but his mother having cancer gave him the excuse to get out I think. Frankly, I'm just glad he's coming home alive!"

"Any news yet about your surgery?" Louella finally found the nerve to ask. She had been troubled ever since receiving her friend's email a month earlier with the news of the lump.

Henry's eyes slowly welled with tears, betraying the answer. But, Delia was resolute. "Yea, it's malignant. No worries, though." She grabbed her husband's hand for comfort – for him not herself.

"Ironic, isn't it?" he remarked. "She's the one with the cancer and I'm the one who needs consoling."

"God's already got this one covered for me," she stated matter-of-factly. "The doctor said the tumor seems to be completely intact. So, I'm scheduled for a double mastectomy on March 15. They're going to do both breasts just to be sure since my mom and grandmother had this also. They found that same gene mutation that took my mom from me. It's likely to show up again and I might not be so lucky next time."

Sensing his friend's stress, Owen felt it was once more time to alter the mood. "So, tell me more about this boy of yours. I just hope he got his mother's looks and sense of humor." The mood relaxed a bit and settled back into laughter and anticipation of a welcome-home celebration.

"Been too long! Nearly two years since his last visit home." Henry stated as he and Delia clicked their tea glasses in a toast to the imminent homecoming. "Only met Allison and Landon a couple times. He was just heading off to basic training when she started working here. They got a little closer during his last visit a couple years ago. She was 19 by then and he just turned 22. All his email to us ask more about her and Landon than his own parents!"

Louella's curiosity peaked. "How does she feel about him?"

"Hard to say," Delia answered. "She was still really messed up then, what with a two-year-old who'd just been diagnosed with autism, parents that refused to talk to her, and a lingering memory that haunted her every night. She asks about him and emails him some, but probably not as often as he'd like."

Glancing at the train clock circling over the counter stations, Owen remarked, "We need to get going pretty quick. But ..." He took his wife's hand and reached for Henry's on the other side. "Would you guys like to pray together before we leave?" he asked. Henry took his wife's hand and, together, the four friends petitioned God for comfort, safe travels, and healing in their lives. By the end of his prayer, all four hearts were blessed by the presence of God's glory – *Shekinah* – reigning down at that moment in that place.

A whistle blew in the distance bringing everyone back to full attention. "Sounds like the lunch crowd is here. Better get ready," Delia noted. Owen and Louella finished their desserts and reluctantly moved out to the platform to catch the train back to their condo in Lakeland.

Each day as the noon whistle echoed in the distance, Delia and Henry could count on a train filled with new and return lunch guests. Those returning were greeted by name with open arms; the newbies were greeted with open arms and, "Welcome to Whistle Stop Honey. We are so glad you're here!" The exchange was 100% heartfelt, whomever the greeter. By 12:15, all 15 tables and 10 stools were usually seated with guests studying the chalkboard menu and eagerly voicing their order. Weather permitting, and if necessary, five patio tables could be set in a few minutes to accommodate an additional 25 guests. Efficiency was a key to success at the Whistle Stop. Therefore, by 12:30 all guests were enjoying fresh popovers with strawberry jam and anticipating a lunch complete with one of Delia's Delicacies. By 12:45 p.m., the room was nearly silent except for the subtle din of clinking silverware, chewing, and the occasional "Oh my gosh this is amazing!" or "I must have this recipe!"

As Allison delivered one order with her typical sparkle to Table 12, she took note of the family seated there – a young boy staring at the #249 in the nearby display case, a little girl about Landon's age with a flattened nose and narrow, slanted blue eyes, and two young parents sitting in absolute silence. Red streaks filled the peripheral whites in contrast to the light green irises of the mother. "You know, they say Delia's soup is sure to cure anything that ails you," Allison said softly as she placed two orders of chicken chowder in front of the couple and a strawberry-jam PBJ for each of their children.

"Thank you," was the soft-spoken reply from the hazel-eyed husband as he held tightly to his wife's hand, exposing their simple gold wedding bands. The couple burdened Allison's heart as she returned to the kitchen for the last tray, completing her tables.

Delia approached with a fresh pot of coffee as the family bowed their heads to pray. "Mind if I join?" she asked.

The five of them clasped hands as the father prayed. "Thank you for this food, O Lord. Work deeply in our hearts so that your joy and love overwhelms even the darkest places. Amen."

Moments later, back behind the counter, Delia couldn't take her eyes off the family. "Hey," she said as Allison rounded the corner and stashed a bucket of dirty dishes out of sight. "They say anything to you?" Delia asked nodding the direction of the group at Table 12.

"Nope," Allison replied glancing at the back table as she refilled two cups of coffee and one iced-tea for counter guests. "The kids seem fine, but the parents are obviously upset."

"Maybe after they finish lunch you should check in with them. Take them all a bowl of strawberry shortcake - on the house. Maybe sit and chat with them for a few minutes." Cordelia had a gift for compassion and an intuitive heart. Allison understood exactly what her friend was implying.

A few minutes later, Allison interjected herself into the couple's silence handing each of them a bowl overflowing with strawberries then adding a quick, "On the house for special guests. And a super-dooper delicious Delia's Hot Fudge Sundae for two adorable kids." She added placing the bowl of ice cream in front of the children.

"Tank yooo bewry mooch," the little girl carefully enunciated as she flashed a huge, flat smile through her pencil-thin lips, revealing a large gap between her two front teeth.

"You are very welcome," Allison replied delighted at the girl's sincere joy at something so simple. "I don't mean to pry," she finally spoke without invitation. "But at The Whistle Stop we have a tradition of sharing stories with our guests. Sometimes our guests share their stories with us." She pointed to the sign over the door, "Even get a discount if you do," she half-jokingly concluded. A slight grimace crossed the mother's face. The father looked up emotionless for only an instant. Allison breathed deeply speaking a silent prayer and then continued. "Okay then. Well we don't force you to share stories. But, hey, I'll still make sure you get the discount if you let me brag a little about my son over there." She pointed to the front window where Landon had long since finished his own lunch and had begun coloring in his ABC workbook.

"He's adorable," the father spoke while twisting a strawberry in whipped cream.

The young mother chimed in. "We'd love to hear all about him," she said. Their own little boy dove into the Sundae, dripping chocolate sauce on his pants due to keeping his eyes focused on the locomotive charging around the tracks instead of his own spoon.

"He's my baby, Landon. I had him when I was 17." Allison paused a moment at that point, generally to give the listeners a chance to ask the obvious questions. The couple chose to remain silent, looking up at her with genuine interest in hearing more. If they'd asked, she would have divulged more about how she got pregnant. But, since they chose to accept her candor without question, she was relieved to not have to go into more detail.

"When he was born, everything seemed perfectly normal. He cried and cooed just like all the babies I'd seen before. He seemed a little withdrawn as a baby, but I just thought it was his personality. You know, he didn't like peek-a-boo or games like that. Wasn't much of a snuggler. He never pointed to what he wanted; he just screamed or banged on his high-chair tray until I guessed right. It got really stressful." Allison sighed deeply at the memories of long, sleepless nights followed by tumultuous days filled with anxiety and questions.

"Then, right around his second birthday, I started noticing things about him that didn't seem right. One day we were at the park when some kids were tossing a ball around. I thought Landon might want to play, but he just sat there staring into space. I thought he was blind or something! So, I walked over to the other little boys and asked if he could play with them. But, Landon just stood there like the other kids were invisible. They would toss him the ball and it would just bounce off his chest or legs. Didn't even flinch.

"Then I started noticing that he never actually looked at me either. He became really sensitive to loud noises. Still is for that matter," she remarked more to herself than the visitors. "He wouldn't really talk much, more like grunts. Finally I took him to the doctor to see if his hearing or vision were messed up. That's when I found out my little boy is autistic."

"Wow. What did you do then?" the mother asked.

"I was devastated at first. I mean, I was a single mom living mostly on welfare, so to have a child with special needs terrified me. I didn't know how to help him, and I couldn't afford therapy or special schools. But that's when God stepped in to help me, for like the millionth time!"

The father spoke up next. "What do you mean?"

"Well, we learned that Landon is autistic, but he's also really smart. He just doesn't have very good social or communication skills. He really needed a therapeutic setting just to get him comfortable around other children his age. So, Shiloh Preschool worked out a payment plan for me to have him go one day a week. He started there about a year ago now. They were so great about understanding my financial issues. And, their program is designed specifically for children with special needs, which was exactly what Landon needed. And me for that matter. They even offered some parenting and support classes.

"He starts Kindergarten in the fall, just like any other five-year-old boy! And, he's reading all his letters and learning new words every day. He loves to practice writing the letters, and he's a really good speller. The pre-school teachers are very impressed with how much he's learned in such a short time. And, well, I'm pretty proud of him myself!" Her face radiated as she finished sharing.

"I feel so lucky because his IQ is actually super high! I had him tested a couple months ago for his Kindergarten entrance and his score was 130! They said that qualifies him for their gifted program even. Imagine, three years ago I thought my son would be disabled for life. Then, a couple of months ago I learn he's gifted. I mean, it's not going to be easy for him with friends and all, but the school thinks he has tremendous potential. They have a really amazing teacher in Kindergarten with lots of experience working with special-needs kids, even. So we already know he'll be in her class. God is so good!"

"But, if God is so good, why did He give you a child with special needs?" The mother spoke with great angst in her voice.

Allison lowered her head to whisper the caustic answer so only the parents could hear. "Well, I was raped. I just couldn't abort the child when it wasn't even his fault. And I really did believe God wanted me to be his momma for some reason. Now I know why. I think God uses Landon every day to help me be a stronger, better person. And I always wonder if an adoptive family would ever love a child with his background as much as his own mother. I don't mean that to sound rude; it's just that I know God has truly blessed my life because of that child. It's not easy, but it is right. I know it in my heart and soul. That's why I can't help but be so proud of him." She paused and looked directly at the couple's daughter, "I thank God every day for Landon. Children are precious gifts from God."

"My sister is weird," the little boy at the table finally contributed to the conversation. "She's ugly and stupid."

"She's beautiful, just like you are so very handsome!" Allison replied without hesitation, as his parents gasped at the spite in their son's voice.

"Kardal, you know that's hurtful," his father spoke in hasty reply. "I've talked to you about speaking that way about your sister." The father's voice became a whisper. "Son, I'm leaving in a week to go a long, long way away. I need you to promise to be the man of the house and take care of your sister, not be mean to her."

Catching her breath for a moment, Allison suddenly understood why God led her to share with this family. Thinking quickly, she turned to Kardal and smiled. "You are so lucky to have a little sister! I have a big brother and he's my very best friend. I always looked up to him as my hero when I was younger, and he always took really good care of me. I bet you'll be your sister's hero someday."

The parents smiled briefly. Then, the father excused Kardal to go visit the train set for a few minutes. After the boy was out of earshot, the father replied, "Thanks. It's so hard for him right now. He's mad that I'm going away again, this time for at least a year. Ever since he turned eight, a month ago, it's like he understands more and hates me for leaving. Takes it out on all of us."

Their mother whispered looking away from the little girl who sat at the end of the table, oblivious to the conversation, indulging in the sundae instead. "It's also hard on him because Skylar needs a lot of our attention right now. She turns six in a couple of months and starts school this fall. He's really upset they'll be at the same school. We've tried and tried to find a way to help him accept her instead of being so embarrassed to have her around."

"I'm sure my being gone so much doesn't help, either," the father admitted. "Boy needs a father around and I'm not able to be there right now. I hate being gone, but we really need the money and insurance now."

"Honey, you're amazing at what you do," his wife began. "He's going to be a fighter pilot someday," she bragged. "Just got accepted for pilot training at Whiting Field. I'm so proud of him, even if it means he'll be gone for almost an entire year now."

"Well," Allison replied softly, "I know how tough it is to be a single mom, but at least your kids have a dad who loves them." She turned her attention to Landon's progress as he worked on the letter book by the window, then continued. "Hey, how about if I introduce Skylar to Landon and maybe they can play together for a little while. That way you two can sit here and talk as long as you like. I'll even get you your own pitcher of tea so none of us disturbs you."

"That would be very nice. Thank you." The father's gratitude and grief mixed together and poured from his eyes as his wife grabbed a tissue to wipe away her own tears. "Skylar, this very nice lady is going to introduce you to a new friend. Would you like that?" The little girl nodded in excitement. Unlike her family, sorrow and stress were infrequent emotions in her life. Down syndrome might have disabled her physically and mentally, but the emotional benefits included a heart full of joy and vigor for life.

***

"So, what happened?" Delia prodded as Allison returned to the kitchen hoisting a full dishpan.

"They need time alone. He's going to Iraq in a week – wants to be an air force fighter pilot. So I found a way to distract their kids. I probably should take the counter area for awhile to keep an eye on them if you don't mind. I'm not really sure how Landon will do with a playmate in his corner. He's not used to that you know."

"You are an angel, Allison." Delia was certain, not speculating.

Allison blushed. "No, I'm just a person with a lot of problems who likes to talk. Sometimes God uses that to help other people for some odd reason."

Delia grimaced as tears filled her eyes with sympathy for the family. Then, she pulled the cap off the purple marker velcroed to the large white board hung on the wall just inside the kitchen doorway. "Family at Table 12," she wrote, adding to the long list titled "Prayer Concerns."

***

"Allison, there's a letter for you," Delia announced as she propped open the front doors a month later, thankful to be able to once more enjoy the early, fresh February breeze. As if on cue, the train clock whistled 10 times as the Travis' strolled in for their weekly visit and fix of Whistle Stop delicacies. "Hey you two! Table 10 is all set for you," she pointed to their favorite corner booth with one hand and handed the letter to Allison with other. Stuffing the note in her pocket, Allison rounded the front bar to greet her friends. The Travis' promptly finished the ritual hugging before moseying back to "their table."

"What's the special today?" Owen asked as Allison happily met them at the table.

"She's been cooking up a storm all weekend. Came out with something spectacular this time! Strawberry gazpacho in a coconut bread bowl! It's to die for!" Allison could barely contain her support of the newest dish freshly written in neon pink on the colossal chalkboard.

Louella laughed. "Well, that will be wasted on Owen, but count me in!"

"Not a fan of cold soup?" Allison asked.

"Not a fan of coconut," Owen replied. "That's for girls. I need something *manly*."

Louella rolled her eyes as he perused the chalkboard for something more suited to his masculine taste buds. Allison tried to help with suggestions, but couldn't stop laughing long enough to speak clearly.

"There!" he paused pointing at a lunch option he'd never tried before. "Give me some of that Meaty Beef Stew. Now that's a man's meal."

"Sure thing," Allison noted jotting down the order, still giggling to herself as she walked back into the kitchen.

Moments later, Delia returned with their food. "Here you go Louella. I know you're going to love this soup, so I went ahead and brought you the recipe," she noted placing an index card with the recipe next to the bowl of soup. Then, she turned her attention to Owen. "So, I understand you wanted something a little more robust today, huh? 'Manly' is the word you used, I believe?"

"You bet! Stew – that's a real meal." He confirmed as she set the steaming bowl in front of him.

"You have good taste, Owen. This is our regular catering order on Fridays for the Catholic church down the road –*Ladies' Bingo night!*" With that, Delia burst out laughing as she pranced off to get coffee. In a rare moment, Owen sat speechless.

A few minutes later, Allison demurely emerged from the kitchen, letter in hand. "You won't believe this," she blushed shuffling toward the front counter as Delia refilled water glasses. For a second, Landon turned his attention from the toys to his mother's voice, then quickly returned to the battle of the tops. Delia gathered a tray with two coffee cups and a full pot and the two women met at the back corner table.

"What ya got there Allison?" Delia requested impatiently as she set down the coffee and pulled up a chair to join the Travis'.

"Remember the family here a month ago? The couple with the little girl who has Down syndrome and the father was getting ready to go back to Iraq?" Delia nodded remembering the incident as Allison continued to fill in the details for Owen and Louella. Once everyone was caught up, she announced, "This letter is from them." Allison unfolded the letter and began reading:

Dear Allison,

We visited the restaurant a few weeks ago. We're the ones with Skylar and Kardal. Skylar has Down's. Thanks for taking some time to tell us about Landon. Your story really moved us to look closer at what God wants for our family. We realized how crazy we'd been in trying to deal with all that stress on our own. Anyway, we wanted to let you know that Adam and I decided it's time to really focus on whatever God has planned for us. We're getting some help for Kardal so he can deal with his dad's work and his sister's disability. And, we enrolled Skylar at Shiloh. Maybe she and Landon will become friends.

Thank you for your courage to share your story. Please pray for us. We know this will not be easy, but with God all things are possible!

Love,

Scarlett, Adam, Kardal, and Skylar Clermont

Allison refolded the letter to carefully place it back in her pocket. "They think I have courage," she whimpered softly. Louella always carried Kleenex whenever they visited The Whistle Stop, which proved handy once more. Owen even snuck a tissue while he continued munching on his manly beef stew.

It wasn't until he spoke that anyone else realized Henry had arrived. "See there! You just never know how God will show up in these things. I'm proud of you, Allison. You made a difference in that family's life."

"Thanks, but I just told a story. God did the rest," Allison was terribly uncomfortable with praise. She was an unwed mother with a lot of baggage that still plagued her on a regular basis. *Scars* – that's how she referred to the lingering memories of her past. While she believed that God was working in her life every day and that somehow, some way, He had plans for her and Landon, she frequently questioned her life and God's provisions. There were plenty of times when her prayers resonated more with anger than gratitude, so for her to be labeled a spiritual helper bore more conviction than joy. One Christmas, Delia had given Allison a plaque that read, "I have special plans for you. I will prosper you, not harm you. I will give you hope and a future. Love, God." Allison reminded herself of His promise every night as she walked through her apartment door and contemplated the personalized version of Jeremiah 29:11.

"Mommy," a dry little voice projected softly from the side of the table. Everyone turned to see Landon standing nearby with an empty plate. "It's time for lunch. The clock says eleven o'clock. My lunch is at eleven o'clock." Allison grinned broadly at her son, bid farewell to her friends, and returned to her favorite role – Mom.

That day, the Noon train brought with it an unexpected guest. Radmund had caught a flight a week earlier than planned. His surprise prompted a celebration The Whistle Stop hadn't seen in years.

Radmund

In addition to her culinary skills, Cordelia also had a God-given gift of hospitality. She could whip up a party with a moment's notice. The day Radmund arrived unannounced, she prepared a soiree like none the Whistle Stop had ever seen. Everyone in town, from the train, and within earshot was invited. Like the loaves and fishes, food poured out of the kitchen for hours as if Jesus himself were the miracle chef.

Visitors disembarking the train did not understand the commotion that erupted when a red-haired young man with vibrant blue eyes, robed in formal air force attire stepped from the train, began walking across the street, and was suddenly attacked by two adults running from the Whistle Stop. A few people wondered if they should help, but it was soon apparent that the commotion was overflowing with emotion. Blessed emotion. Tears, screams of joy, an untethered welcome-home jubilation.

Not since the Strawberry Festival nearly a year earlier had Plant City seen such activity. Just about to ascend the ladder to the train, Owen and Louella noticed the emerging scene. Quickly assessing the reason for the hullabaloo, they jumped off the train steps to stay and join in the reunion. A spontaneous parade marched through the doors of the Whistle Stop Eatery. Cordelia and Henry, with their arms around Radmund, led the procession. Following were numerous friends and strangers, eager to join the celebration of a soldier returned home.

Much to her dismay, Allison had been distracted finishing lunch with Landon when the eruption first broke out. But as the crowd quickly gathered, she snatched up her son and jumped to the cause. This was one of those days, she knew, where the patio tables would be needed. Together, she and Landon quickly snuck out the back door to the patio. "Landon, grab that chair and set it at this table please baby," she begged just as the customers overflowed to the patio. Then, clutching her son to her side, to escape what she knew could be an alarm for his hypersensitive system, they snuck inside through the back door to the seclusion of the kitchen.

It wasn't until a few minutes later, when Delia bounced through the kitchen door frantically barking out orders for the crew to begin cooking this, and get out that, and unthaw the other, that she realized Allison and Landon were huddled in a corner reading one of his favorite books, trying to ignore the noise. "Oh my gosh! Allison I'm so sorry. We are totally caught up in Rad's return. Is he okay?" she asked pausing to check on Landon and give him a quick high-five.

"He's fine," Allison replied. "He didn't really notice. We snuck out to set up the tables on the patio while you brought in the guests. I just thought we'd hang out in here for a few minutes – at least until the noise calms down a little." She leaned forward to whisper so Landon wouldn't hear, "I don't want him messing up the reunion." Deep down, Allison knew she was also using her concern over Landon's possible reaction to avoid her own insecurities. Since she'd learned of Radmund's impending return, her heart sank a little each day. *What if I'm just in the way now*, she told herself. *Delia and Henry will be busy with their own son. Why would they want an autistic kid and his welfare mom hanging around?*

"Allison, what's really bothering you?" Delia asked intuitively.

"Nothing really. I'm just worried about Landon, that's all." Delia and Henry had been so good to her. She couldn't bear the thought of hurting them because of her stupid worries.

"I don't believe you. And you know lying makes your mouth dirty," Delia teased.

"It's just that, well, … oh nothing. Really, it's just silly stuff and you know how I am sometimes. I'll get Landon set up with his toys back here. If you don't mind, I'll just help from the kitchen this time. Maybe Laurabelle can go out there and take orders. That way I don't have to ask someone back here to watch Landon for me." Allison forced her most positive voice, but it fell on wise ears.

"First of all, we are not taking orders today. A grand feast is about to be spread across that entire bar out there and our guests have come to welcome my son home. This is a party and we do not charge guests when they attend a party! And second, you and Landon are absolutely part of our family so get out there and help us greet our guests!" Delia could bark out orders that sounded more like a ballad ringing true and beautiful in the listener's ears.

"Delia, what did I do to deserve someone like you in my life?" Allison asked as she lifted Landon in her arms to go into the dining room and do as she was told.

"You let me in; that's what." Delia winked leaving the kitchen to reenter the Heavenly chaos brewing as the celebration escalated in the dining room.

Having learned from previous experience that earplugs worked wonders for some autistic children, Allison snatched Landon's set from her purse and helped him get them in place. "Now Landon, this is a party. I know it's loud but I want you to be brave for Mommy, okay?" she begged as she lifted him to her hip and he burrowed deep into her shoulder.

"I don't like noise," came his muffled reply.

"You can stay right by me, okay? I'll hold you or your hand the whole time. Then we'll get you back to the kitchen where it's quieter in a few minutes." Landon nodded his agreement and the two of them cautiously emerged into the dining room.

***

Radmund was overwhelmed with the attention. In the air force, everyone looked out for each other equally. It was unacceptable to allow yourself to be the "center of attention." That was reserved for the sergeants, generals, and the President that one time he chose to visit the troops over a year earlier. Now, it was almost more than Rad could handle. But the joy surrounding him and the smiles on his parents' faces made the whole scene bearable, for a little while at least.

When she emerged with Landon, though, everything around him morphed into a slow motion of grey abyss and dull sounds. Many of his lonelier moments from the past two years were comforted with thoughts about her. Her short email notes lifted his spirits for weeks at a time. *If only she knew how I felt*, he'd thought time and again. *I should tell her*, he would convince himself. But the words would never make it to the screen. *It's stupid! We barely know each other*, he would finally convince himself and then write a generic note updating her on the unconfidential things he had been involved with that month.

Friends he'd never met hugged him and spoke of how happy his parents would be now that he'd returned safe and sound. Strangers who stopped by for the free meal were swept up in the emotion, thankful to be included in such a festive day. Each time he made one step closer to Allison, someone would spin him a different direction, physically and mentally. "Yes, I had to shoot my gun a few times, but thankfully, I never had to kill anyone," he answered similar questions over and over again. "We really looked out for each other. I knew my buddies had my back and they knew I had theirs."

Spinning a different direction, he answered, "Yea, we had a couple close calls. No, I wasn't hurt or anything. We did have a car bomb go off right outside our station one night, though. Four soldiers were hurt pretty bad. … It was scary but they prepare you for that stuff, you know?"

There she was in his sight, almost within reach when he was jerked away again. "No, I didn't really get to meet the President. He just stood on a stage and spoke to us. I think he left right after that. One of the guys said he got to shake his hand, but I don't know if that was true or not."

Their eyes met, finally. He was determined to get to her that time. But it was she who turned away then, to a guest who needed directions to the bathroom. By the time she turned back, he was off in another recap. "Drive a tanker?" He stifled the laughter planking his next words, "No, I'm in the air force. We fly planes and helicopters. I actually spent most of my time rescuing wounded soldiers, then treating them until we could get them back to the base hospital. I'm a medic on one of the big C-130s."

"Amputations are probably the most serious surgeries I ever did," was his reply to another guest who joined in the conversation. "There was one time when we helped a little Iraqi boy. He'd been hit by a rogue bullet from one of their soldiers. Luckily, it went straight through the outer part of his arm. We stitched and wrapped the wound, then put a Scooby-Do band aid on top of the gauze. He thought it was great! Came back the next day trying to convince us he needed another Band-Aid for a scratch on his knee. Of course we gave him one and a spare."

Then, all of a sudden, there she was. He sensed her presence before he saw her. Struggling to catch his breath, he turned to take in the beautiful hazel eyes he'd dreamed about all those months. "Hey Rad. How are you?" she asked nonchalantly. Carefully, she lifted Landon from her hip and set him down. He stood stoically at her side, eyes fixed on the floor, clutching tightly to her hand.

"Allison. I've missed you!" He leaned forward kissing her cheek, then stepped back wishing it could have been more. "But who is this young man with you?" He bent down to shake hands; Landon glanced upward, but just stared at the shining brass decorations on Radmund's uniform.

"Landon," she whispered. "It's okay. This is my friend Radmund. Delia and Henry are his mommy and daddy. Shake his hand." With that coaxing, Landon pulled the one free hand from his pocket, looked up only a bit farther as he rigidly shook hands, then shoved his hand right back in the pocket. "Do you remember about Landon's condition?" she whispered, apologetically.

"He's great! I don't see any condition in him at all," Rad responded with a gleam in his eyes that had remained dormant until that very second as he stared into hers. "He's grown up so much. What a little man you have there."

"Yeah, well. He'll be five in March. Starts Kindergarten in September, and I can't figure out how that can be. It's just too fast sometimes."

"How have you been?" he asked. "You never really said much in your emails so I've been wondering if you guys are alright."

"I was a mess when you were home last time. I remember. But, every day I get a little more adjusted to parenting a child with special needs. It's tough, though, when you add 'single' in front of 'parent.' I just didn't want to tell you all that in email. I mean you're out there fighting a war and all. You didn't need my baggage added to the stuff you had on your mind. Besides, I'm doing so much better now. I'm finishing school in December!"

While everyone else whirled around in constant motion, for Radmund, in that one moment, everything faded away except her. As she filled him in on school, his mind flooded with memories of the first time they'd met. He'd come home for a two-week leave over the Christmas holidays, two years after Allison began working at the Whistle Stop. Perhaps it was the warmth of the holiday spirit, or maybe the glistening decorations, or the music filled with themes of love and family; he wasn't sure. But something stirred in his soul as his parents introduced them. He went out the next day to get her and Landon gifts, which later proved a bad idea as she was mortified that he spent money on them, barely even knowing them, and when she had none with which to get him a gift in return.

"Son, you don't know anything about her. You didn't do anything wrong. It's just that she's been through a lot. See, she's very proud but it feels like her whole life is a big charity right now." Cordelia had tried to smooth things over with him. However, it wasn't until Allison figured out a way to offer him a "gift" that he felt relief.

"Here," she said, blandly handing him a card. Inside was a simple inscription. *This certificate is good for one home-cooked meal with Allison and Landon Pershing.* "I know I'm not a great cook like your mom, but I've been told I make pretty good spaghetti and garlic cheese bread. So if you like that sort of thing, we'd like it if you would let us treat you to dinner as our thanks for the gifts and as my way of saying 'I'm sorry' for overacting."

He had showed up at her apartment right on time the next night – one day before he had to return to duty. For him, the entire evening was magical. They hit it off so quickly, laughing and sharing stories like old friends. He thought his parents were overly concerned for no reason. For her, though, Allison was simply determined to make the evening pleasant and avoid sharing any of her burdens with him. He was off to war the next day and she would not allow herself to add one thing to the weight that fighting a war must put on a person's mind. She never realized how much that evening meant to him.

As his thoughts returned to the reunion at hand, he promised himself that this time would be different. He would not let his feelings for her remain secret. But to get the nerve to tell her, that would have to wait until he settled in a bit more. "Oh, I remember that class," Radmund agreed mentally jumping from the past back to the present.

"I survived," Allison concluded. "I really liked learning about triage and the intubation steps, but I'm not sure I have the whole picture yet," she admitted.

"You'll get it. Don't worry," spoke the veteran EMT to the future respiratory therapist.

"Hey, Rad," Henry suddenly appeared eradicating the façade that everyone else had disappeared. "The mayor came by to see you! She's right over here. Don't mind if I tear him away a bit, do you Allison?"

"Of course not," Allison nodded in agreement. Landon tugged on her hand, startling her for a moment. "Hey sweetie, what do you need?"

"Potty," was his simple response. With that, they disappeared down the long corridor leading from the dining room, past the kitchen door, to the set of doors with gender-specific stick figures.

***

By 2:00 p.m., The Whistle Stop quieted as visitors moved on to their next adventure. The Travis' were the final guests to leave that day. "First to arrive, last to leave," Henry teased.

"Free food. You guys never do that when we stop by. Figured we should take advantage of it while we can," Owen retorted.

Delia walked in between her husband and Owen, "And we are honored you chose to spend the day with us in this joyous occasion! Woulda been offended if you hadn't," she confessed sneering at Henry. Radmund reemerged a moment later, thankful for the freedom to finally change out of his dress clothes into more proper February Florida attire – jeans and a navy-blue t-shirt that illuminated his sparkling eyes.

"Radmund, it was an honor to meet you!" Louella remarked noting how strikingly different he looked in street clothes. "Thank you for everything you did to honor and defend our country."

Radmund never quite knew how to accept the public affection for his sacrifice. "You know, it's just something I always thought I should do, Ma'am," he humbly replied as the two embraced.

Louella blushed. "'Ma'am? You are not in the military anymore, so please call me Louella. Makes me feel old to hear such proper titles."

"Sorry, habit," he replied giggling.

"She just had a milestone birthday in December. Hasn't quite accepted it yet,'" Owen jumped in putting his arm around his wife. "The big 'seven-o'," he mouthed Radmund's direction while motioning the numbers on his hands.

"There's no way you're a day over 50," Radmund replied on cue.

"You are so very charming. Totally dishonest, but very charming," Louella joked touching Radmund's shoulder. "Owen, you should take lessons from this young man," she quipped at her husband with a glimmer in her eyes.

"You two always make me smile," Delia finally offered. Then, the women hugged good-bye as the men shook hands. "Next week?" Delia asked as they walked out the front door, her face radiating with joy in all the day had brought them.

"Got it on the calendar!" Louella replied in acceptance.

Picnic in the Park

Despite the constant tugging back and forth during the party, Radmund managed to learn a few things about Allison's schedule from his parents. First, it was Friday and she never had classes on Friday night. Second, the Whistle Stop is a breakfast and lunch spot, which means it always closes no later than 4:00 p.m. So he knew she would be off soon. Third, she and Landon often took leftovers from the restaurant with them for a picnic dinner to enjoy a quiet Friday afternoon at Sansone Park, weather permitting. Finally, the forecast for that afternoon was warm and sunny with a chance of romance.

"Allison," he stammered as she emerged from the kitchen with two boxes of goodies for dinner. "I was wondering if … ummh … if you would mind if I join you and Landon … you know, at the park … um … for your picnic."

"How did you know about that?" She replied sheepishly, then nodded her head in understanding. "Duh. Your parents. Of course you can join us, but don't you think your folks might want you to have your first dinner home with them?"

"Actually, they have theater tickets tonight, and since I surprised them by coming home a week early, I told them not to make any changes. So you see, you'll be doing me a favor. I really hate to think I'd spend my first night back all alone." He did his best to put on a pouty face, but his lower lip was curled too high in a grin to pull off the gesture. "Besides, Dad left his motorcycle out front for me and chose to risk his life riding with Mom in her new convertible. I'd hate to waste a great night for a bike ride."

"Landon, would you mind if Radmund joins us for our picnic tonight?" Landon nodded his approval as he looked up at Radmund, almost making eye contact. "Wow! He never does that. Did you two have a bonding moment while I wasn't looking?"

"His hair is very red," Landon stated matter-of-factly.

"Well, then. That explains it," Radmund laughed. "If that gets his attention, then I'm grateful for the first time in my life to have this ginger mop on top." Together they returned to the kitchen while Radmund retrieved his favorite leftovers.

"Your folks are very good to me," Allison admitted feeling compelled to explain. "They make me take leftovers all the time. I didn't want to at first, but they said they have too much to give to the Food Pantry. So what's left after that gets tossed out if someone doesn't eat it. I didn't believe them at first so I refused. That's when your dad compromised with me, or so he said. I take leftovers for Landon and me most days and that counts as part of my raise." She rambled the entire time he put together a sandwich of Delia's rye bread and chicken salad.

"You know they give what they can to the United Food Bank. We used to throw out so much before that place opened. Now I think Mom actually makes extra to give them sometimes, especially at holidays." He opened the refrigerator to grab some potato salad then finished, "Man! I have so missed this stuff!"

They paused at the fountain behind the front counter to collect three cups of iced tea. Finally, at the front door, she took his arm and confessed, "I'm sure they gave me the same raise they would have even if I didn't accept the leftovers."

He didn't really care what she said. All he knew at that moment was her touch, that his heart was racing a mile a minute, and no matter how much he'd missed his mother's home cooking, there was no room left in his stomach for food now that the butterflies had set in by the droves.

Sansone Community Park was a short walk from her apartment at the Villages. Allison parked her 2000 blue Accord in her regular spot outside the apartment building. Radmund followed on the motorcycle. She had purposefully chosen the complex for its proximity to Hillsborough College and the park. And, just about anything else she could need was within a three-mile radius of the Villages. But most of all, they offered subsidized living, which was one of her greatest needs. "This place is a God-send for Landon and me," she noted as the three of them grabbed their dinner bags and walked across the wooded path to the park. "I mean, there wasn't much chance for me to afford my own place. But the Villages were great and worked with me so I could get a two-bedroom!"

Landon quickly became impatient. Dinner time was 5:30 p.m. and it was quickly approaching 5:45. "Momma, it's five forty-five. I have dinner at five-thirty," he noted pointing at the Lego digital wristwatch Henry and Delia had given him for Christmas.

"I'm sorry baby," Allison replied sweetly as she spread out the contents of his bag on the picnic table. "Here you go. PBJ, plain chips, and a bowl of Delia's coleslaw. Just like you ordered."

Radmund jumped in, "I'm sorry Buddy. It's my fault dinner is late. Don't blame your mom."

Landon looked up at his mother, confused. "Why did he call me Buddy?"

"It means he likes you," Allison answered with a smirk on her face.

"My name is not Buddy," he snapped, obviously not impressed with affectionate terms. His mother, however, felt her heart palpitate just a bit as she contemplated the attention and affection spilling from every pore of Radmund's freckled face.

***

Swinging was a treat Radmund had not enjoyed in five years. With her saddled to his left and Landon safely tucked into the swing on his right, though, he could barely concentrate enough to coordinate his legs to move more than a few feet in the air either way.

"I need a push," Landon demanded as he slowed to a slight sway.

"You got it dude." Radmund quickly jumped to the rescue with a few vigorous pushes resulting in soft gurgling noises – Landon's version of laughter. While many things interfered with his ability to assimilate his environment, swinging was extremely therapeutic. Allison first discovered his delight when she brought home a baby swing she'd proudly purchased for only three dollars at a neighborhood garage sale. The moment he was buckled in, a slight grin of contentment seemed to radiate on his face while the swing swayed rhythmically to the soft music. As soon as he outgrew the baby swing, Allison started the tradition of regular visits to the park on the way home.

"Rad, why are you being so nice to us?" she finally found the courage to ask as Radmund began swinging himself once more.

Caught totally off guard with her sudden poignancy, he dropped his feet, unwittingly dragging himself to a stop with dust flying out in both directions. "Well," he stammered, "why wouldn't I be nice? My folks love you. In fact, they emailed me about you and Landon all the time."

"Really?" The thought of her life spread out over the internet to a man she barely knew was a bit unnerving. "What did they tell you?"

Hearing her concern, he quickly corrected. "Oh, nothing personal. They just bragged about how much Landon was learning and how much they needed you to help keep the Stop going. That's all." He paused and decided the moment had arrived for his confession. "And, I guess I did ask them about *you* sometimes ... a lot," he finally admitted.

Confused, she quit pumping her legs for a moment to sway in the breeze. "Why would you ask about us? You barely know Landon and me."

He began pumping his legs more vigorously, mostly out of anxiety. "Did you just answer your own question?" He didn't mean to be flippant, but that was exactly how she interpreted his reply.

"What?" she responded curtly.

"You asked why I'd ask about someone I barely know. Seems obvious."

"Oh," she giggled. "I guess I did, didn't I?" Allison had purposefully avoided a relationship after the rape. Because of that choice, she was extremely naïve when it came to reading body language or understanding the nuances in the words he chose to say, or not to say. "Why didn't you just ask me? You had my email too."

Suddenly he understood her dovelike responses. "Allison, I wasn't prying. And, I didn't just want to know about you guys because I was searching for a discussion topic. I really wanted to get to know *you* better. Being thousands of miles away, that was a little tough to do in person. And, frankly, I wasn't sure how you felt about me. So, I chickened out and asked the parents instead."

A light bulb suddenly turned on in her brain. "Oh," she replied softly as she buried her face in embarrassment. "Radmund, I'm not very good with guys," she admitted. "I suppose they told you what happened?"

Concerned and confused, he stopped his swing abruptly to look her way. "They mentioned a few things, but only because I bugged them. I promise. They didn't want to hurt you." Guilt overwhelmed him for the constant prying he'd done a year earlier. "Someday you can tell me more, if you want to." He wasn't really sure he wanted to hear what he instinctively knew would infuriate him.

As if on cue, Landon announced, "Another push." Radmund jumped to the rescue once more, then returned to his swing next to Allison.

"I guess I could tell you now, if you want. I mean your folks already told you some of it anyway." She paused her own swing to sit idly by his side as she shared the distant scars still marring her soul. Instinctively, she knew he was safe, which was both extremely comforting and confusing at the same time. Taking a deep breath, she spoke softly so Landon would not overhear. "There was this really cute guy at school and all the girls wanted to go out with him. But he asked me to go to Prom. Me! I couldn't believe he chose me over all those other girls who were way prettier or more popular.

"My family was pretty poor, not terrible, but certainly didn't have any extra dollars lying around for a prom dress. Luckily, my grandmother was a terrific seamstress so she made this gorgeous satiny, turquoise dress. It was strapless with sequins all over the top and stopped at my knees with light blue lace extending to the floor, just like one I'd seen in the Macys' catalog. First time I tried it on I just stared at myself in the mirror thinkin', *That can't be me! That girl looks like a princess*. Then my big brother, Marc, came in the room and just cracked up at me primping and all. But the night of prom, when I came downstairs with my hair all done up perfect and make-up for the first time in my life, Marc stood there like a doofus, mouth wide open. My dad and mom snapped tons of pictures.

"Then my date got there and he walked in and just stood there staring at me, which made me feel so awkward that I wanted to run and hide! But my folks started shooting pictures of the two of us again until we finally just walked out the door and they kept snapping a few last pictures. I was pretty embarrassed at how my family handled the whole thing. Afterall, I was going to prom with the coolest, hottest guy in school! My reputation was on the line … little did I know how true that would be later." She paused a moment, lingering on the last thought.

Radmund shifted in his swing as Allison turned sideways, making eye contact with him finally. Her hazel eyes reflected a cavernous distance, burdened with memories. "Prom was amazing! We danced and laughed and I had the best time in my life. I was sure I was falling in love. He complimented me all night and made sure all the other guys knew how lucky he was to be at the dance with me! It all seemed so surreal. Like it was just too good to be true for some poor girl who'd never even had a boyfriend before.

"After the dance, he asked me if I wanted to go back to his house and meet his parents. I thought it was strange he didn't want to go straight to the after-prom party, but he said he wanted to get to know me better if we were going to start dating. My heart skipped a beat when he said that, so of course I agreed. It wasn't until we got to his house though that he told me his parents were out of town for the weekend. 'Got the place to ourselves,' he flirted. I said we should probably go to the party, then, since my parents would not approve of me being in a boy's house alone. He just made fun of me for being immature. Said if I wanted to be his girlfriend then I needed to grow up and stop worrying about what my parents thought.

"He was really cool after that. Got us some sodas and turned on an old movie. We sat on the couch for a few minutes and chatted like we'd known each other forever. I felt so silly to have suggested we leave. But, then, he started to get pushy and said he wanted to kiss me and stuff. So I let him kiss me, but then he started touching me and ..." she lowered her head. "I told him I wasn't ready for anything serious." Tears were streaming down her cheeks, as she whispered, "I said, 'No.' I yelled, 'No!' He was too strong."

Allison sat quietly wiping away the tears, wishing it would be that easy to eradicate the memory. After a moment, Radmund reached over and gently took her hand in his. "Anyway, it was over in a few minutes, but it seemed like an hour. The beautiful dress my grandma made me had a huge rip and my hair was in total shambles. I could not believe what had just happened. In my shock and shame, I immediately tried to convince myself I'd wanted it as much as he did. At least that way I could pretend it was something beautiful – you know, the way God intended.

"But later that night, when I looked in the mirror, I just wrenched in horror at my reflection. 'You did not willingly give yourself to another and you should not pretend otherwise,' God kept telling me. But another voice, that horrible sinister voice of Satan, kept chiding me. I was riddled with guilt because I believed it was my fault. I shouldn't have put on make-up. Should have worn a more modest dress. Shouldn't have gone in the house with him. Shouldn't have led him on. Should have left the first moment I felt something funny in my gut. I should have known what he expected. Shouldn't have been so naïve." Allison hissed in retrospection. "Why is it that sometimes when we're so down it's easier to hear Satan than God?" The question was rhetorical, so he offered no answer.

"So it took me two weeks before I finally broke down and admitted to my family what really happened. They took me to the police right away but it was too late to collect any evidence. And the guy had already spread rumors about us all over school. Since I didn't deny anything at first, it was assumed to be true. I refused to discuss it with even my closest friends. The police said I could file charges but it would be an ugly court battle, and I'd probably end up looking really bad. Marc wanted to kill the guy, but I made him swear not to do anything. Finally, he promised not talk about it again if I would just erase it from my memory. I promised to try.

"A month later I found out I was pregnant. Thankfully, school was over so I didn't have to deal with more rumors." Allison paused, and got off her swing to walk over and give Landon another push.

"Did you tell the guy?" Radmund asked after she returned.

"I thought about it, but only because I thought it might make him suffer with guilt. I hated him and stupidly thought it would be some sort of revenge. But, my mom said he'd twist it all around to be my fault and portray me as some slut just trying to get him to marry me. Plus he was a senior, off to some Ivy-league college which made it easier for me knowing I would never have to see him again.

"The next week my dad came home and announced he had an appointment for me at the Planned Parenthood way out on the other side of Tampa, where no one we knew would see us. I was mortified. I couldn't even accept the reality of what happened, let alone the fact that I might choose to abort an innocent baby. We had a huge fight that night. Marc ran out. My folks demanded I get the abortion. All I could do was scream at them to leave me alone. Later, I snuck outside to our detached garage and closed the door. Then, I climbed into our family station wagon and turned on the ignition. I hoped starting the engine would end my troubles.

"My brother returned just a couple of minutes after I turned the key. Opening the garage door with his own remote, he accidentally thwarted my plans. But, it was no accident in God's plan. Marc found me sobbing with my head buried in the steering wheel. He grabbed me out of the car and held me in his arms for half an hour at least while we both just sat there crying. No words, just enough tears to flood the valley. Finally we agreed not to tell our folks. He made me swear I'd never do something stupid like that again. But, Marc was always watching out for me after that night.

"I hadn't been to church in a long time, but I felt like it was the right place to go. So a few days later I went out for a walk and ended up down the street at Grace Church. It was just a simple little country church I'd walked by a thousand times before but never noticed until that day."

"Were they helpful?" he asked.

"They saved Landon's and my life. Well, actually God saved us. Of course, Marc followed me even though I told him to go to work. We sat in the church together for a while until the pastor came in and said, 'Hello.' We both nodded back a forced greeting. Then he just sat down by us for a few minutes. We thought he was praying, but couldn't tell for sure. Finally he looked up and said, 'You know, sometimes God has a way of making something amazing out of something really awful. I don't understand how, though. You'd think a minister would get those things, but we don't. It's just that God promised us in the Bible and I know His word is absolutely true.'"

"So he pulled out a Bible and read to us from Jeremiah 29:11. It talks about how God has plans for everybody. 'Plans to prosper you, not harm you. Plans to give you a hope and a future.' Marc put his arm around me and I just broke down and blabbed the whole story to a stranger. He even cried with us as I told him how Marc saved me from the stupid idea of suicide. I thought he would make everything better. But, instead, he just hugged us and prayed that God would help me figure out what to do. I was ticked! I thought for sure a preacher at a church named 'Grace' would fix things.

"But, the next day I went back. It was like a magnet. Something about sitting in that sanctuary made me feel a little better. The pastor, who I learned that time was named Rev. Jerome, sat with me again. Again he just prayed that God would help me figure out what to do. But he wouldn't tell me anything. 'God has an answer for you if you listen,' he kept reassuring me. So, I went back every afternoon all week. Marc went with me every day, and we'd just sit quietly waiting for God to magically give me the answer. I guess I expected some neon sign or big announcement or something." Allison sighed at the notion.

"So anyway. That Sunday Marc and I went to a church service for the first time in years. Rev. Jerome had a baby baptism that day. After they finished the ceremony, the baby's family took the podium to share about how blessed they were to have such a precious gift from God. They married young and didn't really want to start a family for a few more years but now they realized that their baby was an answer to prayer. 'Life is something we can never take for granted,' the baby's mom stated. 'Every child is a miracle created by God. No matter what, God does not make mistakes.'

"To me, it sounded like God was finally yelling at me with His answer! Marc looked at me and we both knew, instantly, what my decision would be. Our folks were furious. They refused to acknowledge that I wanted to raise a child conceived in rape. But, in that moment of God's revelation, He'd softened my heart so much that I fell madly in love with the child growing inside me. It really was a miracle. Marc understood, but our parents never did.

"We really tried to help them accept my decision, but they wouldn't even speak to me anymore. Rev. Jerome even visited one day to try and help, but they used every cuss word in the book and kicked him out. So, that August my folks finally got fed up and kicked me out before I could return to school and embarrass them publicly. Marc helped me find a Bridgeway home in Tampa, then he went back to medical school. I turned 17 on Labor Day that year … and finished my high-school classes through their online program. Got my high school diploma by Christmas. I tried to call my parents to let them know, but the number was changed. I figured they'd changed the locks or wouldn't answer the door if I tried to visit, so I just packed my bag and moved here the week after Christmas. Later that January, a few weeks before Landon was born, I met your dad at a job fair. He hired me on the spot. Didn't blink an eye when he saw me all pregnant without a ring. Your folks were so great! They even went to the hospital with me when Landon was born. I don't know what I'd do without them! That was five years ago already. I love that plaque your mom gave me, reminding me about God's plans and all. I hope it's really true." Her voice trailed off in contemplation of God's promise.

Silence filled the span of the next few seconds, neither quite sure what to say next. Finally Landon interjected, "Hey! I said I have to go potty." Startled back to the moment, they both jumped to rescue him from the swing.

"I'll take him if you like," Radmund offered happy for a chance to take a walk and cool down.

"Landon, would it be okay if Radmund takes you to the boys' potty over there?" she asked assuming his answer would be a resounding 'No!' Instead, her little boy surprised her once more by taking Radmund's hand as they walked together to take care of bodily functions. *Lord, what are you doing here?* she prayed to herself while they were gone. *Why did you bring this man into my life? You know I'm not ready for a relationship.* But even as she worked fervently to convince God that she was not ready, He was softening her heart to understand and accept His plans to prosper her. A few minutes later, she looked up to see Radmund and Landon returning, chatting up a storm as they crossed the playground back to the swing set.

Landon walked right up to his mother, who had returned to the pavilion to clean up the trash from dinner. "Momma, he's weird," he stated as if the whole world were used to blunt honesty.

"Honey, remember how I told you it's not nice to say things like that about people?" she implored for him to restrain, but he continued.

"But, he asked me if it was okay if he asks you out on a date. Why would he ask *me*?"

Radmund immediately blushed a shade brighter than his hair. "Well, I guess I know not to share secrets with that one!" He chuckled trying to mask his embarrassment.

Allison tried to help salvage whatever dignity he had left. "It's fine. He's just very, very literal."

"I'll remember that next time," Radmund responded slowly regaining his composure.

"And, if you had asked me instead of him, the answer would have been 'yes.'" It took a moment for him to register what just happened. Then, he felt his whole body shudder in excitement.

"Okay then," he tried to make sense, but the rest just babbled out with little coherence. "Dinner, uh tomorrow. Night I mean. You know 'cuz dinner is at night. Duh!"

She laughed to herself, trying not to add to his lingering humiliation. "Dinner tomorrow would be terrific."

"Does Landon have to go? Oh, I mean do you want him to go, 'cuz it's fine if you do but my folks could babysit if not but I don't mind either way. I just thought you might want a night off is all." He sat down at the picnic table, wiping his forehead. "It's really hot out here tonight, isn't it?"

She sat next to him, so close he feared she'd be soiled by the vats of sweat dripping from his armpit. "Actually, I think it's a perfect evening," she replied softly. "And, I'm sure Landon would enjoy a night with your folks. He and your dad love playing with the trains."

"Oh man, my dad and the trains! How could I forget?" Then an idea hit him. "Do you work at the Stop tomorrow?"

Puzzled, she looked over to him as they grabbed their boxes and walked through the wooded path back to her apartment. "Umm, yes. I've been working Saturdays this semester since I have classes all day on Mondays. Why?"

"Would you mind if I pick up Landon after lunch? Dad said he's not coming in tomorrow, and I think I hear a train whistle calling our names. It'd be like the 'Three Amigos'." He grinned at the brilliance of the ploy.

"I want to go play with the trains, Momma," Landon interjected making the decision final before Allison could say a word.

"Okay, but only if you make me a promise," she directed the comment right at Radmund.

"Anything you want."

"You will not put Landon on that motorcycle!" She pointed to his dad's bike as they approached her building.

Landon tugged her arm and whispered, "I like motorcycles."

Radmund laughed while Allison fought back her own giggle. "Yes, I know how much you enjoy running your toy motorcycles around, but you are not big enough to ride on one yet."

"Listen Landon, I agree with your mom. Plus, I've been waiting five years to get out my old Camaro! It's way more fun than some old bike." He looked at Allison for approval. After her nod, he finished, "Would that be okay instead?"

"Sure. I eat lunch at 11:00," he reminded everyone.

"Yes, we know," she replied.

"What if I come by early and have lunch with you?" he asked, mostly to Landon but hoping for her acceptance as well.

Details for the next day were finally set to everyone's agreement just as they reached Allison's front door. "I don't mean to be forward, but could I have a tour of your place? I need to move into my own space now that I'm back for good. And, you're not the first person to tell me how great this complex is," he asked hoping she would not think he had any ulterior motives.

Pausing to contemplate the cleanliness of her home, she finally determined it to be in passing condition. "Okay, sure. But, it's probably messy. You know with a little boy and with me working all the time." He didn't care in the least.

The tour lasted only five minutes, just long enough for him to confirm the Villages were exactly where he wanted to live. Nice space, convenient, reasonable rent. It was everything he needed. Oh, and it would be closer to her.

"Landon, say 'good-night' and then go get your pajamas on," she spoke directly to him knowing he only understood expectations, not choices.

"Good night," Landon obliged as he walked over to shake Radmund's hand once more.

"See 'ya tomorrow, Bud … um … I mean Landon," Radmund replied quickly catching himself before repeating the offense from earlier. Allison wasn't certain, but she thought there was the tiniest grin on her little boy's face. "He's so stinkin' cute," Radmund affirmed after Landon left the room.

"He's never reacted that way to a stranger before. It's like you two have been friends all his life or something." She pondered the possibilities as they reached her door. "You probably remind him of your dad and that makes him really comfortable around you."

As they approached the door, his heart sank realizing the night had to come to an end. "I'm really looking forward to tomorrow."

"I'm sure Landon is too," she responded. "He is fixated on those trains, just like your dad!" It wasn't quite the response he'd hoped for.

"Actually, that will be fun, but I was referring to the evening portion of our plans." His eyes lit up like the night sky as they stepped into the hallway.

"Oh, me too," she replied but a hint of queasiness startled her at the thought. Subduing the feeling, she continued, "Where do you want to go?"

"I'd like to surprise you if that's okay. Anything you don't like or are allergic to I should know about?"

"Nope, I like all foods. Remember where I work?" she hoped the joke would lighten the nausea rapidly gurgling in her stomach.

"Great. It's going to be awesome. You'll see," he promised. Then, he leaned in close, hoping that his earlier wish would come true. Instead, she turned her face away just as he approached, causing him to accept another friendly kiss on the cheek. "Well, then, good night. I had a great time tonight!"

"Me too," she replied as her palms dripped sweat on the doorknob. Her words were true enough; it was the next day she feared ... the thought of that word 'date' had finally settled in her mind, making it all just a little too nerve-wracking for her. *What have I done?* she scolded herself after he left. *I'm not ready for any date or stuff or ...*

"Momma, you are talking to yourself," Landon noted as he entered the living room, dressed in red pajamas chugging with trains all over. "It's time for my prayer and song."

"Hey Sweetie." Redirecting her attention to her son, she exclaimed, "Look at how big you are! Ready for bed all by yourself again. Did you brush your teeth?"

"Yes. I brushed two minutes on the top and bottom, just like the dentist told me." *He is a stickler for those details,* she laughed to herself wondering how a little boy with autism had become the 'normal' in her life and the attentions of a handsome gentleman made her want to purge her dinner.

Friends

For the first time in years, nightmares haunted Allison's dreams startling her out of a peaceful slumber. *Why God?* she demanded in prayer. *I thought I was past that and now it's back just because a really nice guy pays attention to me? Why?!* On the other side of town, Radmund enjoyed his first full night's sleep in years. No gunshots in the distance; no middle-of-the-night raids; no 24-hour security detail. *A real mattress with real blankets and a soft pillow*, he muttered before drifting off into deep sleep, which welcomed plain old-fashioned dreams about a beautiful girl and a little boy who liked his red hair.

By the time she got to the restaurant, Allison could hardly breathe; Radmund could hardly wait to get to the restaurant. "Allison, are you okay?" Delia asked as they prepared Saturday breakfast for a restaurant filled with hungry guests.

"I can't figure it out. Radmund and Landon and I had such a great time last night. I even told him all about what happened and he really listened. I mean, it felt like I finally made a friend to talk to about this stuff, and Landon, and whatever. But now I'm terrified to meet him for dinner just because he called it a 'date.' I thought I was over all that other stuff and ready to think about a relationship. Especially with someone as wonderful as your son. But I think I really just need to be friends right now."

"Sweetie, you can think about it all you want, but until you actually take that first step, you'll never really move forward." Words of wisdom came so simply to Cordelia. "Now I know he's my son and I'm biased, but he really is a great catch! However, you need to let him know exactly how you feel or you'll both end up with broken hearts. I can't bear that for either of you."

Allison pondered her options for a moment, then breathed a sigh of relief. "Thanks, Delia. You're right. I know what I have to do." With that she kissed her friend on the cheek and glided back into the dining room with a tray full of pastries, orange juice, and scrambled eggs.

"Hey Mom! What's for breakfast? I'm starved!" Radmund radiated as he strolled through the back door a few moments later.

Delia astutely realized his intentions toward Allison were far greater than those he could expect in return. "Son, help yourself to anything you want. It's on the house!" she joked. After he piled a plate with strawberry pancakes, scrambled eggs, four sausage links, fresh melon, and a ginormous pile of hash browns, Radmund snuggled into a cozy spot at the table in the kitchen reserved for the workers. His mother joined him with her own plate of two strawberry muffins and low-fat yogurt butter. "Listen, Rad, we need to chat."

"Sounds serious. Did I do something wrong after only a few hours back home?" he sneered as syrup dripped from his fork.

Finishing a bit of her muffin, she continued. "Sweetie, I know you really like Allison, but she's still pretty fragile. She hasn't been on a date or even paid attention to a man since the night she was attacked. That's been almost five years now. I think you need to just be her friend right now. If you push it for more, I'm afraid you'll scare her away forever."

"What did she say?" He swallowed a mouthful and continued. "Oh man. I made her uncomfortable last night. I knew it! I shouldn't have asked her to tell me about that jerk. Now I feel like the jerk."

Delia waved a hand to stop his ranting. "Honey, you didn't do anything wrong. She even told me she is thrilled to have someone like you for a *friend* after all these years of being alone. But I think that's where she wants it to stay right now – just friends. It might be wise for you to make sure she knows you're okay with that."

"But I'm not okay with that. I've been in love with her for, well, for a long time. Now you want me to wait another God-knows-how-long?" His fork dropped with a thud on the plate as he shoved the food aside – appetite squelched once more on her account.

"Young man, do not use God's name that way, no matter how upset you are!" she scolded, then continued in a softer voice. "Besides, if you really love her, then you will wait for her until whenever she's ready. Otherwise, you'll lose her forever. Think about it Baby." With that she finished her last muffin, got up from the table, and commenced to the dining room to help take orders, leaving him alone with a heavy heart and plate full of cold food that would not be eaten.

***

"Momma, it's eleven o'clock. I eat lunch at eleven o'clock," came the soft reminder as she finished bussing a deserted table.

"Yes you do," she smiled. "Let me get these dirty dishes to the kitchen and I'll return with your favorite – tuna salad on rye with brussel sprouts!" She grinned at her son, hoping for once he might respond to a joke like other children. Instead, his attention turned to the kitchen door where Radmund finally emerged after hiding for over two hours in turmoil about what he knew he had to do.

"Hi Radmund," Landon waved with a half-smile. "Momma is getting my lunch." Then he looked up at her and took her hand to get her attention. "But it is not going to be tuna and brussel sprouts," he added matter-of-factly. "Then we are going to play with the trains, right?" he redirected to his new friend.

"You bet Sport!" came Radmund's response. "Oops, sorry. Landon."

"You can call me Sport but not Buddy. Buddy is a dog's name."

Allison looked at the two of them in amazement. "I have never seen him engage with someone like he does with you! What is your secret?"

"He told you yesterday; it's the red hair," he smiled pointing to the ginger fringe just beginning to grow out from the standard military haircut.

Landon looked at the two of them but without interest in their conversation, then grabbed his mother's hand again. "Momma, the clock stopped whistling. That means it's past eleven." The adults grinned in response as she excused herself and moved to the kitchen with the bucket of dirty dishes. Having snuck the key from Henry that morning, Radmund carefully unlocked the clear plastic lid protecting the #249 shuffling along the tracks. The two boys immediately began chatting about Henry's story once more. Then, in the middle of a chug-chug along the outside wall, Landon looked over at Radmund and announced, "You're nice to Momma and me. That's why I like you. And your hair is really red."

"Thanks for telling me that, Sport," Radmund acknowledged. "I like you guys too."

Setting lunch down on the table in the back corner, Allison smiled at the sight of the two boys playing together in such sweet innocence. In a moment, the three of them appeared to be any normal family, sitting there munching on sandwiches, chips, and guzzling super-sweet southern iced-tea. Simple, safe conversation about school and trains filled the looming space that hovered over them. Allison bragged about Landon's preschool successes, causing him to look up when he heard his name. Otherwise, his attention was torn between the train and his lunch. Radmund forced his mind to remain only in the moment, breathing in her sweet voice and dreaming of a time when they could be more than just friends. As he ate his last bite, Landon reminded everyone that it was time to go.

"I'll be ready to leave in a few minutes, Sport. I need to chat with your mom for just minute first," Radmund said. Allison was suddenly propelled into a sense of alarm. *What now?* she fretted as he continued. "Allison, I was thinking we might change our dinner plans. After what you told me last night, I can tell this whole *dating* thing is … well …"

"Terrifying," she admitted finishing his thought and clearly relieved.

"Yeah, that." After a deep sigh, he moved forward with his plan. "Anyway, what if Landon and I pick up an Olde Town deep dish pizza and bring it over later? We could all enjoy a relaxing dinner at your place. You know, just a couple of good *friends* getting together for dinner. And, frankly, I missed their pizza more than my mom's cooking," he whispered the last line. "Don't tell her," he motioned with his finger over pursed lips.

He wished she had not looked directly into his eyes. "Thank you Rad." She took his hand, causing his breath to stop short once more. "I was going to ask you if we could just be friends for now, and it's like you read my mind. It would mean so much to me if we could be friends." While her words were genuine and heartfelt, to him they felt like daggers. *Will she ever know how I feel? Will she ever be able to feel that way for me?* he wondered releasing hers and taking Landon's hand as they turned to go. Then, leaving Allison to her work, the boys left to play with their toys.

***

Tossing the dust rag and polish into the hall closet quickly, she grabbed a book trying to pretend she'd been reading instead of frantically cleaning just as the knock came on the front door. "One large Olde Town Special and one kid's pepperoni for the munchkin," he announced in his best delivery-boy tone.

"Oh, hi you two. I was just enjoying some light reading," she lied holding up the book she'd grabbed from the bookshelf. Landon bumped past Radmund's legs, hugged his mother, and then trotted off to his room in search of his favorite Battle Striker Tops. He'd had enough trains for one day. Radmund set the pizzas on her small kitchen table, then looked carefully at the book she still held as part of the charade. Without thinking, he burst out laughing. "What's so funny?!" she demanded.

"Well, let's see. First of all, it's upside down," he giggled helping her reorient the book. "And, second, do you often enjoy a little 'light reading' with *Cardiopulmonary Anatomy and Physiology?*"

Embarrassed to be caught in her scheme, she admitted, "Okay, fine. I was cleaning. This place was a pigsty. But, yes, sometimes I do pick up this book just to make sure I haven't forgotten anything."

He looked around, touched that she'd cleaned for him and hopeful that was a sign of some deeper feelings she harbored for him. "You didn't have to clean just for me," he acknowledged.

"Well, actually, Saturday afternoon really is my dusting day. I just got off a little later than normal today due to a huge crowd. So, it was a rushed job."

"I was just here last night, remember? And it looked fine then," he noted still hopeful for ulterior motives in her expeditious house cleaning.

"Well, I kinda hoped that tour was quick enough that you didn't look closely at the furniture," she gushed.

Still not convinced, he teased her. "Then why try to hide it with the whole book thing? It's perfectly normal to dust furniture."

Finally, in an exasperated tone, she admitted what he longed to hear, "Okay fine. I just wanted the place to be clean for you, that's all. No big deal." *Oh, but it is a big deal!* he thought as he carefully tucked those precious words in his heart. *She wanted to impress me.* Changing the subject as quickly as possible, she exclaimed, "You'd think after working in a restaurant all day I'd be sick of food, but no! I'm starving. Let's eat." With that, she called Landon to the table and the three of them commenced a dinner filled with smiles, pizza sauce dripping onto their chins, twinkling eyes, and lots of chatter from the two adults and an occasional monotone comment from the child.

"That is definitely the best pizza in Plant City!" he declared swallowing the last bite of his fourth slice. "Pizza is one thing my mom doesn't even attempt with competition like this."

She agreed completely. "It's the way they layer it, I think. Sauce on top is such a cool idea." She wiped her mouth just in case any sauce lingered on her chin. "Thanks for getting it. We don't ever splurge on Olde Town, or any other restaurant for that matter," she confessed.

"It's my pleasure," he replied knowing that he'd buy her the moon if she asked. "Besides, what else am I going to do with all that money the government is throwing at me?" To him, it was sarcasm. To her, it was life. Immediately she began gathering the dishes without a response. A moment later it dawned on him. "Oh wow! I am so stupid. I didn't mean anything by that at all. I'm so sorry."

"It's okay. It's just that without the government 'throwing money at us' as you put it, Landon and I would not be where we are today. Thanks to welfare, I'm able to go to college and take care of Landon's medical needs. Don't get me wrong, though. I'm so happy I'll be off the government payroll in a few more months!"

"Allison, you're the kind of person that makes taxpayers proud of the welfare program. You used that money to make a difference in your life and his. You know, the way it was intended. I'm very impressed with how hard you've worked in spite of all the crap life threw at you so early on. You are not a quitter; I admire that immensely."

While he crumpled the cardboard boxes, she wiped down the table. "Everything I do is for him," she noted as Landon and his tops retreated back to his bedroom and the adventures he'd put on hold during dinner.

"That's great and all. But you were only a child when you had him. I think you owe it to yourself to do something just for Allison."

Being selfish was never a part of Allison's personality, even before Landon's birth. However, she often wondered what her life would have been like without a child. And, she had to admit to herself, there were many times she fought off a resentment. "Sometimes I think it would be really different, you know?" she spoke out loud in the middle of her thoughts, confusing Radmund. He shot her a puzzled look as she continued, "Oh, I mean life without him. I mean, I would never give him up for anything. It's just I wonder sometimes. Truthfully, I'm sure I would not be as strong as I am today if not for that child. But, I do wonder why God would let it happen to me ... and to Landon. You know?"

He understood more than she realized. Often, while staked out in the desert wondering if an ambush were near, he wondered what his life might have been like had he chosen a different field. Not that he didn't love serving his country, but he longed for a more sedentary life ... with a family and an 8-5 job. And with his mother's illness, he knew the next battle he was to be involved with would be fought at home. Besides, Brandon Regional Hospital was planning to open a satellite emergency clinic that May. Perhaps they would need a highly skilled medic, he had hoped.

"I know what you mean, sort of. I went into the air force because I thought it sounded so exciting ... like being a hero, you know? But it's so much more serious that anything I imagined."

"That's how I felt when I had Landon. I suppose I thought it was the 'heroic' thing to do. But it was way more than I ever expected, especially after I found he was disabled."

"Except now I can get out of the air force, but you are mother for life. You don't get to step away if it gets too tough."

"Is that why you got out? It was too tough?"

"You seem disappointed. There are tons of guys who barely make it through basic."

"No, it just doesn't seem like you. I mean getting out when something is tough. You seem more like a 'stick-to-it' kind of guy." Together they finished replacing the washed and dried silverware. "Wanna go sit in the living room," she smirked pointing just a few feet away to the space where her couch provided a border magically transitioning the kitchen into a living room. He nodded and then motioned for her to go first. Sheepishly she sat at the far side of the couch while he chose the other, both on purpose.

"I had to get out. Five years fighting in a war that doesn't seem to be going anywhere can be maddening. Besides, I had to come home for Mom. I'm going to switch to the Air Guard for a little while so I can stay home and help around here. She and Dad will need a lot of help after the surgery, especially if she needs chemo treatments for awhile." He paused, then lowered his head and whispered his deepest concern, "Hopefully she'll recover just fine."

"I didn't think it was that bad," Allison asked slightly alarmed. "She said the doctors told her the surgery would get everything and she might not even need any chemo or anything else."

"Allison, you've studied enough biology. Do you believe it's that easy?"

Feeling slightly ashamed at her lack of concern, she admitted, "I guess I didn't really think much beyond what your mom told me. I suppose I didn't want to think about it."

"Well, don't get worked up now. She's been a pillar of faith all along and she wants us to be the same. But she needs us all now. We need to be her troop to help fight this battle together. Even if she won't admit it. She says God will use this to help us all get a little stronger."

The conversation was suddenly interrupted by a melodic, beautiful noise streaming through the ceiling. "I love it when she plays piano," Allison remarked looking upward to the apartment where the harmonious music flowed down releasing them from the elephant hovering in her living room.

"I've never heard piano played like that before," Radmund marveled. "Do you know who that is?"

"That's Miss Goldie, one of the sweetest ladies I've ever met. She's 80 years old but seems to get along just fine for being blind."

"She's blind?!" Now he was astounded. "How does she live by herself … and play piano?"

Allison was taken aback by his naivety that time. "She has a guide dog that helps her around mostly. Still, she seems like a really strong woman. I'm sure it's tough sometimes, but weren't we just talking about how tough times in our lives make us stronger?"

A light bulb flashed on, burning brightly in his mind at that moment. "Hey, do you think she'd be okay with some visitors?"

"I'm sure she'd love it. She's always asking Landon and me to stop by and visit. We do sometimes. And Landon just sits mesmerized, listening to her play. In fact, that's how I learned to play classical CDs for him when he gets so upset about something."

"Then, I think we need to head upstairs." Radmund jumped up ready to initiate another plan.

"What's going on?" she asked preparing to retrieve Landon from his room.

"I'll tell you on the way upstairs," he replied while rapidly dialing his cell phone.

The Perfect Surprise

The Whistle Stop is closed on Sundays – "to give our family time to rest in the Lord" – reads the sign on the front door. But on Monday morning, everything was bustling as usual. Allison rose early for class, dropped off Landon at Shiloh Preschool, then made a quick call to Radmund just to make sure everything was set. "All taken care of," he confirmed. "What time will you be there with our 'guest'?

"Classes end at two. I'll pick her and Landon up right after that. We should be there by two-thirty at the latest."

"Perfect! I have the delivery scheduled for 11:00 a.m. They should be finished by early afternoon." He jumped with excitement on the other end of the line. "I can't wait!"

"Your mother is going to flip!" Goosebumps covered her arms in anticipation she hadn't enjoyed for years. "Are you sure she won't mind moving it to the restaurant?"

"Heck no! She talks about it all the time, but doesn't do anything to make it happen." Radmund couldn't decide which was better – the fact that this was definitely the greatest Valentine's gift he could ever give his mother or that he and Allison had teamed up together to make it happen.

***

Delia turned abruptly, startled by her son's arrival before 9:00 a.m. "Mom, I got your shift covered today! You get the day off all to yourself," he announced grabbing her in a deep bear hug. "I know you got all that bread baked and ready to go already. Could smell it half way down the road. Besides, Dad said you've been talking about taking a day to go to the mall for a 'color bath.'" A color bath was the name they used to describe a therapeutic session where all the bright colors, lights, and sounds helped release endorphins in the brain, causing a little harmony and equilibrium to replace stress … at least for a little while. "Why don't you drive on over to that outlet mall you love so much in St. Pete?"

"Son, I can't breathe," she half-groaned releasing herself from his grip. "What's going on?" she demanded.

"You need a day to yourself. I need you to leave. Seems like those two things work out quite nicely, now doesn't it?"

"My birthday isn't until Friday, remember? You came home early and that was the best gift ever, so please don't go spending your money on anything else for me."

"Well, it's not for your birthday. It's for Valentine's Day for the whole place. Geesh! You're so self-centered!" he teased. "And, you are not to return until three o'clock. Is that clear?"

Intrigued, she relented, grabbed her purse, kissed her son and walked off to enjoy her first vacation day in over three years. "This better be good!" she called back exiting through the back door.

"Oh it will be," he whispered to himself.

***

The delivery crew arrived exactly at 11:00 a.m., just as Landon sat down to his regular lunch of PBJ and chips in the front window. He and all the other patrons were enthralled as the men quickly rolled the upright baby-grand piano into the dining room. "Where ya want it?" chomped out one man while slurping a large wad of gum.

"Over there," Radmund replied, pointing to the perfect place he and Henry chose. It was just a bit off-centered, to the left of the floor-to-ceiling fireplace. The perfect location – not in the middle of everything, but not back in a corner either. Two support columns stood in that spot, making it impossible for a table with more than one guest to remain there, so the area just sat starkly empty compared to the rest of the room designed around the strategic placement of the other tables. "It's perfect for the width of the piano. The bench can go right here," he pointed to the space between the two columns. "And, since it's an upright, it won't take up too much floor space beyond the columns."

"Plus," Henry added, "this will be the best spot for acoustics, I think." He looked at his son, then couldn't help but give him a huge bear hug. "Son, your mother is going to love this idea!"

"I know, right?" he acknowledged in pride. "She's kept this thing sparkling white all these years! And listen to that tone," he added as the tuner began his work. "Hardly needs any tuning at all as far as I can tell."

"After your grandparents died in the car accident, this was all she wanted. It's priceless as far as she's concerned. You know she sits at it sometimes and makes the most horrible racket, pretending she's in Carnegie Hall." They both laughed at memories of Delia's failed attempts with piano lessons. "Do not tell your mother I said that!" he commanded. "Besides," Henry continued, "it's like a portal to her parents."

Radmund stood in reflection a moment as the tuner worked on the bridge under the soundboard of the artistic vintage Chauncey. "It's kinda weird, Dad. I can clearly hear Grandma and Grandpa pounding out those songs in perfect rhythm. But I can't see their faces in my memories, no matter how hard I try."

Henry smiled at his own thoughts. "You were only four when they died. I'm not surprised you remember the sounds, though. Whenever we couldn't get you to sleep, we'd either go to their house or just call them and they'd sit there together and play something until you were out cold."

"Why didn't I ever take lessons?" Radmund asked.

Laughing out loud, Henry replied, "Oh we tried. We desperately wanted you to learn, but you stomped your little foot and defied us every time we took you to a lesson. 'I want to play football, not piano!' you declared pounding your little eight-year-old fists on the keys." He paused looking at his son, "Then, not so funny … now, hysterical!"

"I'm sorry. I wish I could play now," Rad admitted with regret for his youthful obstinance.

Raising his head from under the soundboard, the tuner noted, "Well, this baby is solid! She's been tuned regularly in the past so hardly a string out of place even with the move. You got yourself a nice instrument here," he concluded putting away his precision tools. Henry shook his hand as Radmund wrote the check for final payment of the delivery and tuning.

Radmund escorted the crew back to their truck, thanking them for being available on such short notice. Upon his return, he noticed the train clock. "It's only noon," he muttered in disappointment. "We have to wait three more hours for her to get here."

"Is she really as good as you described?" Henry asked.

"Better," Radmund affirmed.

"Well, then, I guess you can pass the time by covering your mother's shift like you promised," teased his father as the train whistle blew in the distance.

***

Allison and their special guest arrived at 2:30 p.m. as if on cue. "Wow!" she exclaimed walking through the front door to eye the glistening white in the back of the room. "It is perfect right there!" Turning Landon's attention to the piano, she said, "Look at that!"

"It's a piano," he offered as if there had been a question.

"Miss Goldie, welcome to The Whistle Stop." Allison beamed extending her arm so the two could find their way to a table near the piano. Goldie's guide dog strolled faithfully at her side. Only a handful of customers remained at the late afternoon hour, mostly out of curiosity at the blind lady, her guide dog, and the piano.

It was the first time Goldie ventured anywhere that far from her apartment since driving was not an option. Walking with a guide dog, however, she was able to go nearly everywhere she needed. Like Allison, she chose to live in the Villages for their walking proximity to so many needs and wants. Finally reaching the piano, her dog lay down at his owner's feet. "Good boy, Buddy," she praised patting his head.

"See! I told you Buddy is a dog's name," Landon exclaimed pulling out his own chair at the table. The comment held such emotion that both Allison and Radmund sat frozen for a moment. Then, simultaneously cracked up. "It's not funny," Landon demanded.

"Did my dog do something?" Goldie asked in confusion.

"Oh no, Miss Goldie," Allison replied. As Allison finished explaining the inside joke to Goldie, their anticipated Guest of Honor strolled in the front door visibly relaxed due to her leisurely color bath – several bags in tow.

In a moment of realization, all her bags dropped abruptly to the floor. Her mouth fell open in shock, but no words escaped. Henry rushed to his wife's side, picking up the bags and setting them in the front corner window by Landon's toys. Radmund moved quickly to his mother's other side, taking her hand and leading the way to the family heirloom. "What is going on here?" she gasped.

"Happy early ValBirthentine Day Mom!" Radmund wrapped his arms around his mother as she stood motionless, arms dangling at her sides. Henry returned to join the hug while Allison sat by Goldie narrating the events unfolding moment by moment.

"Dad said you've been wishing you could move this here for over a year. I just happened to have some old school friends in the piano-moving business now. So, *whola*," he waved his arms magically, "wish granted!"

Henry chimed in, "And I believe Allison has a bonus gift for you darling." Turning to Miss Goldie and Allison, he said, "Allison, you're up!"

"Well, Delia, I know how much you talk about this piano and you wish you could hear it like when your folks used to play. I'd like you to meet my neighbor, Miss Goldie. She is the best pianist I've ever heard." Right on cue, Goldie stood to her feet, extended her hand outward, and waited for Delia's touch to complete the greeting.

As dear friends might do, Goldie reached her other hand to cover Delia's as they shook. "My dear. I've heard all about you and this piano. And, frankly, I've been anxiously waiting to give it a try if you don't mind." Still speechless, Delia nodded her head not yet registering her new friend's disability. Allison escorted Goldie to the piano bench while Buddy remained slumbering on the floor at the nearby table. "A little birdie told me this was one of your favorites," Goldie introduced as she intricately fingered the keys in perfect rhythm.

Delia sat motionless. "Here you go sweetheart. Looks like you might need something to wet that dry throat," Henry chuckled offering a glass of fresh lemonade. After gulping half the glass, she nodded in agreement, then sat back, eyes closed, savoring every measure of *How Great Thou Art*. The notes floated off the soundboard and resonated through every square inch of the restaurant. Delia was certain the Heavenly choir would descend at any moment to harmonize with music so extraordinary. The few guests who'd postponed their departure were greatly rewarded for their patience as they were immediately taken aback by the concert.

Ringing the high octave chord to signify the ending, Miss Goldie turned in the direction she believed Allison to be. "Allison?"

She quickly moved to the piano touching Goldie's hand. "Yes Ma'am. I'm right here."

"Sweetie, would you sing with me this time like you did the other day when you and Landon visited? It was so lovely."

Allison nearly fell backward. "Oh, Miss Goldie. I ... I ... no way," she blushed crimson red. Then she whispered in her ear, "Not here in front of everyone. That was just for you and Landon."

"What's this?" Radmund jumped to the chance. "You can sing? I definitely want to hear this!"

Henry sat next to his wife and chimed in, "Me too! You been holdin' out on us, huh?" Delia nodded vigorously.

"No, really. I'm not good. It was just for fun." She turned to Radmund who moved by her side, egging her on. "Please don't make me do this."

"Momma, you sing to me every night. I like it." There was no way she could turn down that adorable face, even though he was simply making a statement, not a plea.

"Fine. But don't laugh." Turning to Goldie, she asked, "Shall we do *Amazing Grace*, Miss Goldie?"

Delia clapped her hands with excitement finally forcing out a few words. "Oh that's my other favorite!" Radmund sat in the only empty chair at the table with his parents as the performance began. Landon shuffled over to Delia and climbed into her lap. Allison closed her eyes and began singing as Goldie masterfully wove the notes together in perfect synchronization.

"Amazing grace, how sweet the sound that saved a wretch like me."

Yep, there's the Heavenly choir, Delia thought to herself.

"I once was lost but now I'm found. 'Twas blind but now I see." By the time Allison began the second verse, she was completely enveloped in the song, unaware she and Goldie had mesmerized an entire restaurant. Not even chewing continued, even though the special of the day was a town favorite – On-The-Tracks BLT Salad.

Normal closing time came and went that day in order to accommodate the five remaining requests from entranced patrons. By 4:30 p.m. Delia reluctantly said 'good-bye' to the last customer and locked the front doors. "This is truly the most amazing gift you guys have ever given me!" she exclaimed falling exhausted into a nearby chair. Goldie grabbed hold of Buddy's harness and carefully ambled her way through the new environment to sit near Delia's voice.

"Miss Delia, this has been a highlight for me also!" she chimed in. "I haven't had that much fun in over five years now. Since I lost my Paul."

"Then, this is one of those gifts that just keeps on giving!" Henry contributed. "Would you consider playing here on a regular basis, Miss Goldie?"

Goldie's smile personified her name, radiating throughout the room. "Why, I'd be honored!"

"Of course, we'll pay you for your time," Delia nodded enthusiastically.

"No need for that my dear," Goldie waved off the offer. "I'd much prefer some of your home cooking. I hear you're the best cook this side of Tampa!"

Delia blushed at the compliment, then glanced at her extended family sitting nearby. "I think your sources might be a bit biased, Miss Goldie. But you would be welcome to stop by and eat whenever and whatever you like."

Radmund and Allison glowed at the success of their plan. "What about right now?" Radmund spoke up quickly. "Seems like the perfect time for one of your huge family dinners, Mom."

As if on cue, Allison jumped to take over. "However, this time you sit and relax while we get things ready!" She motioned for Radmund and Landon to join her in the kitchen. Delia, Henry, and Goldie happily sat back to relax and cherish the joyous moment when God brings fresh blessings and new friends into your life.

Miss Goldie

Landon licked his lips after consuming the last bite of super-crispy Southern-Fried Chicken – a recipe his own mother had perfected thanks to the years working with her mentor. "Momma, you make good chicken," he commented setting the leg bone on his plate to wipe his mouth.

"I must agree with this young man," Goldie agreed wiping her own mouth free of chicken crumbs. "And, Miss Delia, my sources did not do justice describing the spices and flavors you masterfully weave into this world-famous potato salad!"

Embarrassed by the attention, Delia changed the subject immediately. "Miss Goldie, if you don't mind, we have a tradition of sharing stories here at the Whistle Stop. Would you mind telling us a little about your life? I'm not prying or anything. You just seem like a fascinating woman. And, I've learned that women with your sparkle usually have an amazing story," she concluded.

While the others shoveled remaining morsels of chicken, potato salad, and fresh-picked green beans, Goldie took her place in the rocker and gladly reflected on her life. "Well, first of all, thank you for asking. I have truly been blessed by God," she began. "And, you know, while it isn't all roses, I thank God because I know that He never gives more than we can bear. But, those blessings He pours out on us, oh those make it all worthwhile! Like meeting each of you and playing that extraordinary instrument! I haven't played for anyone outside of my home since my husband passed on to Heaven.

"I used to play piano in church, many years ago. Paul and I led the singing every Sunday morning. Oh, he had such a lovely voice!" She emphasized the point by patting her knee, then turned to Allison, "Like you do my dear. Such a sweet sound!" Allison lowered her head, blushing.

"Back then, I still had my eyesight. But I never used sheet music anyway. I learned to play by ear when I was a little girl, listening to my mother play every night after dinner was cleaned up. Most of the time, my dad would get out his violin and fiddle along with Mother. We'd all end up singing together for what seemed like hours."

Because he'd been sitting so quietly, Goldie wasn't sure which way to turn to find Landon. "Landon, sweetheart. Where are you?" she asked holding out her hand. Allison nudged her son toward the elderly woman. "There you are. Landon, do you like television?" she asked. He nodded slightly.

"Landon, remember, Miss Goldie can't see you. You have to speak your answer to her," Allison prompted.

Landon looked her direction, but not directly up at the old woman. "I like *Myth Busters* and the *Discovery Channel*, but Momma only lets me watch it one hour each night." Everyone except Landon laughed. To him, gadgets and technology were fascinating, not funny.

"Well, when I was your age we didn't have any TV at all! But we had our music. And we had each other. When Paul and I first met, my folks were thrilled to have a real singer join the fun." She paused a moment basking in her memories. "Oh he could croon out a tune like nobody! Right after he met Paul, my father was certain Paul and I would be married someday. But it would be two more years, when I was 18 and he was 20, before I was ready to say 'I do'. January 9, 1950." She closed her eyes a moment as a small tear rolled down her cheek.

"I grew up in Benton, Tennessee. Oh it was such a sweet little town," she paused in retrospect. "Rustic … that's how you would describe it today. But after Paul and I married, we bought a lovely little farm near Dayton, Tennessee. Paul started his studies in theology at Bryan College. After he graduated, they hired him to work as an Assistant Professor. He was so good and teaching those young men and women about God. Then, on Sundays we would lead the singing at the university chapel."

"He must have been a very Godly man," Delia noted with a wink at her own husband. "You just glow when you talk about him."

Goldie confirmed, "He was my soul mate. Lost him five years ago, rest his soul." She paused as if a moment of silence were always appropriate when pondering his death, then picked up the story. "I'm not sure if God only has one person in mind for each of us or not, but I know that my Paul was a most precious gift. We had 57 glorious years together, and I wouldn't trade one moment of it for anything in the world."

"Do you have any children, Miss Goldie?" Allison asked.

"My yes we do! You might say we were 'prolific' in that department," she giggled. "We had nine children by our twelfth wedding anniversary! The twins were our first-born – Martha and Steven. We thought it was pretty funny that God gave us two babies exactly on our second anniversary!

"Then, I popped out four more within the next seven years – Rachel, Jonathan, David, and Lydia. Some days those children kept me so busy I would escape to the chicken coop just for some quiet time to study the Bible! But we loved children so much that it didn't matter how many diapers I had to change in a day. God must have known because he just kept blessing us with more children. I got pregnant with another set of twins only six months after Lydia was born." A quiet sadness returned to her voice at that point.

"I didn't know I'd contracted histoplasmosis until after about two months. By then, it was difficult to treat the virus and not harm the babies. But, it was too dangerous for me to go without any treatment. So, when my labor started twelve weeks early, we knew something was wrong." She lowered her head as Delia held her hand in comfort. "Joseph was stillborn. James was born alive, but he was too little and weak to survive on his own. We lost him the next day." Tears streamed down her wrinkled 80-year-old cheeks.

"And, that horrible virus didn't just take my babies from me. The trauma of the whole thing caused me to have a retinal detachment right after the babies were born. Took away my eyesight in the left eye."

Radmund placed a Kleenex in Goldie's hand as Delia and Allison grabbed one for themselves. "Here you go Miss Goldie," he said. "The box is on your right if you need more."

"Thank you Sweetie," she muttered. After a sip of iced-tea and one more dab of the eyes, she continued. "But, anyway, you know how I said God was so good to us? Well a year after the twins died, God surprised us with Peter. We were afraid to have any more children due to the retinal concerns for my other eye, but God knew it would be okay. Peter brought a whole lot of excitement to that house, let me tell you! Maybe 'raucous' is a better way to describe that child! Thank goodness the twins were old enough to help out or I think we would have just given up. That one child caused more trouble in his first five years than all my other kids together. My mom came to live with us that first summer just to help out. Paul's summer schedule was lighter since classes were cut back then, so between the three of us and the twins, we survived. But it was only by God's grace that we made it without shipping that boy off to boarding school!"

"Miss Goldie," Henry interjected. "If you don't mind my asking, how did you lose eyesight in your other eye?"

"Oh yes. That was another of God's blessings in disguise. Twenty years later, just after I turned 50, I had another terrible issue with my right eye. It's called giant cell arteritis, which is how I ended up totally blind. But, I don't mean to complain. After all, God gave me 50 years to enjoy this amazing world He created. And now, I have the most vivid memories of everything, and an amazing sense of hearing for an old woman! Better than all of you, I bet!" A few laughs forced their way into the room, slightly alleviating the mood. But Goldie quieted for a moment. "See, I stopped playing the piano after the twins died and I lost my left eye. Didn't think I could do it anymore, which was just me pouting mostly. But something about going totally blind got my rump back in gear … so to speak," she grinned. "That piano was calling my name every day. So, one day I just sat down and started banging out old hymns. It was my therapy. The kids would gather around and sing along with Paul and me. I guess it was God's way of showing me that eyesight is not what makes a person happy. It's the love of your family." She waved her arm to gesture those in the room. "And you people clearly have that love also. I can see it in my heart. I am truly blessed to be here with you today!"

"Miss Goldie, that's amazing. I bet you were a fabulous mother," Allison said as she checked on her own little prodigy.

"Thank you my dear, but I'm sure I made plenty of mistakes. Oh there were so many problems those kids caused me; it's a wonder I didn't lose my religion! But those are stories for another day. This one is getting late and I'm suddenly very tired. Must be recalling all those births!" she laughed.

"Of course. We should get you home then," Radmund invited. "Thank you for spending your afternoon and evening with us! I knew this would be a great gift for my mom, but it appears," he began looking around the room, "that every one of us has been blessed by your presence."

"Before we go, though, I have a request for you all," she said grabbing Buddy's harness and working her way back to the piano. "I'm not sure why God allowed me to lose so much in life, but I'm certain that He is in control and blesses my life richly every single day. And I know I am a rich woman because of what God has helped me through. Today I still have seven wonderful children who are all happily married, eighteen grandchildren, and I'm about to be Great-Grandma for the fifteenth time! Now don't get me wrong. Sometimes it still hurts to think about what I've lost in life. But I've learned to cherish the happy memories and not dwell on the sad stuff." She began fingering a tune on the baby grand.

"I heard this beautiful song a few weeks ago and had to learn it." Not sure where everyone was seated anymore, she directed the question into the air above the piano, "Allison, do you know the song *10,000 Reasons* by Matt Redman?"

"Of course I do! It's one of my favorites!" Allison said jumping to join her friend at the piano. "And, I'm certain everyone here knows it also. We sang it at church yesterday. And, I do recall a certain tenor and his wife belting it out with rather nice harmony." She grinned looking at Henry and Delia.

"Excellent, then would you all do me the honor of singing together as we praise God for the memories and blessings He gives so abundantly?" Together, they moved around the piano and raised their voices to Heaven in ultimate gratitude for all that happened that day and all days before and yet to come.

Bless the Lord, O my soul
O my soul
Worship His holy name
Sing like never before
O my soul
I'll worship Your holy name

The sun comes up, it's a new day dawning
It's time to sing Your song again
Whatever may pass, and whatever lies before me
Let me be singing when the evening comes

Bless the Lord, O my soul
O my soul
Worship His holy name
Sing like never before
O my soul
I'll worship Your holy name

For a moment, Henry and Delia completely forgot about a surgery scheduled just about a month hence. Radmund couldn't take his eyes off Allison as she poured out her heart in music. Allison smiled broadly when she noticed that even Landon had joined in the celebration by the last chorus. And Goldie knew that, once again, God had reinvigorated her life just when she needed Him most. Shekinah – the glory of God – truly reigned down upon The Whistle Stop that day.

Valentine's Day

By Friday, nearly everyone in town had heard of the musical addition to The Whistle Stop. Miss Goldie began showing up around 10:30 a.m. to entertain the lunch crowd. Radmund picked her up every day. Other apartment renters began to gossip about the handsome red-head and elderly woman walking arm-in-arm to his car each morning. Buddy even resorted to following instead of leading during that time. Once at the restaurant, Radmund then made it a habit to hang out with Landon during lunch and play with the trains or other toys for awhile afterward. Allison often wondered who the real child was as she observed the two in the front window clanging tops, battling transformers, or chug-chugging with the trains.

Delia always made sure to feed Goldie and send home plenty of extras as compensation since she refused to accept a nickel for her performances. She would not even allow a tip jar to be placed on the piano. "God gave me this gift," she said adamantly. "That's far greater than any money you could offer! No offense." Henry and Delia chuckled at her defiance, but respected her feelings enough not to ask again.

Soon after the doors opened that morning, Owen and Louella hopped off the train for their weekly fix of coffee, company, and great food. "Happy Valentine's Day! And welcome to the new-and-improved Whistle Stop," Delia remarked in grandeur as she regally waved her arm motioning their attention to the rear of the restaurant.

"Well, what have we here?" Louella asked intrigued.

"That is my parents' old artistic vintage Chauncey baby grand piano," she beamed with pride. "Radmund and Allison had it moved here to surprise me for my birthday."

Owen walked right to the piano and began picking out *Chopsticks* using only the pointer finger on each hand. "Need a player?" he asked. "I'm pretty good you know."

"Owen, the only piano you've ever played is that little Fisher Price toy you got Elijah this year for Christmas. And even his banging was better than you!" Louella said, quickly nudging her husband away from the instrument. "Don't break it!"

The front door bell rang as Miss Goldie and Radmund ambled in, as if on cue. "Besides," Delia commented walking up to guide Goldie over to meet the Travis', "we have a piano player." Radmund released his charge, waved at the Travis', and then moved quickly to conspire with Henry and Allison in the kitchen. Delia continued, "Miss Goldie, I'd like you to meet our favorite Whistle Stop regulars – Owen and Louella Travis. Owen and Louella, this is Miss Goldie, the best piano player you will ever meet in your life!" Goldie extended both hands as her two new friends each eagerly took hold of one and greeted her.

"Miss Goldie, it is an honor to meet you," Louella said.

Owen reiterated, "Very nice to meet you. I guess this means I don't get the job, huh?" He grinned at Delia.

After a moment, Goldie excused herself and easily found the way to the piano. Despite her age, Goldie learned to compensate for her lack of vision by using her incredible memory to "visualize" her surroundings from touch and sound. Generally it only took one visit for her to find her way around a place with little help from Buddy. However, he was always by her side just in case. Before she sat down, Goldie addressed the restaurant, already full due to the holiday. "Ladies and Gentlemen, today is Miss Delia Edmond's birthday, and we have prepared a little concert in her honor. Allison, Henry, Radmund … are you ready?" Delia stared in amazement, then in horror, at the thought of her husband joining the trio.

"We're all here," Allison grinned waltzing up to the piano and waving hello to the Travis' at the same time. "You ready you guys?" she turned addressing Henry and Radmund.

"You know we are. Let's get this party started!" the two men responded in unison. With a kick in her spirit, and the word from her singers, Goldie began pounding out *Fever* as Henry led the group in a rousing, but often off-key, rendition of Peggy Lee's hit. Luckily, Goldie's piano forte rose above Henry's solo.

> *Never know how much I love you*
> *Never know how much I care*
> *When you put your arms around me*
> *I get a fever that's so hard to bear*

Delia stood nearby, stunned at her husband's outing of courage and wishing it had not manifested itself in such a public way. But, when Henry dramatically broke out into the chorus, mixed with a little impromptu dance with his still-stunned wife, she couldn't help but throw her dishtowel on the counter and jump into the action – singing and dancing as if they were teenagers again. Allison and Radmund snapped in time, occasionally offering a background harmony on the word "fever." Several of the guests even started singing and joined in the cavorting.

> *You give me fever, when you kiss me*
> *Fever when you hold me tight*
> *Fever in the mornin', a fever all through the night*

Finally, Henry danced Delia toward the counter as the song ended. Delia collapsed, leaning on the end of the counter, while Henry poured each of them a glass of water, as Allison retook her place by the piano. "Delia, in case you haven't figured it out yet, we've put together a few songs that have transformed you through life," she explained.

"Oh, please tell me you're singing this time," Delia pleaded in jest.

"Yep, just me. But get a good drink of water because Radmund has a request for you on this one." She paused as Radmund gallantly approached his mother, hand extended in formal gesture. When he signaled ready, Allison asked rhetorically, "Miss Goldie, I got *Georgia on My Mind*. What about you?" Goldie nodded in full agreement and began picking out the beautiful ballad.

"May I have this dance?" Radmund requested as his mother stood in immediate acceptance of the invitation.

> *Other arms reach out to me*
> *Other eyes smile tenderly*
> *Still in the peaceful dreams I see*
> *The road leads back to you*

Waltzing around the dining room, she was entranced in cherished memories of the days a little girl danced with her father's arms around her; the sweet smell of his cologne wafted through her senses; his soft sing-along echoed sweetly in her ears.

"Just an old sweet song, keeps Georgia on my mind." Allison sang softly as the song ended, much to the chagrin of everyone in the room. Radmund bowed thanking his mother for the dance. She hugged him intensely, tears pouring down her cheeks. The entire dining room stood in ovation for the song and dancers.

After a moment to regain his own composure, Radmund announced, "Now, we all know you are a huge Beatles fan." He grinned knowingly at his father. "And considering everything you've been through these last few weeks, we thought this one would be a great way to celebrate your birthday … and many more to come!" He emphasized the last phrase, his mother in full understanding of the implication and hope in his tone. Then, he nodded for Allison to continue.

Allison motioned for Landon to meet her at the piano. He reluctantly obeyed. "I think Landon might even help me with this one," she stated, looking into his eyes begging for cooperation.

He nodded, "I know my part."

"Great!" she exclaimed hugging him and lifting him to stand alongside Miss Goldie on the piano bench. "Look, Miss Goldie! *Here Comes the Sun*!" she declared pointing out the window to the typical Florida sunny day.

"Cordelia, it's been a long cold lonely winter. Oh Delia, it feels like years since it's been here. Here comes the sun. Here comes the sun, and I say. It's all right," Allison began singing softly and grinning at Radmund acknowledging their teamed cleverness in modifying the lyrics. "Oh Delia, the smiles returning to the faces. Cordelia, it seems like years since it's been here."

"But look!" she spoke, then continued singing, "Here comes the sun. Here comes the sun, and I say, It's all right." Hugging her little boy, she rallied, "Take it away Landon!"

Too bashful to look up, but determined to please his mother, Landon softly began the chorus in his own monotone key, "Sun, sun, sun, here it comes. Sun, sun, sun, here it comes. Sun, sun, sun, here it comes." The end of the song brought another rousing standing ovation from the audience. Delia jumped to her feet, hugging Landon and Allison.

"Thank you so much! Landon, that was awesome. It was the best birthday present you could ever give me!" she declared, causing him to turn rigid at such attention.

"You're welcome," he stated simply as his mother helped him down from the bench. He quickly retreated to the comfort of his front window still uncertain as to why his help was needed or even appreciated.

Allison called Radmund and Henry back to the piano. "We have one more song for you," they chimed in together.

"Oh great," Delia laughed. "Couldn't you just leave it with the last one, you know … when it was *beautiful*." Radmund and Henry feigned hurt.

"And, we'd love it if all of you would join us as well," Miss Goldie announced standing momentarily behind the piano. "Since Delia is such a Beatles fan, we thought this version of *Happy Birthday* to be the best way to top off our little concerto." Together the trio, all the patrons, and even an infrequent howl from Buddy sang *They Say It's Your Birthday*. As the song began, two other servers emerged from the kitchen with a full sheet cake decorated with roses, proper lettering, and 48 candles in all the primary colors. A ceremonious parade through the crowd ended with the cake mounted on a huge cake platter displayed for all to see on the center of the front counter bar.

"Blow them out, honey," Henry urged, "before the smoke alarms go off!" Delia elbowed her husband then blew three times to get all the candles. "Okay. We have red velvet or white cake. Everybody gets a piece if you like." The servers began cutting pieces as Henry, Radmund, and Allison delivered to all the guests.

"Well, we thought we would celebrate a nice, romantic Valentine's Day here," Owen teased as they prepared to leave two hours later. "Didn't know we'd end up stuck in the middle of some noisy party for an old lady."

Louella blushed, even though she was used to her husband's taunting. "Owen!" Turning to her friend, she apologized. "Delia you look absolutely beautiful. Ignore him."

"Louella, if he didn't joke, I'd think he was ill," Delia antagonized in return. "This was the best birthday I've ever had!" she declared. "I'm so happy you chose to be here today and share it with me. Did you know?"

"It's possible a little birdie emailed me a note," Louella admitted.

"Would that little birdie be named Allison?"

"Perhaps. But we had no idea about Goldie or the piano. She is a gem, and a fabulous pianist! She reminds me of my own mother in so many ways," Louella smiled thinking back to her childhood days. The train whistle signaled her back to the moment, forcing the friends to bid adieu once more with lightened hearts and heavy stomachs.

***

As they cleaned up the restaurant that afternoon, Radmund asked for a moment alone with Allison. Henry obliged by distracting Landon at the #249 for awhile. Delia and Goldie sat near the piano chatting on and on comparing stories about their children.

"Hey Allison, you got a minute?" Radmund asked grabbing a rag to help her finish wiping down the counter. "I wanted to give you something for Valentine's Day," he noted handing her a rectangular shoe box wrapped in a red ribbon.

Suddenly reminded of the Christmas a few years back, Allison became frustrated. "Radmund, you know I don't want you to get me gifts. It makes me feel awkward and I don't have anything for you."

"Get over that will you? If a person wants to give you a gift, they want to give you a gift! It's not because I want anything back. In fact, I want to give you this because it makes me feel good too. So, if you get all funny about it, then you make me feel bad. We wouldn't want that now, would we?" He was only half-teasing.

"I suppose not," she admitted feeling guilty for her social ineptness. *Maybe Landon comes by it naturally*, she thought. "Chocolate-covered strawberries," she giggled opening the gift. "And I thought it was something unusual." She was surprised at her own disappointment.

"Oh, those are just because I needed an excuse to steal some from Mom's stash … for myself," he kidded grabbing a strawberry from the box. "The real gift is below." He began slurping the chocolate off the berry as Allison uncovered a brochure at the bottom of the box.

"It's a brochure. How sweet," she teased. "Get it? 'Sweet'?"

"Duh," he responded trying to sound offended. "That was so obvious!" Then, he opened the brochure and handed it to her, pointing at the important information. "This is actually a gift for both of us. So, see, you're kind of giving me something anyway. There's this conference at church next Saturday night. It's called 'The Silver Ring Thing.' It's all about purity and saving yourself for marriage. I really want to go, and I'd like you to go with me. Just as friends, of course."

Her defenses went into full rage as she shoved the brochure back at him. "I heard them announce this last week. You think I should go to a purity conference?" Her volume rose with every word. "Is this some sick joke? Because I'm not finding it funny at all."

"What? Of course not," he stammered, taken off guard by her sudden animosity. "You know, in God's eyes, you're as pure as the day He created you. Why not celebrate that? And, after what you've been through, I thought you would like the idea. I just think this conference is a cool way to promise to keep that purity. It's the greatest gift we can give to our future spouses. God designed it that way." He cautiously took her hand in his. "I'm so sorry to have upset you."

Taking a deep breath, she responded, "Rad, you really are a good friend. I guess I'm just still really defensive. It has nothing to do with you. May I see that again, please?" She carefully reviewed the brochure after he cautiously handed it back. "I have to admit, it did catch my attention. I like the idea of thinking of it as a celebration." She looked back up at him and grinned. "We'll probably be the elders in the group. According to this photo," she pointed to the crowd pictured in the brochure, "the average age is a few years younger than us."

A smile slowly spread across his face, relieved to see the tension between them lifting. "I don't think anyone cares about age at this conference. Besides, you might look old, but I'm still confused for sixteen all the time!"

"In your dreams," she joked in response. "Okay, I'll go with you. Thanks." With that she hugged him before moving on to the kitchen to finish putting things away for the night. He should be thrilled, he knew. But it was obvious she accepted the invitation just as he offered – friends and nothing more.

That Sunday brought with it Allison's turn to give Radmund a gift. After church they all gathered at Cordelia and Henry's house for a family-style pot-roast – Henry's specialty which he happily made every Sunday to ensure his wife did no cooking at least one day a week. When they'd all eaten in abundance, Allison offered Radmund an envelope simply addressed: *To Rad, my best friend. I'm sorry for letting the scars of my past interfere sometimes. Love, Allison*

"Well, open it!" his mother demanded feigning curiosity. "This family is getting really good at conspiracy," she'd told her husband the evening before, just after Allison secretly met with them to divulge her plan and get their cooperation.

Radmund anxiously slit open the envelope to reveal a two-page, double-sided contract, single-spaced in ten-point font. Squinting to read it carefully, he broke out into a wide grin. "You got me an apartment? However will you afford that, my dear?" he teased Allison hugging her in gratitude. He'd made no secret about his desire to rent an apartment at the Villages, ever since his first tour of her place. But, when he checked only two weeks earlier, the landlord regretted to inform him they had no vacancies.

"I was in the office paying my rent Saturday morning when another resident stopped by to turn in his keys. The landlord told me the guy had just given them notice on Wednesday. He got some awesome job transfer to Tampa and had to move right away. Naturally I thought you might want the space. But, it's only one building over from where we live, so I can understand if you want to wait for something on the other side of the complex to open." She was baiting him.

"That does present a problem," he replied sarcastically. "Yet, it's such a great deal. I think this might become the best bachelor pad in Plant City!"

His mother joined in the fun. "Darling, you will not have any wild parties there. Look here," she pointed to the lease. "It's against the rules. You could get kicked out for making too much noise, and we will not have you moving back in with us if that happens!" Delia winked at her compatriots.

Henry handed his son another paper for consideration. "You need to check out this last contract, son. It could be a deal-breaker, I'm afraid," he snickered.

Reading it carefully, Radmund cracked up laughing. "Contract between Lessee and Parents," he began aloud for all to enjoy. "By signing this contract, the Parents agree to help the Lessee move all of his belongings to the new apartment. The Lessee agrees to move ALL of his belongings to the apartment, leaving none of his toys, furniture, clothing, or other sundries behind. If this contract is fulfilled by the 17th of February (two days hence), the Parents also agree to help the Lessee clean and organize his new apartment and leave Lessee with a fully-stocked refrigerator."

"Think carefully, son. By signing that contract, you are bound by the Edmunds' law to get all your crap out of our house!" Henry then further provoked his son by shoving an ink pen in his hand and pushing him to sign the contract immediately.

"Gee Dad, I kinda feel like you guys don't want me around anymore," Radmund forced his best pouty face. Landon looked at him, clearly confused. Noticing his young friend's concern, Radmund whispered in his ear, "I'm just kidding."

"Are they making you leave again?" Landon queried.

Delia picked him up and snuggled him close to her, which he only tolerated from her and his mother. "No Landon. We're just teasing. Rad is going to move to an apartment near you and your momma! Isn't that exciting?"

Landon looked over at his mother, then at Radmund. "Can we go play at the park more when you move?"

"You bet Sport! And, you can teach me how to work those magnetic tops you love so much while I teach you how to toss a Frisbee and build a humongous fort with my Lego kits." He winked at Allison who shook her head in dismay.

"Are you sure he can't leave his toys here?" Allison begged Henry and Delia.

Apologies and Commitments

The Whistle Stop closed early that Tuesday to give the family time for the big move. A sign on the door read, "Closed early today because we are kicking our son out of the house. If you are parents of an adult, we're sure you'll understand."

Delia organized all of his kitchenware and pantry items into categories, feeling compelled to fulfill her motherly duties. What he didn't have, she and Henry gladly donated, using him as an excuse to clean out their extras. By 8:00 p.m. that Tuesday, the only thing Radmund needed was time. By that Saturday, the night of the conference, Radmund, Allison, and Landon had enjoyed dinner together two more times, once at her place and once in his new space.

She and Landon surprised him with home-made spaghetti and garlic bread on Wednesday as a "Welcome to the Neighborhood" gift. "No classes tonight – cancelled," she noted as they barged in, Landon bearing the foil-wrapped bread and she carrying the steaming pot of pasta that sent spicy aromas of basil and oregano wafting into the air, causing his stomach to instantly emit loud rumblings.

Shortly after dinner, Landon found Radmund's Legos sticking out of a still-packed box. Together, the two boys masterfully constructed a two-foot skyscraper. Admiring his work, Radmund stood up to find Allison nearby enthralled in the playtime. "Hey Allison, I was thinking. If you didn't mind, could Landon come to my place sometimes instead of the co-op during your night classes? I mean until I get a real job that is."

"I'm sure he'd love that!" she concluded from the intensity in his attraction to the new toys. "It's really cool to watch the two of you together. Sometimes frightening, but mostly cool. You guys remind me of when Marc and I would play together as kids. We always had to use his toys because he refused to play with dolls!"

On cue, but without looking up, Landon interjected, "Dolls! Yuck!" Allison's eyes glimmered in amusement. Radmund stole a moment's secret stare, enthralled by her radiance.

As Landon destroyed and rebuilt his new-and-improved (but much smaller) skyscraper, Allison told Radmund all about her childhood. Most of the time, though, she talked about her brother and how he was always there for her. "You remind me of my brother," she noted twice, sending those familiar daggers into Radmund's heart. "The two of you are my heroes, really. Even after he went back to med school and I moved here, it was like he instinctively knew when I needed some encouragement and I'd get an email or phone call that night. You've been like that to me ever since you got home." She touched his hand, "Thanks for that." His heart melted.

He surprised her on Friday with more Olde Town pizza. "I had a terrible hankerin' for this stuff again, and I have no willpower. Got this huge pizza on the way home, and realized that was really silly 'cuz you know I can't eat it all by myself. I was hoping you might help me so I don't waste it." *You are a terrible liar*, he thought reprimanding himself.

"Really? You just had a hankerin' that happened to include …" she rummaged through the boxes to reveal a second pizza, "a kid's cheese pizza also huh?" She held up the evidence, glaring at him with that twinkle in her eyes. "Landon," she called out to him, beckoning him from his room, "the delivery boy just brought you some yummy cheese pizza."

"Hey, what about my tip?" he requested. "Seems in order now I think since you just gave away my favorite pizza."

"Yea, well, how's this for a tip. 'If you find yourself in a hole, it's time to stop digging'." Then, unknowingly sweeping him off his feet, she gently laid a hand on his right cheek and gingerly kissed him on the other. As she moved to the kitchen to retrieve utensils and plates, he remained in the doorway a moment, frozen. "What's wrong with you?" she asked returning to set the table.

"Why did you do that?" he asked in all seriousness.

"Well, I figured it was better than eating with our hands like savages. But, you don't have to use a fork if you don't want to," she answered completely oblivious.

"Not that. Why did you just kiss me?"

Allison blushed four shades of red. "I'm so sorry! I didn't even think about it. It's just something I'm used to with Marc. Nothing personal, I promise."

"Could it be personal?" he asked hopefully. "I mean, not with Marc, but with me?" Allison stood silent.

Landon walked in ruining the moment Rad longed to explore further. "He's not a delivery boy, Momma. Hi Rad," Landon stated literally. Then he plunked down at the table and began devouring the pizza reserved for children under 12. Allison and Radmund continued to stand stoic a moment longer before quietly seating themselves to dine on the Olde Town Special. Other than saying grace, little conversation occurred during that meal. It wasn't until Landon moved to the living room for his daily dose of *Mythbusters* that Radmund broke the silence.

"I didn't mean to make you uncomfortable," he finally admitted. "It's just that I think you know how I feel about you. And, well …"

"I wasn't thinking," she interrupted.

"Maybe that's the problem. Maybe you think too much to let yourself feel something."

"Please don't make more out of this than it is," she implored him. "I'm not sure what else I can offer you right now, and I do not want to lead you on when I know my heart isn't ready for a commitment."

"Do me a favor, then, please." He knew he shouldn't ask, but it came out anyway. "Kiss me again and then tell me it means nothing more than friendship."

She motioned for him to whisper, pointing to the little boy only a few feet away engrossed in his favorite television show. "Let's go on the patio please. I don't think he needs to hear this kind of talk."

Once safely removed from listening ears, Radmund made his request again moving closer than her comfort level allowed. "I can't do this," she simply stated backing up. "It's too soon."

"Too soon? It's been almost five years in my book. Just admit it. It's me isn't it? The thought of us dating is repulsive to you because of me. At least be honest and stop blaming an old wound." He didn't mean to offend her, but the red-headed temper got the best of him.

Furious at the implication, she stepped right in his face, and without thinking, kissed him with full intent that time. He wrapped his arms around her waist and happily complied. Then, as suddenly as she initiated the embrace, she backed off. "I'm … I'm … sorry," she stammered backing up to the porch rail post for support. "That was so wrong of me. You just made me so angry insinuating that something is wrong with you and that I'm not capable of actually liking a guy … liking you … oh, you know what I mean."

He was genuinely confused. "I really don't know what to think," he responded. "I would do anything for you, and yet there isn't anything I can do to help you." He thought of all she'd told him about her life so far, then braced himself for the answer, "Is that the first time you've kissed a guy since … since that night?"

She began crying, taken aback at the realization of what she'd just done. "Yes," she sobbed. "I'm an idiot. And tomorrow we're going to some conference on saving yourself for marriage and this is what I do to myself and my best friend."

"Well, first of all, it's not like we just had sex or anything, so stop berating yourself! And, second, that was pretty intense … in a good way I thought." He grinned, gently lifting her chin to look into her eyes. "Did it really mean nothing to you?"

"Rad, I can't pretend. Sometimes I do wish it were more. Really, I do. But I just don't feel that way about you. I kissed you because it was like proving a point or something. That's all." Deep down, though, she began to question why she continued to push him away. "I really need you to be my friend. Could we forget that kiss, please?!"

He promised to try, but he knew he would not forget that kiss or her wish. *Someday I hope your wish comes true,* he thought.

Together, they rejoined Landon for the last minutes of *Mythbusters*. The rest of that evening was filled with conversation on Radmund's childhood. No further mention of the kiss was voiced, but it remained deeply embedded in their thoughts.

***

"Would you like to eat here, after we close, before the conference?" he asked springing into the restaurant the next morning as Allison poured fresh coffee for the counter guests. "My folks are taking Landon home with them, right?"

"Last I heard, the three of them are taking off early to get a couple hours in at the Dinosaur Museum. Then, I believe your father is planning to initiate his new grill with a good old-fashioned BBQ of chicken legs – one of Landon's favorites next to the PBJ." She glanced at the front window to find Landon happily playing with a box of Legos Henry had brought in. "They spoil him like he was their own grandson."

"Can't say as I blame them," he agreed walking from the other end of the counter to where Landon sat playing. "Hey Landon, what's shakin' bacon?" Landon looked up at Radmund and wrinkled his nose.

"I don't like bacon." As usual, Landon was confused by Radmund's colloquialism. Allison laughed as she bent down to explain the phrase to her son. "But, Momma, if he wants to know what I'm doing, why didn't he just say, 'What are you doing?' He uses weird words."

"Yes, sweetheart, but that's because he's a weird man." She stood back up and playfully punched Radmund on the arm. "You know he doesn't understand that stuff. Why do you do that to him?"

"Ouch!" he jokingly complained rubbing his arm. "I'm just trying to help the kid expand his literal mind, that's all."

She pulled him aside, out of earshot and whispered, "I told you. The doctors said we need to be very straight-forward with him. He doesn't get jargon. Remember … autistic?"

"Really? I think you underestimate your son. Check this out," he coaxed. "Hey Sport. What happened the other day when Henry 'lost his train of thought' while we were playing with the trains?"

Landon looked up again. He tilted his head slightly and closed his eyes in purposeful recall. "He didn't lose the trains. He forgot what he wanted to say, like old people do." To Landon, it was simple recall. To Allison, it was a breakthrough. To Radmund, it was pure joy.

"See there! Taught him that myself," he bragged. "Just wish he didn't have to repeat that 'old people' part. Kind of irked my dad with that one, especially since Landon put the two concepts together in his brilliant little memory."

"Yep, that's right. Teaching that boy to speak disrespectfully of his elders; that's what he's doing to your son, Allison," Henry taunted as he rounded the bar from the other side. The three of them were still chiding each other when Cordelia suddenly emerged from the kitchen, covered in white powder. "Honey, are you in there somewhere?" Henry quipped turning his attention to her as she approached them brushing the powder from her cheeks.

"Mom, it's not Halloween yet. What's with your ghostly look?" Radmund teased back.

"It's powdered sugar," she emphasized while tossing a handful at his chest; he futilely attempted to bat away the dust. "I'll have you know the best cooking accident just happened in there. Laurabelle and I were trying to make puppy chow, but we accidentally burnt the chocolate chips, so the consistency was weird. Couldn't bear to throw out the candy, so we got inventive. We mixed the chips with butter and peanut butter, crushed up some Chex cereal and stirred it all together. Finally, we rolled them in balls, then in powdered sugar and put them in the fridge to chill. They are amazing if I say so myself! Here. Try a sample and let me know what you think." She handed each of them a piece of the powdery candy, of which they all happily obliged. Approval was fervently offered in unison along with requests from three of the customers at the counter.

"What are they called?" one counter customer asked ordering a large baggie to go.

"These are the 'WaThump Candy Balls,'" she answered.

"Oh, this has got to be good," Henry laughed. "Tell us. How did you get that name?"

"See, when we spooned out the dough it made this really awesome sucking sound coming off the spoon. Then the dough kind of went 'thump' as it splatted on the cookie sheet. All-in-all, it was sort of a rhythmical sound – wa-thump, wa-thump. Thus, 'WaThump Candy Balls.'"

Henry shook his head. "This is going to be really difficult to describe on the chalkboard."

***

"Now Landon, you mind Cordelia and Henry. And no touching the trains unless Henry is with you." Allison sat with her son giving final directions. "The conference is supposed to be over by nine, so we'll be back in plenty of time to get him before bed," she confirmed with Landon's sitters.

"Allison, we raised one boy already. I'm sure we'll be fine." Delia insisted.

"Besides, it's not like he hasn't stayed with us before," Henry added.

"But it's several hours this time, and over dinner. He's never been away from me that long before." She wrung her hands visibly stressed. It was Landon who finally alleviated her concerns.

"Momma, I'll be good as gold," he said giving Radmund a "thumbs up" at the same time.

"See there! Taught him another one," Radmund proudly proclaimed nodding his head.

"At least it's not insulting to anyone this time," Henry goaded. "Now I believe we have a date with some dinosaurs, young man." He and Delia each took one of Landon's hands and strolled out for the afternoon.

The restaurant cleared out a bit early that day, leaving Allison and Radmund with ample time to enjoy a leisurely dinner together before embarking on to the conference. He purposefully kept the conversation light-hearted with humorous stories about his troop's antics when they got bored hanging out in the desert for days on end. She noticed, and was secretly grateful.

First Baptist Church is the largest Christian venue in Plant City, boasting over 3,000 members. And, true to their reputation, The Silver Ring Thing filled the sanctuary with visitors ranging from early teens to young adults. "Wow! They never fill up like this on Sundays!" she smirked as they made their way into the crowded auditorium. "In case I forget to tell you later," she whispered leaning to Radmund soon after they found their seats, "thanks for tonight. I'm sure it will be wonderful." As the lights dimmed, he prayed she would find it to be so much more.

She sat entranced as various speakers shared their most personal stories about mistakes with a boy/girl friend and the risks of teen pregnancy and sexually transmitted diseases. Finally, a young woman took the stage to speak. Radmund and Allison sat frozen in their seats as she began her story. "When I was 15, my uncle raped me. I was too ashamed to tell anyone until he did it again." Allison immediately took his hand, holding so tightly that Radmund thought his fingers would go numb. The speaker continued to share how that act of incest changed her young life. "I felt like trash. When I finally told my parents, they accused me of lying just to get attention. So, I pushed it to the back of my mind. School was a blur. I started failing my classes. I even started cutting myself and drinking my folks' beer. It all made me feel numb.

"Then one summer day when he knew my parents were at work, my uncle came over and I freaked out. Thankfully, my dad came home early that day, just in time to catch my uncle trying to convince me that we had a 'special' relationship and I was making a big deal out of it because I wasn't mature enough to understand." Tears streamed down the speaker's cheeks. Allison sobbed. "Well, he ended up going to jail for what he did, but I had to tell all about it in court, which was so awful! So one day, I decided to make it all go away. Thankfully, I was too chicken to take more than a few pills. I spent three hours in the bathroom, 'bowing to the porcelain god,' as they say." She paused for strained laughter from a few in the crowd.

"While on my knees, I also begged the real God to make it all go away. But I didn't really believe He was interested in me anymore. I felt like my soul was like my arms, riddled with scars. That was when my best friend invited me to The Silver Ring Thing at her church. They played this song by Johnny Diaz that just bored right into my heart and I knew God had not given up on me. He would forgive me and make me pure again if I trusted Him.

"The first thing I had to do, however, was forgive my uncle for what he did to me. So I started praying for him. Let me tell you, that was tough! Praying for someone you hate is probably the most difficult ... and most faith-building thing you'll ever do. If someone has hurt you, try it. You'll be amazed at how God works in your heart and begins to help you to find mercy for the person. Anyway, here I am eight years later and I know that I am pure in God's eyes. I've been dating an amazing man for a year now. He gave me this beautiful ring at Christmas!" She extended her left hand as the camera focused on her engagement ring. "We're getting married in July, and I will proudly wear a white dress on our wedding day." The audience erupted into thunderous applause and cheers as the young woman radiated, standing there in God's glorious redemption.

"The band is going to play that song for you now. It's called *Scars,*" she concluded. "If you've been hurt by someone, I challenge you this day to put it in your past and start praying that God will help you forgive whoever scarred you. Or maybe you need to forgive yourself for the scars you've allowed at your own hand. Especially never forget, there are no scars God can't heal. And there is nothing He won't forgive!" Her voice rose to emphasize the point. The audience began to applaud once more. And then the song began, sending absolute silence across the entire auditorium.

Praise God we don't have to hide scars
They just strengthen our wounds, and they soften our hearts.
They remind us of where we have been, but not who we are
So praise God, praise God we don't have to hide scars

The entire time, Allison felt as if she were holding her breath. Her heart thumped so loudly in her chest, she was certain Radmund could hear it over the crowd. Releasing his hand, she discovered her own was drenched in sweat. There were other speakers that night. They talked about the sanctity of marriage and God's will for people to save themselves for their spouse. But all Allison could do was pray. Right there, with her best friend, they began begging God to help her forgive her attacker and to help him, wherever he was and whatever he was doing, to confess and seek God's forgiveness as well. She wasn't sure how she could ever really forgive him, but she knew she had to at least try.

When the conference ended, so did their prayer time. "Rad, I was wrong earlier about this being a wonderful evening." She choked out the words.

"Really? I don't understand," he replied, concerned and confused.

"It was life-changing," she affirmed. Shivers rose from his head to toes. "Listen, Rad, I really need to hit the Ladies' Room before the crowd, you know? I'll meet you at the car in a few minutes," she said abruptly turning away and pushing her way through the row of people, disappearing into the aisle crowd.

"Guess she had to go really bad," he commented to the young man Allison shoved out of her way during her hurried exit.

He reached the car at least five minutes before she emerged from the crowd through the front doors. She'd cleaned up the smeared mascara, not that he cared or even noticed. Yet, her eyes still gave away the sentiment pouring from them moments earlier. "Guess there was a big line for the bathroom, huh?" he asked.

"Well, actually, I didn't really have to go. Sorry," she admitted sheepishly. "I needed the excuse to get you something. And for me too."

"I told you, you don't need to get me anything in return. I think what we just shared is the greatest gift of all! Just let that be enough," he pleaded.

But she insisted. "Nope. This is really important. Hold out your hand," she requested gently. He obliged without further question. Carefully, she placed a small silver object in his palm and held up the same item in her other hand. "These are the Silver Rings. I'm going to make this commitment and wear mine until the day I replace it with a wedding band. I got you one too because I'd like to make this commitment with my best friend."

He looked up at the moon and sniffled. "This has been the greatest night of my life," was all he could choke out. Under the radiance of the moon in full Shekinah, they innocently embraced, celebrating a moment in time when their friendship was sealed with a precious vow.

Radmund strolled in the back door around 3:00 p.m. the following Monday. Delia and Henry finished wiping down the front counter just as their son ambled into the dining room, head hung low. "Oh honey, you didn't get the job? I'm so sorry. But, hey, there's lots of places around here that need a good EMT." His mother consoled him, adding a hug for good measure. It was then he began chuckling.

"Not funny!" Henry complained in jest. "You know your mother is fragile right now. Don't do that to her," he demanded.

Delia flicked him with her dishtowel. "Stop that. I'm not fragile. I've got 17 more days before the surgery. I might be a little tender for a few weeks after that, but now I'm strong as an ox!" She turned to her son, hands on her hips. "So, did you get the job or not?"

"Of course I did!" he taunted. "You think they'd pass up on a prime candidate such as *Moi*?" he declared pointing to himself for emphasis on the last word.

"Oh honey, arrogance does not become you," Delia bantered right back. Then being unable to contain her excitement a moment longer, she threw her arms around his neck. "I'm so proud of you!"

Henry shook Radmund's hand. "Brandon Regional **is** extremely lucky to have someone with your talent working on their EMT set!" Then he whispered, "Now don't let that go to your head."

"Now wait, here's the best part of all," Radmund continued his news. "I was kind of hoping not to start until June, to be here and help at the Stop while you recover, Mom."

Before he could finish she interrupted, "Rad! I told you not to let that interfere! I'll be fine and this restaurant will run without me. Besides, the Strawberry Festival starts in four days so I've already hired two new people to help out then." She sneered at her husband, eyes twinkling. "Hopefully no one will scare them away so they'll stay on after the festival. We could use the summer help."

"Mom, let me finish!" He said when he finally managed to get a word in the midst of her rambling. "As I was saying, June. Yea, so after the interview … of which I *blew* them away recounting my many awesome talents … ," his eyes flickered as his parents rolled their own. "… they told me they did want me, but the ambulance service would not be ready to start until … drum roll please …," to make sure of the effect he patted rhythmically on the counter. "June! That's when I knew God was in charge. I didn't even have to ask for the delay. It was already part of the plan."

"It's a good thing God overlooked your attitude!" Henry ribbed.

"There's one drawback though," he confessed with a bit of chagrin tainting the news. "I got word that my request for a delay in the Air Guard summer rotation was denied. They didn't have anything open late summer. But, they were willing to compromise and gave me an earlier time."

Noting the downturn in her son's eyes, Delia sighed. "How much earlier?"

"Tomorrow."

"Tomorrow?!" Allison whimpered from the hall unwittingly walking right into the conversation.

A bit startled at her stealthy appearance, the other three turned abruptly. "Yep, tomorrow," Radmund confirmed. "But it is only for a couple of weeks. And, it's just over in Orlando. It'll be here and over before we know it." He turned back to his mother. "That way I'll be back at least three days before your surgery. So it really works out all the way around."

"Honey, it's fine. Really." She took his hand in reassurance. "I'm just happy you'll be back in two weeks this time, instead of two years."

"Me too," Allison chimed in much to the surprise of everyone else in the room, especially one.

***

"I'm so glad you got the job!" Allison congratulated him later that afternoon as they picnicked at Sansone once more before his departure. "I start my clinicals there late May. Luckily it's only one day a week so I'll still be able to help around the Stop like normal until your mom is back on her feet.

As the two discussed typical duties of an air force rotation, Landon sat quietly eating his chicken-noodle soup, unusually quiet even for an autistic child. Finally he spoke up. "Radmund, are you going to miss my birthday party?"

That was the first moment Allison realized he would, indeed, miss Landon's birthday that coming Sunday. "I'm afraid so. But, I did get you something. I think I have it somewhere here in my pocket," he teased fishing around for the gift. "Oh yea, here it is. One neon-green Battle Striker just like you ordered, right?" Landon's eyes lit up with excitement, a rare expression for him.

"Radmund, that was not necessary," Allison mentioned, but inwardly she was terribly impressed that he not only remembered her son's birthday but that he had actually taken time to find out exactly what Landon wanted.

Landon admired his present for a few minutes then returned with another question. "Radmund, are you leaving us?"

"No Sport. I'm just going away for a couple of weeks. It's something I have to do with the air force. But, I'll be back really soon, I promise! And as soon as I get back, we'll spend an entire afternoon with the trains and Legos and whatever other toys you want, okay?"

"Okay." And that was all the explanation Landon needed to be pacified. *Sometimes this disability is a blessing in disguise*, Allison thought to herself.

"Is there anything I can do for you while you're gone?" she asked.

"Yes. Make sure Miss Goldie gets to the Stop for her daily entertainment. You and I both know she needs that as much as my mother and, frankly, everyone else who visits the place. I've already told her you'll probably be picking her up sometimes. You just need to tell her what time so she can adjust her schedule. If you can't get her, then call Dad. He's already got Mondays on his schedule since you've got classes."

"Got it. Anything else?"

"Nope, that does it. I'm only gone for a few days. It's not any different than when folks leave for vacation." Even though all of that was true, he could sense her sadness. "Are you going to miss me?" he hoped.

"Of course!" she responded way too quickly, afraid she'd given him the wrong impression. "You know how much Landon and I enjoy hanging out with you. And he's doing so well memorizing those stupid idioms you teach him. What if he relapses?" She knew two weeks would be very quick, so it confused her as to why she felt the need to joke and pretend it didn't hurt so much.

Landon tugged his mother's arm and spoke up. "But Momma. Don't worry. It will go by at a good clip." No intonation in his voice, but a little grin directed toward Radmund that verified his purposeful use of the language.

"What?" she beamed. Turning to Radmund, she asked, "Why in the world would you teach him *that* one?"

"Trains. We learn all our idioms by the trains. The train speeds by 'at a good clip' don't you know?"

"Oh, shoulda thought of that one I suppose," she admitted in retrospect.

"I'm really going to miss him. He's a stitch! Do you think he realizes how funny he is?"

Allison grinned at his attention to her son. "Not always. But lately, thanks to you, I think he's looking for times to make jokes. Which reminds me … Are you the one who taught him the joke about the most intelligent insect?"

"Ah yes. The spelling bee. That is a good one," he chuckled nodding his head at the memory.

"Then, should I assume you are also the one that taught him that 'pee' rhymes with 'bee'?"

"What? No, couldn't have been me. Must've been that little preschool buddy of his. What's his name? Oh yea. Johnny. Definitely. Sounds like preschool boys to me," he rambled in feigned defense.

"He told me that spelling bee joke last night, cracked up laughing at himself – which hardly ever happens by the way – and then started running around the house saying, 'Pee. Bee rhymes with pee.' It took me 10 minutes to get him calmed down, thank you very much!"

Radmund looked sheepishly at his partner in crime. "Hey Sport. I thought we agreed that little rhyme would stay a secret. Why'd you go and get me in trouble now?"

Landon looked quizzically at his mother. "Is he in trouble Momma? You laughed too."

"Yes, I did. But I did not laugh at your running around the house afterward, now did I?"

"Not while he was in the room at least, I bet," Radmund jibed. For the next half hour the three of them played on the swings, relaxing and enjoying those rare moments when everything in the world fits perfectly into place and seems so peaceful.

Then the sun set literally and figuratively on their evening. "Well, I guess I need to go visit with the parents for awhile. Gotta leave at o-six-hundred in the morning." He walked them back to her apartment, hugged Landon with reassurance that he'd be back in 14 days, then hugged her with the same assurance. "I am going to miss you," he repeated. "Try not to go too crazy missing me." She smiled up at him and promised to abide, not knowing that crazy was just about to spill into her life.

PART 2
March – April

Yet I still belong to you;
you hold my right hand.
You guide me with your counsel,
leading me to a glorious destiny.
Whom have I in heaven but you?
I desire you more than anything on earth.
My health may fail, and my spirit may grow weak,
but God remains the strength of my heart.
Psalm 73:23-26 (NLT)

Festivals and Romance

Each year in Plant City, February sneaks out the back door and March bombards the town bringing with it the renowned Strawberry Festival. Although the name implies a focus on strawberries, this festival also brings thousands of visitors from all over the country for the rides, activities, food, and headliner music. Fresh strawberry recipes are cooked up with hundreds of unique culinary delights available for all visitors to sample. Delia entered at least one of her delicacies each year in the contest. This year she planned to enter her Strawberry Gazpacho in a Coconut Bread Bowl. Since its debut, the soup had become one of the most requested items from the chalkboard.

"Sweetheart, it's Friday. The Festival starts tomorrow! When are you going to finalize this recipe?" Henry pushed.

"Stop pressuring me! I have to get it just right," she implored him. "Here, taste this and tell me what you think."

He obliged, sipping the cold soup from the spoon shaking in her trembling hands. "It's perfect!" he reiterated for the third time that morning. "If you ask me to taste that again, I won't need lunch! It's awesome just like that. Do not change a thing."

"I'm so nervous. I always enter desserts. This is such a change for me. And, I really want to win this time, just in case."

"Just in case, what?" he asked, although he easily read her mind. "In case you can't enter next year? Is that what you were thinking?"

She set the soup pot on the counter and buried her head in her hands. "Okay. It's been on my mind. I thought I was so strong. I think I'm just emotionally more fragile right now with Radmund being gone right now and all." Henry gently took his wife in his arms, caressing her long silky hair.

"You're going to be fine. You've been drilling that into my head for weeks. Do not start questioning God now." Just being in his arms reassured her.

Allison, Goldie, Landon, and Buddy rounded the hallway into the dining room a moment later. "Good morning," Delia announced forcing her nerves to retreat. "I'm so happy to see you guys!"

Henry moved on to pour refills for the table guests. Topping off the cups, he worked his way over to the piano as Goldie seated herself on the bench. Allison walked up right behind him having situated Landon in his usual spot with his usual toys. "Hey, Delia could use a pick-me-up right now if you don't mind," he requested.

"Love to! I thought I sensed something in her voice," Goldie astutely noticed. As the music commenced, a gentle breeze blew through the restaurant as several guests opened the front door. Unbeknownst to Allison or Goldie, that breeze blew in far more than just a relaxing breath of fresh air.

Allison waved as she sang, noticing the Travis' meandering to their usual table, but something was different. They had a stranger with them – an extremely handsome, dark-haired, muscular stranger with piercing green eyes that captivated her attention as soon as he walked through the doorway. He, likewise, could not help but return her stare as they sat down. Her elegance clearly penetrated through her physical beauty into her soul. He saw it first in her eyes as she stared at him, then heard it through the intensity of her singing. Right behind the Travis' came another stranger – an elderly man still quite handsome for his age with a sparkling white smile like the Northern snows from which he was escaping. He first chose a stool at the counter, mesmerized by the talents of the statuesque pianist.

Allison eventually forced herself to look away, goose bumps rippling down her arms after she noticed her stare was being reciprocated by the young, dark-haired stranger. Goldie poured her heart into the music, completely unaware of her own elderly admirer.

Applause, as usual, erupted when the song ended. Before the last note stopped resonating off the walls, Allison escaped to the kitchen. Sensing her songstress' sudden departure, Miss Goldie politely announced, "Well, I guess I'll just play a couple of tunes by myself now." The elderly gentleman moved from the counter to the table closest to the pianist. Buddy, lying on the floor at her feet, shifted his head from one paw to the other.

"Wow! What's got you all jittery?" Delia asked as Allison entered breathlessly.

Allison struggled a moment to understand herself. "I'm not sure. I was just singing when the Travis' walked in and I waved to them like normal. No big deal. But they brought someone with them today," she recounted.

Delia cautiously opened the kitchen door, just enough to scan the dining room. She paused a moment perusing Table 10 where their friends sat giving orders to Henry. "I think I understand the problem," she nodded, intuitive as ever. "Perhaps I should go greet our friends."

"Sounds like a good idea. Tell them I said 'hello.'"

"Why don't you come with me?"

"No, I think Laurabelle needs me to help get the lunch orders going. It's half full out there and the noon train isn't even here yet."

"Okay, suit yourself." Then, she paused mid-door, "Oh by the way, if he asks your name, shall I tell him?" Allison blushed deep crimson and turned away. "I'll take that as a 'yes,'" Delia concluded skipping through as the door swung shut behind her. On her way to greet the Travis' she paused a moment noting a handsome elderly gentleman entranced with a seemingly unaware piano player.

"Darling," she whispered passing her husband between tables, "there seems to be romance in the air today." He had no idea to what she was referring, but the return of her beautiful smile convinced him that the stresses of earlier had subsided, at least for the moment. She floated on past, not waiting for a reply. He paused, watching her saunter to the Travis' table, shaking his head in jovial dismay.

"Good morning!" She spoke far more exuberantly than normal. "I see you've brought a visitor."

"This is Kholby Brown. His grandparents are good friends of ours," Louella explained. "Kholby, this is Cordelia Edmunds. She and her husband, Henry, are owners of this amazing place."

"Delia is the best cook you'll ever meet," Owen interjected. "And, definitely the better looking of the two!" he threw in loudly as Henry returned with a coffee pot.

"Kholby, I understand if your grandparents are saddled with this old guy for a friend, but surely you had a choice?" Henry quipped in response as he joined the introductions, then elbowed Owen. "Next time you get cold coffee." He winked at Kholby and Louella, but forced a scour on his face when turning to Owen.

Kholby stood up and shook their hands. "I have heard a great deal about you two and this place. Mr. and Mrs. Edmunds, it is very nice to finally meet you," he respectfully added with a twinkle in his emerald eyes.

"Hopefully from Louella and not Owen," Delia kidded. "And, it's *Delia* and *Henry*. Not that we're retro hippies or anything. It's just that I turned 48 a couple weeks ago and anything that makes either of us sound older is not allowed."

"Yes, Ma'am," he consented retaking his seat at the table.

"Okay, I can live with 'Ma'am' but only because our son just got out of the air force and he's called me that out of habit at least a dozen times. I've grown fond of it now." Her award-winning smile brightened the entire corner.

Owen looked around a bit then asked, "Where is he anyway? I have some questions about this mole on my arm."

Henry pulled up a chair next to his friend, pretending to examine the spot. "First of all, if you want my son to diagnose or treat you, it's not free! And, second, that's called an age spot. *Old* men get them all the time." He held out his own peaked white arms. "See, none on me!"

Louella had to put her coffee cup down to avoid a spill. "Henry, you are so good for him! Keep him in line just fine!"

Delia finally answered the lingering question. "Rad left on Tuesday morning for his first rotation in the Air Guard. They let him take the summer stint early so he could be back by my surgery."

"That was very nice of them," Louella replied. "Are you holding up okay? I could come over to help you if you like."

"Things are going to be just fine," Delia conceded in response. "I would love your continued prayers, though."

"Absolutely," Louella affirmed. "I will bring you some food a week or two after your surgery. Just because you're a brilliant cook doesn't mean a friend can't help out a little."

Henry forced a smile, "I'd love that. She won't be up to cooking for awhile and we all know what happens when I try to follow a recipe."

Owen could not resist. "We sure do. Just look out back in the trash can!"

Allison sheepishly approached the table at that point, tray balanced on her shoulders, filled with their orders. As she handed the plates to each person, an obvious connection between the two young adults seemed to scream out with no voice.

"Allison, why don't you join us?" Henry invited. "Looks like we've got all the other tables covered for now anyway."

"Alright. Thanks. I guess we have everything under control for a few minutes anyway." Allison felt as if her skin would jump off and run away at any point as she scuttled the chair out to sit down.

"So, Kholby, what brings you to town?" Henry asked.

First he had to try a huge bite of chicken salad, then he answered. "I just finished my Bachelor's degree at University of Miami. Majored in English, but I've been working for a contracting business. And there's a couple of Habitat for Humanity projects we're building here in Plant City. Heard about it at church and decided God wanted me in on this one. Worked out well since my grandparents have the trailer over in Lakeland. I moved into their place while I'm on this project."

Owen continued the story. "His grandfather is having surgery back in Illinois, so we knew they wouldn't be down this spring. But we didn't know about Kholby, so I thought he was a burglar when I saw him coming out of the place a few days ago with a big box!"

Kholby laughed in compliance. "That's right. Lucky for him I was not a thief. He just walked up and introduced himself with a very stern 'Hey, what are you doing in that trailer?' reprimand. Scared me so badly I dropped the box of trash I was simply trying to get to the curb. If I'd been a criminal, though, he would have been mincemeat!"

Henry couldn't resist. "You're right. Old man like Owen wouldn't stand a chance against a buff young guy like you!"

"Still called his grandmother to verify, though," Owen retorted. "Just look at him. He's got mischief written all over his face."

Louella gave Kholby a sympathy hug with one arm. "Ignore him. He's full of it, you know."

"Yep, I learned that very quickly. Doesn't bother me, though. You remind me of my grandparents." Delia couldn't help notice that although Kholby spoke of things directed to everyone at the table, his eyes rarely ventured away from one who sat across from him shyly staring back.

***

As conversation progressed at Table 10, Goldie continued to entertain the early lunch crowd, instinctively growing more and more aware of the silent attention just to her right side. The high "C" was her favorite key on the piano; its ring was pure delight to the sophisticated hearing of a blind person. She ended her favorite jazzy version of *The Sweet By and By* with a clink of the high note then turned to her right. "Are you a piano enthusiast?" she asked, startling him.

"I beg your pardon?" he responded.

"Do you like the piano? You've been sitting there obsessed with it for at least three songs now." Her voice was gentle, but curt at the same time.

He could tell her eyesight was impaired, but to what degree he couldn't be certain. "How did you know I was here? I attempted to be ever so quiet."

"My hearing is quite good, in spite of my age. Now, sir, why would you sneak up and stalk an old woman without so much as an introduction to alert her to your presence? You are lucky I don't carry pepper spray."

"Oh no. Quite the contrary. I simply did not wish to interrupt such extraordinary talent in motion. Watching your fingers flutter on those keys is equally as magical as the sounds you produce while doing so."

Buddy looked up from resting as she reached for his harness. "But, you assumed I wouldn't know you were there, right?" Her tone began to lighten as she fully turned herself on the bench to face the gentleman's table.

"I did assume as such, but only due to your companion's red jacket," he began. "Pardon my asking, but wouldn't your husband be a fine escort as well?"

She felt her cheeks warming in what was certain to be a wrinkled blush. "Not likely. My Paul passed on five years ago. Someday, though, I suspect he'll be there to escort me through those Pearly Gates. You still have not answered my question. Why is it exactly that you should feel the need to hover so close when there are any number of other tables in this place?"

He stared at her trying to discern sarcasm from serious. "Forgive me my dear woman, but this is a public place. And, there are so many people here, likely to come and enjoy the rapturous melodies as well as the fine food. Why would you presume a gentleman's attentions to be anything other than honorable?"

At that point, she giggled giving away her theatrics. "I suppose so. I would still like to know why you've been sitting there staring at me for some time now. It was a bit unnerving as I played. And at my age, I don't need any distractions."

"And what age would that be?" he asked. "Sixty perhaps?"

She fluttered her hand in the air. "Sir, but you are a sweet talker. It is quite apparent that I'm well over seventy. Just turned eighty in December."

The elderly flirting continued. "Madam, since it is impossible for you to see your beauty in the mirror, you must trust me that your appearance is truly not that of a woman beyond 70." She couldn't see his lovely white smile, but she clearly understood the genuine warmth radiating from his presence. "I am so sorry to hear of your husband's passing. I truly am, so please do not think me forward if I ask if you might consider accompanying me to dinner tonight?"

Goldie reached down to scratch Buddy's ears. "Dinner, with a man whose name I do not even know yet? I think that would be most inappropriate."

"Let me fix that then," he stated. "My name is George Picardy. And I am most pleased to make your acquaintance Miss …"

"Goldie Bingham. Likewise," she responded reaching outward for him to shake her hand.

***

The first of 11 chimes found Landon at his mother's side just as she delivered shortcake to her friends at Table 10. Alerted to the tugging on her shirt, she smiled looking down at him. "I know honey. Lunchtime. I'll get it right away."

"Hey Landon! What do you have there?" Louella paused from her shortcake to acknowledge the little boy.

"This top is brand-spanking new," he replied showing off his neon-green Battle Striker. "Radmund gave it to me."

"He's learning idioms," Allison laughed as she explained. "Apparently, he's got a knack for memorizing them afterall." She grinned, taking her son's hand, "It was great to see you two again, and to meet you Kholby." Goosebumps rose once more along her arms as his name escaped her lips for the first time.

"You too," the three guests replied, nearly in unison.

"She has a child?" Kholby asked after she was out of earshot. Delia and Henry had left the table a few minutes earlier to serve new customers, and Louella and Owen felt it was out of line to give much detail to his question.

"Yes," Louella replied hesitantly. "Kholby, why don't you go talk to her?" Taking the hint, he excused himself, then walked to the front of the room where Allison and Landon were enjoying their lunch break.

"Hello. Mind if I join you for a couple minutes?" he asked timidly. Landon ignored him completely. Allison quickly chewed her bite, unable to get out a response before he assumed her answer and sat down anyway. "My name is Kholby. I hear you are Landon." He held out his hand for a moment, then retracted when he realized there would be no handshake.

Finally swallowing, she spoke. "He's very intent on his lunch."

"I see that." Kholby watched him carefully, trying to understand. "There's nothing like a great PBJ, huh Sport?"

Landon's attention was immediately diverted from the food to the stranger. "My name is Landon. Only Radmund calls me Sport. Not you."

"Okay, then …" she replied, nervously fidgeting with her cup. "Well, I'm going to get some more tea. Would you like anything sweetheart?" she asked Landon, then motioned for Kholby to follow her. Landon shook his cup to verify it was still full. "I'll be right back then." She waited until they were a few feet away to answer his unsaid questions. "He's autistic. But, he really is adorable. Just doesn't take quickly to strangers is all."

"I thought so," he confirmed out loud. "He is really cute. I can see he has your hair, but does he look more like you … or … your husband?" His fishing was not nearly as smooth as George Picardy.

She looked up at him, then returned her focus to avoid an overflow. Almost rhythmically, she curtly replied, "I'm not married. I'm 21. Yes, I'm a single parent. I had him when I was 17. He looks like me. Anything else floating around in there you want to ask?" It never occurred to her to think about her son looking anything like the man who raped her.

"Um, I don't think so," he responded astutely. "Hey, I didn't mean to upset you. I'm sorry."

She set the glass on the counter and looked at Kholby, then her son. "It's okay. I'm just a little defensive about him is all."

"Landon or his father?"

"Both. But for different reasons." *He does not need to know all the details of my life*, she decided. "I'd be happy to tell you all about my son, but that's it."

"Okay, message received loud and clear." They returned to the table to find Landon finished with his lunch and having returned to the battle of the tops. The brand-spanking new neon-green top appeared to be victorious in the round ending as they sat down. Kholby was not used to feeling so out-of-place. But she had him tongue-tied. "Um, I … was wondering … well … Would you have tonight … I mean dinner … with me … tonight? I mean, we have to go back to Lakeland in a little while but I could come back. I have a car and I'd pick you up … if you're off work by then ... seven-ish I mean." He babbled on, "I'm not so hard to talk. I mean it's not hard to say things for me. I mean … oh geesh."

She couldn't help but laugh. It wasn't intentional; he was just very amusing and so cute. "I have an online seminar for one of my classes tonight. Sorry." His head dropped at her rejection. "But, tomorrow is when the Strawberry Festival begins. And I get off early most Saturdays." Her eyes twinkled as his heart palpitated.

"Hmm, Strawberry Festival. Sounds like something I should investigate if I'm going to be working here for awhile."

"One thing." She turned her attention to her son. "He goes with us. We've been looking forward to opening night for a month."

Kholby was not used to being around little kids, let alone one with a disability. "Aren't noises and stuff supposed to be a problem for kids … like him. Will he be okay?"

The humor and cuteness she found in him only a moment earlier vanished. She set her cup on the table and looked him squarely in the eyes. "He is a little boy. If you have to put his disability in front of that, then we have nothing further to say." She stacked the lunch dishes together and abruptly turned to go, nearly bumping into the Travis'. "Owen, Louella … it was nice to see you again," she said scurrying by without another word.

"See you Sunday afternoon for the party," Louella quickly responded.

In a split-second she was out of sight. "Well, I see you worked your magical charms with her," Owen teased.

"Owen, I don't think now is the time for jokes," his wife chided noticing the dismay on their young friend's face. "What happened Kholby?"

He glanced at Landon then back at the door to the kitchen where Allison vanished. "I'm an idiot," he admitted.

***

The next morning a delivery man arrived with a dozen white roses and a card. "Says it's to Allison and Landon," he stated setting the vase on the counter as Delia signed the form. "Tip included already."

"Thank you," she smiled. "I'll make sure they get these. They're lovely." Allison and Landon came in through the back just as the delivery man exited through the front. "Hey, Allison," Delia called. "Something for you up here."

"Really? Why would I … get … um …," She noticed the bouquet from across the room. " flowers?" A curious twinkle reflected in her eyes as she wrinkled her freckled nose in disbelief.

"Perhaps this card will explain," Delia grinned handing her the small envelope attached to the vase.

Allison was shocked. She hadn't ever received a flower, let alone an entire vase filled with roses. She carefully opened the envelope and took out a purple card; a huge grin grew across her face as she read the note. "They're from Kholby."

"Well I think that boy is smitten with you, my dear. To send you flowers the day after he met you. Very sweet."

"Actually, they're an apology gift. He was a jerk and he knows it apparently." She handed the card to Delia. "Go ahead. You can read it if you like."

Delia began reading. "Dear Allison and Landon, I'm so sorry for the dumb stuff I said yesterday. If you will forgive me, I'd really like to have lunch with Landon today and get to know him a little better. Then maybe we could still have our date tonight – the three of us I mean." She set the card aside and breathed deeply, inhaling the sweet scent of the flowers. "What did he do?"

"Nothing really. I'm just very defensive with Landon and my past." She sat down. "Delia, what should I do? I'm so confused."

"Well, Sweetie, do you think he deserves a second chance?"

"Probably. I was pretty short with him, I suppose. But I just want to meet a guy and not have to explain Landon or what happened."

"Think about it from his point. He doesn't know anything about you, so what do you think he'd assume?"

"I know. But I didn't want to tell him anything. And he was kind of freaked out about Landon."

"Can you blame him for being a little freaked out? All he knows is you are a single parent of an autistic child."

"Radmund wasn't bothered at all. He was totally great from the first time we met." A strange guilty sensation rolled through her body for a fleeting moment.

"Well, Radmund is a one-of-a-kind," she paused to let the concept sink in. "Plus he wasn't really a stranger either. Maybe not the whole story, but he did know something happened in your past. I think it's time you followed your heart and not your fears, Allison."

"You're right as usual, Delia. I should call him, just to thank him at least," she agreed.

Delia handed the card back to her. "It appears that was his goal since his phone number is highlighted in yellow." Secretly Delia wanted to yell out 'NO! He's probably a jerk just like you think! Don't fall for the new guy!' Yet, something warned her to keep those thoughts to herself.

When Kholby showed up two hours later for his lunch date with Landon, Delia started to regret having had any part in encouraging Allison to "follow her heart." A few minutes later, Goldie and George ambled in for lunch. "Miss Goldie, what a pleasant surprise!" Delia announced meeting them a few feet inside. Noticing her arm-in-arm with the gentleman, Delia quickly surmised she was not there to entertain that day. "To what do we owe this honor, on a weekend no less?"

"Delia, this is my new friend, George Picardy." She turned slightly to George. "George, this is my dear friend, Cordelia Edmunds. She's the fabulous chef and owner of this restaurant."

George reached out a hand to shake Delia's. "Very nice to meet you. I truly enjoyed my lunch yesterday and had to return for more of your delicious larder."

"Mr. Picardy ..."

"George," he interrupted.

"George. It is an honor to have return guests! I do remember seeing you here yesterday. I believe my husband waited on you then." The memory quickly became clear. *Ah yes, you're the one who was sweet-talking Goldie*, she thought to herself. *Must've worked,* she giggled silently. "I have a lovely, quiet spot over by the fireplace if you like," she remarked out loud escorting them to their table.

In the meantime, Kholby settled himself in the front window with Landon. "Hi Landon. What are you doing?" His nerves were on full alert between Allison's presence and the intimidation of a little boy.

Completely monotone and with only a halfway glance, Landon replied, "Watch these tops. They are magnetic. See, they bang together and have a war."

"That's really cool!" Kholby was intrigued. "They didn't have toys like that when I was your age."

"You used to be five?" Landon asked in surprise, looking up that time. "I'm going to be five tomorrow."

Kholby began to relax. "No kidding? Tomorrow, huh?" He looked over at Allison.

"Having a party over at Sansone Park at four," she invited. "Owen and Louella are coming over if you want to join us."

He turned back to Landon. "Would that be okay with you? I mean if I come to your party?"

The tops began battling once more as he answered. "Sure. Radmund won't be there though. That makes me sad."

Allison set their lunches on the table as Kholby stood up. "He's mentioned this 'Radmund' at least three times now. Is that one of his little friends or something?"

"Sort of. Radmund is Delia and Henry's son. He's our age, but he and Landon are really tight. Rad's in the Air Force Guard, on a summer rotation right now. He'll be back next week."

Kholby took in all she said, and didn't say, before he replied. "Is this ... Radmund ... *your* friend ... also?"

"He's my best friend," she answered matter-of-factly.

"Okay then." He wasn't sure if she had been totally honest with him or herself. "Well, Landon, that looks like an awesome lunch. I'm starved." Together, they enjoyed a "get-to-know-you" lunch while Allison turned her attention to the cute older couple in the back corner.

"Miss Goldie? Hello!" she said alarmed to see her friend with a date.

"Allison, dear. This is my new friend, George Picardy. We met yesterday when he stopped by for lunch."

"Allison, your singing yesterday was sheer delight to my ears!" he said profusely as they shook hands.

"Thank you Mr. Picardy," she replied brightening the quaint corner with her grin. "What can I get you two for lunch?"

"It's George, if you don't mind," he replied. "And, I hear the Track BLT Salad is the dish to have today." Allison jotted down his order, grin growing brighter each second as she snuck repeated glances at the two of them.

"The usual for you, Miss Goldie?" she queried. Goldie nodded her head. Then, pausing before taking their order to the kitchen, she muttered, "Um, Miss Goldie, there's a key on the piano that I don't think is quite right. I was wondering if you'd listen to see if you think we should call a tuner."

The pair walked to the piano where Allison pretended to find 'the key' and pluck away at it a moment. "Okay, the key is fine," she whispered. "I just had to ask you about the handsome suitor you've picked up there."

Goldie smirked. "Is he handsome? I thought he sounded like it. And he smells nice too, don't you think?"

"Yes, he is handsome. And, yes he does smell very nice," she agreed.

"We met yesterday. He was stalking me after you left so abruptly. He's quite the sweet talker."

"Miss Goldie, how do you know he's safe?" Allison was a little concerned, but truthfully, more curious. She knew Buddy would eat up anyone who tried to hurt his mistress. And if the dog didn't succeed, Goldie's friends would.

"Silly child. I may be blind, but I'm not stupid. Does he look dangerous to you?"

Allison shrugged, spying on the thin, elderly gentleman in question. "I suppose not. But, how well do you know him really?"

"Not well. We did have dinner together last night, but then he took me straight home. And, he was a gentleman the entire time."

"Oh, that's why you said you didn't need a ride. I wondered!" she grinned in reflection. "So, what are you two doing today? Besides lunch I mean."

"We're heading to the parade and the opening of the festival later." Goldie's face radiated as she spoke.

"No way! Me too. And, I have a date also! Actually, Landon and I are going with a friend of Owen and Louella's. His name is Kholby Brown."

"A date? What about Radmund?"

"Miss Goldie, you know we're just friends," Allison replied fidgeting on the piano bench. "Besides, he's away now."

Goldie shook her head. "Are you sure my dear? Like I said, I may be blind but I'm not stupid."

"You are one of the two wisest women I know," Allison agreed. "But, I promise. Rad and I are really close – best-friends close. Nothing else."

"Um hum. If you say so," she said with a hint of sarcasm. "Well, if we are all going to the festival this evening, would you like to double-date? That way you can see for yourself that George is a decent man … and I can check out your date."

Allison clapped in excited agreement. "That would be wonderful! I was a little nervous anyway." She whispered, "This is actually my first date since … well, you know."

"Settled then! We girls just have to stick together in times like this, don't you know?" They were still giggling as Allison helped her friend back to the table where George sat by curiously wondering how two women of contrasting generations could sneak off to the side and kibitz like equals.

Kholby was less than enthusiastic about including two additional people on their first date. Having learned his lesson earlier, though, he said nothing and smiled gallantly as she supported her idea. "Kholby," she'd begun. "Goldie is blind and vulnerable. I can't just let her go with a stranger. It's not like they'll go on rides or anything with us. Oh, and if we want to go on a ride, then Landon could stay with them since he doesn't do well with that type of stimulation." By the end of her argument, he was mollified.

The six of them were a most interesting group exiting The Whistle Stop that night. Two young people nervously separated by one little boy as they each took one of his hands, two senior citizens holding hands like kids, and a dog leading the way. "What have I done?" Delia stewed to her husband after bidding the group a good evening. "Why did I encourage her to go out with him? Radmund is going to be devastated."

"Stop worrying! It's a simple date. Maybe this will help her figure things out with Rad." Henry contributed in hopeful spirit.

"She swears they're just friends, though, Henry."

"So she says, but I think there's more she doesn't see yet. Let's hope this kid is a diversion."

"Or it could be that she and Rad are just meant to be friends." As much as Delia would love to see the two of them together, she also wanted the very best for both of them. And she knew that meant to let God handle it instead of trying to step in herself. Delia locked the front door and turned back to her husband's waiting, open arms. "Even after all these years, I still love the way your arms feel around me," she cooed wrapping her arms around his neck. A quiet moment passed as they kissed under the dim lights, and then she suddenly broke away in awkward laughter.

Henry was slightly offended. "That's not really the mood I was going for," he admitted.

"Oh, honey. Don't take it personally," she giggled. "I was thinking of Goldie and George. They're so cute together! Apparently our Strawberry Festival is the impetus for romance in Plant City, not Valentine's Day."

"Well, I don't need a festival or a holiday to be romantic with my wife," he whispered in her ear.

"I think we should go home," she agreed staring deeply into her husband's eyes.

Growing New Memories

The Strawberry Festival commemorates each year with a new theme. Allison grinned as they approached the main gates that night. "Growing New Memories," the banner read. *Perfect*, she thought. *Get rid of old haunts and fill the space with new memories.* She snuck a quick glance at her date; he was busy helping Landon get a curbside seat for the parade. *I can do this, right God?* she whispered to herself. Then she sat on the curb next to Landon, taking his hand. "Sweetheart, I'm so excited about the parade!" she said hugging him.

Kholby sat next to her, very close. Her heart skipped a beat as their arms brushed against each other. "I haven't been to a carnival in years," he said wringing his hands in nervous habit.

"It's a festival," she corrected.

"Oh," he smirked. "And the difference would be?"

She looked up at him, smirking right back. "A festival is a celebration of happiness. A carnival is just an excuse to eat junk food and pay lots of money to go on death rides and play rigged games. And ... a carnival fits in the mall parking lot. This thing spans several city blocks."

"Something against carnivals, I sense," he teased nudging her arm.

"Didn't you see the sign when we came in? It's the theme! 'Growing New Memories.' See. Their goal is to help people make all kinds of great memories." She paused and then reiterated, emphasizing her point, "Celebration." At that moment, the floats and bands could be heard a block away. Indeed, the celebration was beginning.

"Momma, I hear music. Will they have candy?" Landon asked.

"Of course! But don't go jumping in the street. You know the rules. I'll help you get the candy if it doesn't come close enough. And, no eating anything until after I inspect it. Got it?"

"Clear as a bell, Momma." He looked up at her making sure she noticed his newest phrase.

"Now where did you learn that one?" Her eyes sparkled taking in her son's progress.

"From me, of course," Kholby interjected, accepting the credit. "You didn't think we just played tops without talking at lunch did you?" She looked back and forth between the two boys. "You said he liked learning new phrases. He explained the rules for that top game he loves so much, then asked if I 'got it'. I thought I did."

"Let me guess. He still won."

"Every game. I think maybe he didn't tell me everything."

She laughed. "He never does when it comes to winning. He's very competitive."

"I know. That was 'clear as a bell' to me," Kholby chuckled.

Goldie and George stood back a ways since crowds and candy were of no interest to either of them. Besides, as Goldie put it, "I'm here for the sounds anyway." George gently took her hand in his as the marching bands came by. "I can hear the saxophones!" she clapped joyfully, inadvertently pulling away from his touch. In a moment, she realized what happened and subtly reached out to find his hand in the spot she'd left it a second earlier. His smile lit up the entire street corner. "Oh, I loved playing alto in high school. That was actually my first instrument," she noted as their fingers entwined.

"My lady, but I, too, played in the high school band. My instrument, however, was the tuba. You know – ooopma looopma." He imitated as he explained how it was his job to keep the underlying rhythm. "They made me play it because I was the only boy large enough to carry the contraption."

"Oh my. I do remember our tuba player. He was a little wisp of a thing. Could barely carry that horn three feet without stopping for a breath." She smiled brightly as old memories filled her heart with joy while the new ones she and George were growing filled her heart with hope.

When the last float rolled by, everyone waved to the lovely Strawberry Festival Queen. Everyone except Landon; he'd had enough. His bag for collecting candy was sufficiently filled to last at least a week and the Sea Lion Splash Show was starting at 8:00 p.m. – in 20 minutes according to his Lego wrist watch. The group reassembled and headed to the aquarium. Allison noticed that Landon reluctantly took Kholby's hand as they wormed through the crowded streets. She spotted Goldie and George walking hand-in-hand just a few feet ahead. Surprising as it was to both of them, she took hold of Kholby's free hand in hers. He, of course, happily reciprocated by clasping her fingers gently within his sweating palm.

***

It was nearly 10:00 p.m. when the group finally made their way back to the Villages. "My darling, thank you for a grand evening. I have not had that much fun in years," George commented as he kissed Goldie's hand. "I shall look forward to our birthday party date tomorrow afternoon." He stood close by until he was assured that Goldie was safely inside her own apartment. Then, he winked at the others and meandered down the steps and out to his car.

Kholby agreed to escort one very tired little boy to his apartment downstairs per Allison's request so that she might have a couple of moments alone with Goldie. "He's very sweet, Miss Goldie," she reassured her friend. "And he is extremely handsome."

"Honey, I think Kholby is a gentleman as well. And I can hear a beautiful smile spread across his face when he speaks about you and Landon," she teased.

"He's cute," Allison reassured her. "His eyes sparkle just like George's."

"That's good, but I'm confused. What about Radmund?"

"Oh Miss Goldie, please don't go there again. I told you we are just friends," she asserted.

"Sweetheart, blindness often gives the other senses an extra 'boost'. In my case, I've developed a keen sense of intuition as well."

Allison was unnerved at her friend's perception. "No, I promise. I really don't have any other feelings for Rad, hidden or not. He's my best friend." She paused a moment then continued. "And Kholby makes me feel alive again like I did when I was a teenager. It's like with him I'm able to go back and capture the dating years I was robbed of earlier."

"Allison, does Kholby know about your past?"

"Of course not. I just met him."

"How long had you known Radmund before you told him about what happened?" Goldie asked preparing a pot of hot tea.

The memory stopped Allison cold for a moment. "I think that was different because I knew we were only friends. It was safe telling him since I didn't expect him to think of me in any other way, you know. And his folks treat me so well – like their own daughter. So it felt kinda like talking to my own brother."

"But how did you know you would only be friends?" Goldie asked.

"I don't know. How do you ever know that when you are really getting to know someone? What about George? Do you think he'll be more than your friend?"

"I'm sorry to pry my dear," she paused motioning for Allison to sit down a moment. "Do you have a moment for me to tell you a story?" Allison nodded as she took a seat on the couch. "When I met Paul, I thought he was the most intelligent and wonderful man ever. And, it only took a moment for me to feel like he had become my very best friend. We spent all our free time together and we talked about everything. I mean everything. He was even willing to go to the store to buy feminine products for me!" She giggled at the memories. "Remember, though, how I said the other day that it took two years for us to get married?"

"Sure."

Goldie continued. "Well, I was madly in love with another boy – Finnigan O'Shannon. Oh he was a beautiful Irish boy with gorgeous green eyes. And he made me feel like a princess."

"Why did you end up marrying Paul then?" Allison asked.

"Because after a few months I realized that Finnigan made my heart flutter, but Paul made my soul dance. And you know what was most precious about my Paul?"

"I give," she responded pondering Goldie's story.

"He just stood by patiently watching me make a fool of myself with the Irishman. But whenever I needed him, Paul was there for me."

"Didn't he get upset about you and Finnigan?"

"Of course he did! Drove him crazy. But Paul was a very wise man. He knew he'd push me away forever if he tried to interfere. So, he dated a bit here and there, but mostly he waited for me to get my 'wild oats' out."

"Miss Goldie," Allison replied timidly, "I can't imagine you sowing any 'wild oats.'"

"Sweetie, I went to all the sock-hops, soda fountains, and drive-in movies in my day. That's what wild oats were back then." Goldie reached out for Allison's hand. "Not like today, is it?"

"No Ma'am," she replied in retrospect of all her elderly friend had said. "Miss Goldie, thank you for your story. But, I promise you, Rad and I are friends. And he's good with that too. He understands how I feel."

"If you insist. I'm so sorry dear. I need to let you back to that handsome date and your son," she replied. Hugging once more, they bid each other good night, then Allison scampered down the steps to her own apartment. *She's an interesting old woman,* she contemplated all the way.

"I was beginning to think you'd left us," Kholby quipped when she came through the door.

"Momma, Kholby gave me milk before bed. I might wet the bed now," Landon admitted.

"Did he pour the milk down your throat?" she asked as a slight irritation rose in her voice. Landon shook his head. "Then I think it's your fault, isn't it?" He looked confused at the accusation. Exasperated, Allison motioned toward the bathroom. "Go potty right now, then I'll be there to tuck you in and sing a song." Landon obliged completely unaware that he had done anything wrong.

Kholby quickly apologized when Landon was out of range. "I thought you always gave little kids milk before bed. My mistake."

"He's so interesting. He knew it was wrong if he got the milk himself. But he doesn't understand that if someone else initiates it, it's still wrong. I worry about how he'll handle that in school. In fact, that's my biggest fear for him in life."

"But he's so smart. I don't get how he can be that smart and autistic.

"Many autistic children actually have very high IQ's. It's the social stuff they don't usually master. That's why it's neat he's learning some slang phrases. That's one way for him to pick up on social conventions most of us just get. I hope he'll learn how to read the body language of his friends more once he's in school."

"Momma, I'm ready now," Landon called from his bedroom. She excused herself and meandered down the hall to complete the nightly ritual – tuck in the sheets, sing a song of his choice, and say their prayers. Kholby followed, but stood in the doorway entranced as he observed the process.

"He likes *The Barney Song,* huh?" he asked as they quietly retreated from Landon's room a moment later.

"Ha! He acts like he randomly picks songs, but they are the exact same order every week. He's a stickler for predictability and routines. Saturday's song is always that one. Tomorrow it will be *Jesus Loves Me*." She turned to face him, one knee tucked under the other leg. "Speaking of tomorrow. You don't need to bring him a gift, if you are coming to the party that is."

"I wouldn't miss it!" he confirmed. "And, we'll see about the gift. Not sure I can compete with that top your friend gave him already, though."

She sensed a concern in his voice. "Well, I told you. He and Rad are really tight. But I think he's getting more comfortable with you. Look, he didn't object to you bringing him on down for bed while I talked with Goldie for a moment, did he?"

"Hmm, guess you're right. Speaking of that, what were you two girls jabbering about for so long?" Like George, Kholby did not understand how two such different women could enjoy 'girl talk'.

"We talked about you guys, of course," Allison flirted in honest admission.

Kholby twitched at the thought of what they might have said. "Good stuff? About me at least. I mean George is an odd duck, but I'm normal, right?" he teased half-heartedly.

Allison laughed. "George is the most eloquent gentleman I've ever met. At first I thought it was for show, but now I see he's the real deal. But not in an arrogant way, you know? He's really funny. And did you see how he made her light up, like a little girl again?"

"I noticed. And, … what did you two say about me?" he asked again, hopeful.

"She thinks you're a diversion," Allison admitted curious about his response.

Unnerved, he twitched again. "A diversion from what?"

"From Radmund."

"Oh, *him* again." He turned to her making full eye contact. "We barely know each other. But I already know I like you a lot, and I'd like get to know you and Landon much better if you'll let me. So, I think we need to clear up this whole Radmund thing right now." His voice was stern. She understood.

"Radmund is my best friend. I told you that. I told her that. I told him that."

"Who are you trying to convince? Us ... or yourself?" He was beginning to realize the competition might not be another man, but the girl's struggle in her own heart instead.

She took his hand, sat up straight, and confessed. "I love Radmund ... like my brother. Yes, he mentioned that he wanted it to be more at one time, but we've moved past that now. He understands that I need to date other guys. He knows ...," *why I need to do this. He's the only one that would understand why I need to date like a normal girl.* The last of her thought remained silent.

"*Other* guys? Not just one, then?" His attention perked up on the plurality of her statement, which caused him to totally miss the unstated portion.

"No. Not like that. I just meant that he understands I want to date someone else."

"Are you telling me everything? I feel like there's a whole story here I don't know."

She was not about to confess anything else to him that night – not on their first date. "We just met. I know very little about you, and you know very little about me. I think we'll leave it at that for now. You know, to make the next date more interesting." Her eyes sparkled as she teased him with her words.

"Next date?" He was pleased. "You want to plan something then?"

"Well, there's Landon's birthday tomorrow, but that's not really a date. So, if you're not too busy, I was hoping you could join Landon and me for dinner on Monday. I have classes all day, and I know it's your first day on the job with Habitat. But, you still need dinner, right? So, if you're not too tired, maybe you could come over around six?"

"We should be done around four each day for a little while, they told us. But I'll be gross after a day's work and need time to get cleaned up." He paused to calculate the timing in his head, then confirmed. "Six should be perfect. I'll call you if I'm later than that."

With that, the next date was set and small talk commenced for another half hour. She told him about Marc and their childhood joys, but all her stories stopped at age 16. He failed to pick up on that unspoken detail as well.

He told her all about how he first felt the call to the mission field at a senior-high camp. The message had been so clear, he thought, spoken just to him even though there were over 100 students in attendance. His heart raced as he visited the CRAM Ministries booth that night to get more information. Then when he started college that fall his roommate began talking about how he planned to go this mission school and teach English to the Chinese students. "Before long," Kholby said, "I just knew that was where God was leading me. The rest of college I focused on a major in teaching English and Bible studies."

"Aren't you afraid to go over there? Or what if God wants you to go to a third-world country? That's really scary," she admitted as he finished his story.

"That's the coolest part. People think if they accept Christ that He'll make them go to someplace really dangerous. But if God wants you to be a missionary, He puts it in your heart as a passion so that you can't wait to go. And He fills you with courage so you know it's going to be okay. That's what God did for me. And now, I can't wait until my opening comes. I know God has amazing things planned for me and the students I will teach. I truly cannot wait!" She sat quietly listening, confused as to how he could be so excited about going so far away and yet so interested in a relationship with her at the same time.

"It's nearly eleven already," he suddenly noted. "I've got a 30-minute drive back to Lakeland so I should get going. I promised Owen and Louella I'd go with them to the early service tomorrow. Not sure why I did that now in hindsight!" he grinned. "But they're nice people and they take good care of my grandparents, so I suppose one early morning won't kill me."

"You're a good man, Kholby Brown," she stated more to herself than him. "I'm looking forward to seeing you again tomorrow at the party ... and Monday for dinner." She lowered her head bashfully. Noticing, he gently lifted her chin upwards making eye contact again. They leaned in to each other, closer and closer – yet both unsure if it was the right time or not. At the last second, she turned away. "Not yet, Kholby," she apologized in hushed whisper. "I don't think I want to be a girl who kisses on the first date." She twirled the silver ring on her finger as she hugged him goodnight instead.

"Hmm, lots of things to wonder about then for the second date, huh?" He quickly turned and walked away, smirking to himself.

***

Sunday afternoon rolled around with a party fit for a prince. Banners hung from the pavilion support beams announcing the five-year-old's birthday celebration. Computer-generated pictures draped the ends of each picnic table. A table near one end of the building held a rectangular cake nestled right in the midst of an array of Delia's famous homemade cookies – chocolate chip, peanut butter, and oatmeal raisin. All of Landon's favorites. Along the cake's perimeter ran icing tracks with a Thomas Train Engine poised directly above the "Happy 5th Birthday Landon." The table next to the cake included Delia's famous coleslaw, BBQ pork roast, and Jacked-up baked beans – another of her famous recipes which simply included a quarter cup of Jack Daniels and a heaping scoop of brown sugar mixed in the baked beans before cooking. By the time the beans finished baking, the whiskey cooked off leaving a succulent flavor of sweet corn in the midst of the sugar, onions, and other seasonings.

Setting large jugs of tea and water on one end of the food table, Allison looked around in joy and exclaimed, "Thank you so much for helping get everything ready! It's perfect, Delia. Landon's going to love this!" Landon had gone home with Henry after church so the ladies could sneak over and get the party all set up. "And thank you so much for the food. It would have been just fine to have cake and ice cream, though."

"Consider that as part of our gift for his birthday. Besides, we invited so many friends and family over that we wanted to provide dinner for them as well."

"You guys are so good to us. Landon and I thank God for you two every night in our prayers!" Henry and Landon walked up as if on cue. "Landon! Happy Birthday!" His mother stated nervously as she explained for the fourth time, "Some of our friends will be here today for your birthday. Jonathan and Skylar are coming just to play with you, though! But, the adults will leave you guys alone so you can have your fun time on the swings, or the sandbox, or the slides, okay?"

"I understand, Momma. You worry too much." She thought a snicker crossed his sweet little face.

Returning to where Delia and Henry finished lining up plates and utensils, she moved in close. "I think he's okay with being the center of attention. He's so excited for Jonathan and Skylar to get here. Apparently they hang out together at Shiloh all the time. Maybe having his little friends here will take his mind off Radmund's absence. He's asked four times today if I thought Radmund might surprise him." She looked around, sadly, internalizing her own disappointment in his absence.

"It's really neat how he and Skylar became friends so fast," Delia noted. "Who knew that family's little visit a few weeks ago would turn out like this? It's a small world."

"It's been great for Scarlett, also, especially since Adam left. I see her once in awhile and we've even started emailing a little," Allison trailed off a moment in thought. "I wish they weren't moving to the base so soon. I think we could become good friends."

Scarlett and Skylar arrived a few minutes later. "I can't stay," Scarlett admitted. "Kardal has a soccer game today and I promised to be there for him. Seems this sport is really helping him mature and feel a little less angry about life."

"No problem," Allison replied. "We'll keep an eye on Skylar. Plenty of people around here to help. Besides," she noted pointing to the swings where Skylar was already aloft, "I don't think she'll be lacking for things to do."

"She loves swinging!" Scarlett confirmed. "I'll be back in a couple of hours to pick her up."

As Allison walked with Scarlett to her car, Owen and Louella arrived, followed closely by Kholby in his own car. Allison quickly said goodbye to her friend and turned her attention to the incoming guest.

George met Goldie at her place and then they ambled over together from the apartment. Jonathan and his parents, and a few other families from church all showed up within a few more minutes. Food, fun, and a festival commenced for the afternoon. But Allison found it difficult to focus on any of the guests except one.

Best Weekend Ever

She balked at first, but Allison finally consented to take the leftover food as long as Goldie split it with her. After packing up the last morsels, Goldie and Buddy led the way as Kholby and George helped carry leftovers to the apartments. In the meantime, Owen and Louella, Delia and Henry, and Allison cleaned up at the pavilion while Landon, Skylar, and Jonathan stole a few more minutes playing together.

At his parents beckoning, Jonathan reluctantly left the swings and said goodbye. "Thank you for coming to my party," Landon remarked. "Thank you for the present."

"He's growing up so fast," Allison whispered to Delia. "Sometimes he's just perfectly normal."

Delia put her arm around Allison's shoulders and replied, "Sweetie, that child is exactly the way God made him – perfect. Don't ever forget that."

A few minutes later and Scarlett returned to collect Skylar. "They lost," she commented to Allison while nodding toward her son who chose to remain in the car. "He's not very sociable now."

"No problem. Thanks for letting Skylar come over. I think she had a great time," Allison remarked, then bent down to chat with Skylar a moment. "Hey sweetheart. Thanks for coming to the party and for Landon's present! I'll see you tomorrow at Shiloh."

Scarlett hugged Allison. "Thank you for inviting her. It's the first time anyone asked her to a party."

"We loved having her here. She's such a precious child! I wish you guys weren't moving so soon. But, we can still email. I'd really like it if we could be friends, and maybe you'll be back here someday."

"Thanks, Allison. After Adam's rotation ends, we plan to move back around here somewhere. In the meantime, I'd love an email buddy!" With that, Scarlett took Skylar's hand as they waved a final farewell.

"Bye Skylar," Landon chimed in waving from afar in the pavilion. Skylar waved to them all even as she resumed jabbering nonstop to her mother about the fun she'd had at the party.

Owen and Louella hugged Landon, wishing him one more "Happy Birthday" before they took off for home. "Landon you are growing up so fast," Louella commented as Landon stood by dutifully.

Returning to his side, Allison took his hand. "What do you say?" she nudged her son.

"Thank you for the Train Transformer and for coming to the party." His delight in the toy could not be detected in his tone but was obvious earlier when he had ripped opened the box and begged to play with it immediately. But per his mother's urging, he reluctantly opened his last gift – the one from Kholby – tossed it aside and grabbed his new transformer so he and Jonathan and Skylar could commence a war in the sandbox.

"You're very welcome," Owen replied. "And, thanks for showing me how it works. I think I might get one of those for myself." He winked at the birthday boy who totally missed the connection. "Hey Allison, Kholby talked on and on about the festival last night." Owen snickered slyly turning his attention to teasing her a moment. "Well, actually the festival was only a teeny-tiny little piece of our conversation this morning."

"Ignore him as usual," Louella contributed. "And, you ...," she directed to her husband, "mind your own business!" As they walked off, Landon tugged his mother's shirt while doing the 'potty dance.' Understanding his urgency, they made a beeline for the bathroom up the hill.

Delia and Henry had everything packed or cleaned up by the time they returned. Kholby reemerged from the path between the park and the apartment complex. His grin lit up the area as dusk set in. "Those two are adorable together," he announced walking up to the tables. "George opened the door for her, made sure to put all the food away and tell her exactly where it was in the fridge, and then poured them both a glass of wine. They totally forgot I was even in the room."

"I bet we'll still be that romantic when we're 80!" Henry postulated with one arm around his wife's slim waist. She giggled in response, then blushed.

"Okay, well, with that thought, it's time we got home," Allison muttered. Kholby heartily agreed as they each took a bag of gifts in one hand and one of Landon's hands in the other. "Thanks again, you two!" she called back as the three of them moseyed through the park and down the path to her apartment.

"That was an awesome party! He had a blast!" Kholby noted once they had Landon tucked in bed for the night.

"Um, yea. He was asleep before his head hit the pillow," she agreed. "So, you really think George is okay for Goldie?"

"Oh man. He's so cute with her. Did you notice how he sat with his arm around her at the park? And she snuggled right up next to his shoulder. Adorable!"

"They do seem really good together, don't they?" she confirmed.

"And get this. I overheard them making plans for tomorrow night. He's taking her to the 'early-bird' special at Fred's Market."

"Their early-bird ends at four. That's like lunch," she said amused.

"For you and me, maybe, but for old people that's dinner." He laughed, then continued. "She was so excited. Said it was her favorite buffet. Especially loves their boiled cabbage. And then they're going to a movie. Dinner and a movie, just like teenagers but with different hours."

Kholby picked up the Transformers Bullet Train and began playing with it. Concerned, Allison commented, "I bet Landon will want to play with the Cars Lego set you got him tomorrow, you know, when he has more energy. I know he loves Legos! He was just distracted today with his friends and that transformer that Owen found."

"It's fine. I want to play with this thing myself!" he replied, manipulating the train. "How do you get the missile thing to work?" he wondered out loud, then realizing she was laughing at him, he set the toy down and put on a façade of maturity once more. "We'll find a way to put the two together tomorrow night, which, by the way, I am really looking forward to. What can I bring?"

"Bring? Are you serious? Did you see all the leftovers they sent home with me? I hope you don't mind, but we are having the same dinner and dessert tomorrow as we did tonight."

"That's great with me. I bet nobody can compete with Delia's cooking. ... Um, although, I'm sure you're a great cook," he quickly added trying to cover his faux pas.

She laughed, walking him to the door. "I don't even pretend to hold a candle to her. That's why I wouldn't dream of cooking for you the night after having her food. Plus, it's a long day of classes so I'll be lucky to get home in time to microwave." They reached the door and paused a moment. Both knew they were contemplating the same thing as the night before. That time, though, it was he who moved away.

"I'm exhausted and have a very early morning. Start the foundation for the house at seven a.m.," he yawned. Then, he brushed her hair from the side of her face and softly kissed her cheek. "Until tomorrow," he offered walking away. A foggy memory of another's kiss on her cheek fluttered way to the back of her mind, but she savored the new memories from the weekend even more, brewing with hopes for more tomorrow.

***

"Dinner was just as amazing tonight as it was last night!" he agreed as they cleaned up together. "I always love leftovers, but her stuff is amazing," he exclaimed.

Landon obliged his mother's request to help load the dishwasher. "It's time for *Mythbusters*. Can I go now? I'm done with the dishes just like you asked."

"Sure. Thanks for your help," she praised tussling his hair as he walked away.

Kholby went in to join Landon in the living room while Allison prepared dessert – leftover birthday cake and vanilla ice cream. "Hey Landon. Mind if I watch with you? I love this show!" Landon nodded his permission as Allison brought out dessert plates. Then, the three of them sat together for the entire hour, engrossed in whether paper-made battle armor would compare to steel or not. Once over, Allison nudged Landon, motioning for him to retrieve his new Lego set from the bedroom. Kholby quickly surmised a set-up, but he didn't mind in the least.

"Allison, I'm so sorry for the things I thought about him when we first met. I was a jerk." He apologized for at least the fifth time since they'd met only a few days prior. "I can see how smart he really is, and how much he loves you."

"Thanks," she replied. "Now don't apologize again. I'm sick of hearing it!" She was joking, he thought. Landon entered the room dragging the box with the pieces to his new Cars Lego set. "Landon, would you like Kholby to put that together with you?" She already knew his answer. They'd rehearsed it earlier.

"Yes, please," he replied exactly as the script directed. The pieces assembled quickly, and the builders were quite proud of their efforts. Finally Landon looked up very serious and said, "I'm an apple in my Momma's eyes."

Kholby smirked as he responded knowingly, "I absolutely believe it!"

She tried to stifle the laughter, but a snort resulted and she couldn't contain it any longer. "Honey, I said you are the 'apple of my eye.' It means you are the most precious person in the whole world to me. Why do you memorize them so well for Radmund and Kholby, but not me?"

"You didn't explain it to me right," he replied curtly. He'd been doing so well that she forgot he still needed things explained in very literal terms. "You laughed at me," he pouted angrily.

"Baby, I'm very sorry. You are so cute and funny sometimes." Her cheeks blushed with embarrassment in front of her guest. "Won't happen again for at least 20 minutes, promise."

"I'm going to play with the train transformer in my room now." Landon shoved the Cars Lego set under the coffee table and sauntered off, still pouting.

"Wow, he takes it pretty seriously, huh?" Kholby remarked.

"Nah, he's just trying to make me feel bad. I'm used to it. You should see when he gets his real pouty lip going! He can make it droop down to his collarbone!" She tried to imitate her son's gesture which only served to move them both to fits of laughter once more.

"Stop laughing!" Landon stomped into the room, hands on his hips, lip drooping to his collarbone. Allison quickly hugged her son, reassuring him that they were sorry.

"We really were not laughing at you, Landon. Your mom just made a funny face. That's all," Kholby added. "But you gotta admit. You do *try* to be funny sometimes, don't you?"

Landon forced the pouting lip to return. Keeping his head hung low, he raised only his eyes, looking up at them both trying to be very serious. "It's only funny with Radmund. I don't like it this way!"

"Honey, I think it might be way past your bedtime now. You had such a long day yesterday and you're still very cranky tonight." She'd had enough of his attitude in front of their guest. In the quiet of his room, just by themselves, she asked, "Landon, why were you so rude out there? It's not like you to do that."

"You hurt my feelings," he explained.

"But sweetheart. You have to understand that sometimes people say things that are funny, even when they don't mean to. It's not laughing at you in a bad way. We were laughing because you are so cute. I love that about you."

She tucked his covers in as the ritual began. "It's not the same with *him* here. I miss Radmund," he finally admitted, pouty lip returning.

"Me too. But Kholby is a really nice man. And, he liked watching TV and playing with you tonight. Didn't you enjoy it also?" She tilted her head as she spoke, hoping for his agreement.

"He's okay. I like Radmund better. We talk about stuff when he plays with me."

"Well, you just met Kholby. I know you talked to him at lunch the other day, teaching him about your tops. I bet you two will start chatting more if you give him a chance. Now what song would you like tonight?" As if she didn't already know. It was Monday – *Bingo* – except their version used L-A-N-DO-N instead (running the DO together with just the right slur on the beat). It was definitely a family favorite. Prayer time followed with the usual requests for Delia and Henry, Momma, Jonathan, Skylar, Miss Goldie and her *friend*, and Radmund. Those were followed by a special "thank you" for Mr. Owen and Miss Louella and the cool toy they gave him for his birthday. "Would you like to pray for Kholby also?" she asked as he concluded.

"I suppose so," he sighed reluctantly. "And, please help Kholby to go back to his house and stay there. Amen." It wasn't what she expected at all. In fact, she didn't even realize he had the capacity for such strong sentiment until that moment.

"That's some ritual you got there. Takes a long time," Kholby whined as she returned. "I don't know how you do it, being a single parent and all."

"Why do you keep bringing that up?" she quipped, suddenly irritated herself. "It is what it is, now drop it." *Apparently Landon is not the only one who is tired and cranky,* she thought.

Kholby had never been good at guarding his words, and he was very slow in the learning process with her. *Idiot! Think before you speak*, he reprimanded himself. "I just want to know more about you, that's all."

"You know everything you need to; it's in my past and there is nothing more to say. Besides, I'm not asking you to divulge your past relationships, am I?"

"No, but I'd tell you whatever you wanted to know if you cared to find out."

"I don't need to know those things. I want to know you *now*, what you like and dislike, your thoughts on life. That stuff."

"Hmm, okay then. Well, first of all, I love this chocolate cake!" He grinned holding up the empty plate. "I don't like classical music, but if Miss Goldie played it, then I'd probably learn to love it. I love roller coasters, especially the one I rode with you on Saturday." He put his arm around her as they nestled into the couch for more comfortable conversation. "Actually, I think I liked it because of my riding partner." She melted at his words and his touch. "Hey, I told you three things. It's your turn."

She couldn't argue with equality in conversation. "Okay. Well, I really like red-velvet cake best, but chocolate is Landon's favorite. I'm graduating in December with a degree in respiratory therapy, which will be great. I love my classes, but I'm terrified about actually working with patients. I start my clinicals in June, one day a week." She paused to count. "Okay, your turn again. Tell me more about China."

He sat back, snuggling in closer. "Did you know the Chinese people have to sneak church services in their own apartments?" She shook her head, already engrossed. "Well, they do. They have churches in China, but the government actually tells the pastors what they can say. But people still line up for blocks just to get in and hear a little bit about Jesus. My group gets to work with young college students who are learning English, but that's just a façade for them actually attending a Christian school. I really hope I get a chance to share God's word with some of them. They have to ask me first, though. I could be arrested if I bring it up to them."

"So if you want to go to China, how'd you end up working with Habitat?" she asked.

"Oh, that's for now. I just got my degree in December, so I'm hoping they call me to China sometime soon. Habitat was nice enough to give me a steady job during school. I really like seeing the people light up when they walk in their house for the first time. It's pretty cool!" He paused and held up the hand not around her shoulders. "Okay. Your turn again. You're amazing with Landon. How'd you do it?"

"What do you mean?" she replied as he took her hand to hold in his. Both hearts fluttered.

"I've never met anyone with an autistic child before. I thought they were really tough to handle but you seem to be so calm. And it's obvious he adores you. Is it as easy as you make it look?"

Warmth flooded her whole body as she pondered his compliment. "First of all, it was really tough when I found out. I'd only read the worst-case scenarios about the kids who scream or never talk. So, I freaked out. He wasn't talking yet, even though he was two. I thought I'd never hear my son ask for a bedtime song, or be able to tell me what he needed," she paused. "Or, that he'd never tell me he loved me." They both sat a moment in silence.

"But by his third birthday, the doctors reassured me he was on the very high-functioning end of the spectrum. And, one day he just started talking in simple sentences, I was so relieved. It was still tough. He would throw a fit if anything startled him, which was awful since he had to be at the restaurant with me most of the time. Delia and Henry were wonderful. They've always treated us like family and helped me deal with it all. In fact, they're the ones that really helped me learn how to help my son.

God knew exactly where I needed to be when he brought me here." She stopped short, realizing how close she came to divulging facts she swore not to share with him. "We got him on some medicine a few months ago that really has helped his anxiety so much. Landon deserves most of the credit, though. He's got an amazingly sweet personality, and he's taught me so much about being patient. Not because he's difficult, but because he's just really basic about life. If it's logical or literal, he's fine. If not, it doesn't really matter to him. I've learned to look at life in an analytical, but unique, way thanks to him."

"I love how your face glows when you talk about him," Kholby noted staring at her, moving his arm from around her shoulders and lightly touching her cheek. All her nerves shuddered as he leaned closer and whispered. "It's our second date. Technically, third if you count the birthday party."

"Yea," she squeaked. "I'd say third since you came over after the party. But that was just a few minutes, so I don't know if it counts. Then there was also the day we met at the restau ..."

He stopped her mid-word, gently putting his finger over her lips. "You talk a lot when you're nervous," he smiled.

"I talk a lot all the time," she whispered. "But I can be quiet if necessary."

"I think now is necessary," he acknowledged leaning in so close their noses brushed together.

"Okay," she breathed as their lips finally met for the first time. Moments later, she slowly opened her eyes, still assimilating all the senses from the kiss. It was as if the warmth of his touch spread across her entire body in an instant. The scent of his cologne lingered in her mind, sweet mixed with a hint of cinnamon. Her lips, still moist, twitched a tiny bit in excited response. But most of all, she sat frozen, staring into his eyes, only inches away.

He sat motionless, sorting through the mass responses in his own brain. Her soft, innocent touch left him breathless. Sounds of his heartbeat echoed in his head, pounding rhythmically with the fireworks still accelerating in the distance of his conscience. And her eyes, focused on his, reflected an intensity that made him tremble with joy.

"Um, well, um ..." he tried to speak. She just sat, remaining motionless. "I think I should go now. It's another early morning at the house," he finally stammered out the words.

Jerked back to reality, she muttered. "Huh? Oh yeah. I guess so. Early morning. Yeah." He never let go of her hand, from the couch to the door. Even though it was only a few steps in her small apartment, she felt as if they floated through the air for hours. "I, um, I ... I had an amazing time tonight. Thanks for coming over."

"Me too," he agreed still focused on the depth of her eyes. "Any chance we can get together again this week? I'm here every day, you know."

She paused to consider her schedule, certain she would find another night free. "What about Friday. I know it's a long way off, but it's the only other night I don't have classes this week. Maybe we could have another picnic. That's Landon's and my usual Friday date, if you would like to join us. And, we get some awesome leftovers from the Stop for dinner."

"Hmm, Delia's cooking again. Another chance to play on the slide with Landon. And, an evening under the stars with you. Nothing could keep me away!"

"See!" She grinned regaining her normal composure. "I knew you liked that slide yesterday! You said you were just going down to help Landon, but he didn't need any help. You used my son as an excuse to play on the toys!"

"Guilty," he smirked holding his hand up as if swearing in testimony. "And, I can't wait to see both of you again. Slide or no slide." Finally he leaned toward her, brushed her hair aside, and kissed her on the cheek, much to her dismay.

"Kholby," she said as he started through the doorway. "This was the greatest weekend ever."

"For me too," he agreed, then waved moving quickly out of the building, resisting the urge to run back into her arms.

Surprise!

The week moved at a snail's pace as far as she could tell. Classes dragged forever, and her shifts at the Stop seemed an eternity. A constant highlight, however, were his daily visits for a quick lunch. At least that's why he said he came by, even though they all knew that Habitat had ample church volunteers bringing in lunch for the workers. Thursday brought the first surprise of the week when the professor in her Cardiopulmonary Patient Assessment class collected the report assigned that previous Tuesday – the assignment she'd completely missed hearing about due to her texting instead of taking notes. Luckily, Allison was an excellent student with a straight-A reputation. "Thank you for the extension, Professor Ridgely. I promise it won't happen again." Then she'd spent the rest of the night researching and drafting the report, at the same time berating herself for allowing such flagrancy in her academics.

"I still can't believe I let that slip by me," she complained at dinner on Friday. "Thankfully, I got it all done last night after class and turned it in first thing this morning, before I went in to work."

"You must have been up all night," he worried.

"Only until two. It's all good. I didn't have to be at work until nine, so it was fine," she yawned as she tried to convince them both. "And I don't have classes again until Monday. So time to relax!" With that, she poured herself another glass of tea and turned around leaning her back against the picnic table to get a better view of Landon as he played on the swings. "He actually asked if we were seeing you tonight. I think that's a good sign, don't you?"

Kholby looked fondly at the little boy. "I'm trying. We talked a little at lunch this week, when he wasn't too busy with those tops or trains. But, he's kind of a hard kid to get to know. Mostly he just tells me how Radmund would do it – whatever it is we're playing with at the time," he noted not realizing the envy slipping through his tone.

She thought a moment on how to respond, but decided it was probably best if she just changed the subject. "So, would you like to go the Festival again before it ends on Sunday? Toby Mac is the final concert. He's one of my favorites!"

"Me too! I'd love to go!" Looking back at the swings, he approached the taboo topic   still oblivious of his parameters. "Do you think maybe Landon could stay with Delia? I mean, a concert might not be that easy for him to sit through. Plus, it'd be nicer for you if you weren't distracted, don't you think?"

Sometimes, when he looked into her eyes, it was an abyss of emotion into the deepest realm of her soul. Other times, it was a cold, double-edged sword. That time, he saw the sword and immediately realized she was about to strike. "First of all, Landon loves Toby Mac," she began with a sharpness in her voice that dulled the stare. "Second, do not ever use me as your excuse to get rid of Landon for a date. I'm perfectly capable of choosing to bring him or have him stay with someone else."

"Wow. I'm sorry. Didn't mean to hit a nerve," he replied a bit miffed and fed up with her instant defense about life and the boy. "Look, I'm not trying to be rude. I really like Landon. But it would be nice if you and I could spend some time alone." She looked at him again, the edge in her stare beginning to soften. Before she could respond, he continued. "I know part of this is just a way you protect him because of his disability. But, it's like you're holding back other stuff too. Look, it's okay if you don't want to tell me about your past. But, please do not hold it against me when I mess up and say things that offend you for the very thing you refuse to tell me about."

She completely averted his gaze at that point. "I'm really sorry," she sighed. "You are exactly right. About everything. I'll really try to be less defensive. Landon is a special kid, so it's hard not to be overly sensitive about him right now. When he's older and learns to stand up for himself, then maybe it'll be easier for me. But for now, I'm a mom and a bodyguard. He deserves nothing less." She took his hand, returning warm shivers to both their arms. "But I will assume you have the best intentions from now on, instead of jumping down your throat."

"And, I promise to try and think more about your feelings before I stick my foot in my mouth again," he grinned.

Unbeknownst to them, Landon stood nearby, his face contorted in question. "Momma, you can't fit down his throat. But, I can stick my foot in my mouth," he simply stated as he attempted to test his theory while sitting on the ground and taking off his left shoe.

"Hey Landon," Kholby replied, slightly alerted to his presence and wondering just how much of the conversation he had understood. "I can't stick my foot in my mouth, but obviously you can!" They all laughed, including Landon that time, as he succeeded. "It means I said something that wasn't very nice."

"Oh," Landon said in retrospect, replacing his foot back on dirty concrete. Allison grimaced at the thought of what he'd just done.

"Jumping down your throat means you got angry with someone." Allison wished those were not the idioms he overheard. They were not fun or positive like the others he'd learned.

"You guys were fighting," he concluded astutely.

The two adults stared in disbelief. "How did you know that?" she asked.

"He wasn't very nice and you got angry with him."

"Exactly," they both concurred.

Looking at him, then each other, they broke out in simultaneous laughter. "We are not laughing at you," she promised as Landon looked on confused. "You are so smart! We were fighting over something really silly. You made us happy again. Thanks!"

"Okay," he agreed, although not the least bit interested in what really happened. "I have to go potty."

"Would you like me to take him?" Kholby asked.

"No. Only Radmund or Momma takes me to the bathroom at the park." Allison shot an apologetic look at Kholby as she quickly escorted her son to the bathroom.

"Momma, are you still mad at Kholby?" Landon asked as they emerged from the restroom.

"No. It was a silly argument," she replied. "Why?"

"If you are mad at him, he might go away. Maybe Radmund will come home if Kholby goes away."

She stopped walking a moment, picked up her son, and then whispered in his ear. "Sweetheart, Radmund isn't staying away because of Kholby. Remember, he had to go to work for a couple of weeks. He'll be home soon. Besides, I think you can have just as much fun with Kholby as you do with Radmund. But, it won't happen unless you are willing to try." Putting him down, she finished, "It would be a really special present for me if you tried to like Kholby as much as you like Radmund."

136

In spite of his disability, Landon loved his mother very much. He truly wanted to please her, probably more than anyone else in the world. "Okay, I'll try for you," he agreed.

A noise was brewing in the distance when they returned to the pavilion where Kholby sat waiting. "What's that? Sounds so familiar," she said. Landon moved on to another table to play with his Cars Legos Set, which happened to be the only toy Allison "remembered" to bring that night. "It's the Charlie Daniels Band. I forgot they are performing tonight at the Festival."

"How cool! It's like free lawn seats," Kholby concurred. As they focused, the sounds were stronger and clearer. "I know this one! *Simple Man*. Great song!" He turned to her and extended his right arm, motioning for her to join him. "May I have this dance?"

She snuggled easily into his open arms as they began moving rhythmically to the music. Both became completely lost in the moment as they swayed in perfect unison. The moon hung full and bright in the sky, sending a warm glow into the dusk of the evening.

"Excuse me. May I cut in?" came a voice startling them both back to reality. Allison turned in what seemed like slow motion as the voice registered in the back of her brain. "Hey Al," he greeted her with his own arms open wide.

"No way!" she screamed. "You're here! Landon! Look who's here! I can't believe it!" She lunged into his arms, hugging him so tightly he thought his ribs might crack. Landon immediately jerked, disturbed by his mother's reaction.

Kholby finally found the moment to interrupt, but could barely speak over the knot in his throat. "Hi. You must be Radmund," he said hesitantly.

"What?!" he laughed. "No, I thought *you* were Radmund."

Allison jumped in to clear up the mess. "Well, this isn't awkward," she joked sarcastically. "Kholby, this is my big brother Marc. Marc, this is Kholby. You know," she muttered out of the side of her mouth, "I emailed you about him."

"Oh, you're Marc!" Kholby sighed in great relief as he reached out his hand in greeting. "It's very nice to meet you."

"You too," Marc acknowledged shaking his hand.

Still unnerved by her shrieking, Landon sat frozen, rocking his body in resistance at her beckoning. Finally, Allison had to hold her son in her arms as she coaxed him to greet his uncle. "Landon, this is your Uncle Marc. I know you don't remember him. But he's my big brother. I talk about him all the time." Landon wiggled on her hip, lifting his head from her shoulder to look at the stranger. "It'd mean a lot to me if you shook his hand," she encouraged.

Landon limply reached out his hand in greeting of the uncle he'd met only as a baby. "Hi. I'm five now."

"I know. I'm sorry I couldn't be here in time for your birthday. But, I did bring you a gift. If, of course, you're still accepting them being so late and all." He reached in his pocket, took out a small box, and handed it to his nephew.

Landon checked for a visual cue from his mother before accepting the gift. "It's okay. Open it," she responded setting him back on the ground knowing he was calm again.

In a moment his conquest was complete, but the puzzled look on his face clearly indicated his lack of enthusiasm. "What is it?"

Marc laughed, reassuring his sister that he expected that response. "This is called 'Kanoodle.' It is an awesome puzzle game where you use the pieces to build pyramids! It's only for kids who are super smart, though, which is exactly why I knew it was the perfect gift for you." Allison and Kholby both looked on in the same bewilderment as Landon. "Okay, then. How about I show you *all* how it works?" Marc offered. Landon watched carefully as Marc demonstrated the steps to follow while using the guidebook patterns for help.

With one pyramid successfully completed, Landon was hooked. "My turn. I understand now." He quickly turned the page to the next pattern and worked feverishly until the second pyramid was completed. Only a minute passed by. Not much for facial gestures, Landon's grin was the best he could do to show his delight in the new game. "Thank you Uncle Marc. I like it."

"Yea. Thanks Uncle Marc," Allison agreed. "When do I get my turn?"

"I know, right? It's like the most addictive game I've ever seen. Frankly, he was my excuse to buy one. Do you think he'll let me play it sometimes, seeing how I'll be living here now?"

"What!? You're moving here?" Once more she threw her arms around his neck, hugging with all her might.

"Sis, you're going to break my neck! Please," he snickered. "I got my residency right here at Brandon Regional. They have a new clinic opening in two weeks. You are looking at the resident ER doc! I leased a condo in Hillsborough, but can't move in for a week yet. Figured I'd see if I could bunk with my little sister a few days 'til then."

"Are you kidding? Of course you can stay with us ... forever if you want!"

"No, that would be kinda stifling, I think," he smirked looking over at Kholby. "But I can't wait to catch up ... if you can spare an evening or two for your big bro. And I can't wait to get to know my nephew better!"

"I have to work tomorrow, but no plans after four. Ooh, would you come to The Whistle Stop tomorrow and see Delia and Henry? They're going to be so excited to see you again. It's been almost four years already. And we could have lunch together!" She stopped to look at Kholby, acknowledging his presence for the first time in several minutes. "Would you like to join us also?" she asked, more of obligation than anticipation.

"Actually, I was going to tell you. I'm off tomorrow so I won't be around like usual. Owen and I are going to fix some of the windows and siding on my grandparents' trailer. It got hit hard in the hail storm a few days ago."

"Even on your day off you still work on someone else's house," she said in utter respect. An idea suddenly lit up in her mind. "Hey, Marc. Do you really want to get to know Landon better?" She grinned in Kholby's direction.

"You bet! What'd you have in mind?"

"Kholby and I were hoping to go to the Toby Mac concert on Sunday. Any chance you'd be free to spend the evening with Landon? I mean you could take him to the Festival as well if you like. He loves it there. But he would probably prefer to walk around and play games than sit that long, even at a concert he likes." Kholby put his arm around her, rubbing her shoulder gently to show his approval.

Marc turned to his nephew, who was mid-way through Level Three by that point. "What do you think, Sport? Wanna hang out with your Uncle Marc on Sunday?"

Kholby anticipated Landon's response, but was taken aback when all Landon said was, "Okay." *Apparently I'm the **only** one who **cannot** call him Sport,* he reflected in slight irritation.

"Marc, where's all your stuff? How'd you get here?" Allison began interrogating him.

"I have a car, you know. Not in the best of shape, but it runs, even after all these years, and from the Northeast all the way down here in two days." He pointed to the white Ford Escape in the parking lot.

"You do not still have Matilda! I can't believe it."

"Hey now. Don't criticize her. She hasn't let me down yet."

"Matilda? You named your car Matilda?" Kholby cracked up.

"Matilda was our neighbor growing up. Remember her?" he asked his sister.

"Oh yeah! She had more energy than anybody I knew. She must have been 110, but still out there mowing the lawn, weeding the garden, and fighting off those stupid dogs whenever they came around yippin' at us!" Allison nodded as the memory brought a huge smile to her face.

"Darn tootin'! She was a fighter, filled with energy." He looked back at Kholby. "And that car is named in her memory. Keeps on working and fightin' no matter what!"

"Momma, it's 8:30," Landon pointed to his watch. They were all startled at how quickly the evening flew by. "It's bedtime."

"He is a stickler for routine," she agreed. "Marc, you remember? I live right over there," she pointed the direction of her apartment building.

"Yep, I know right where it is. Me and Matilda will meet you there in a few if you're sure it's okay." He looked at his car and back at them. "I'd offer you guys a ride, but everything I own is in the backseat."

"We always walk anyway. Lots of exercise is great for your heart," Kholby replied trying to impress his girlfriend's doctor-brother with the emphasis on health. *I'm an idiot,* he thought. *That was totally obvious.* When they got to his car, Kholby felt it best to leave Allison and her brother to their reunion.

"You don't have to go," she insisted.

"Yes, I think I do," he replied. "I know you want some time with Marc. Besides, I don't want to embarrass myself anymore." He moved in closer, feeling awkward as Landon stood at her side. "I want you to have some time with your brother. It's important to you. And, I get you all to myself on Sunday!" With one hand on her cheek and the other gently nuzzling her waist, he leaned in for a light kiss, hoping Landon would not notice.

"There's Marc," Landon commented nonchalantly. "Let's go." He grabbed his mother's free hand and began tugging her away from the one place she desperately wanted to remain for a bit longer.

"Sunday," she beamed waving as Kholby got in his car to leave.

**

Together they sang the Friday song to Landon – *You Are My Sunshine*. But Landon's eyes were shut in sweet dreams before the duet finished singing "away" in perfect harmony.

"So that was weird earlier," Marc commented as she set up the couch for his bed. "I mean both of us thinking the other was Radmund."

"It's okay. I thought it was kinda funny," she snickered. "Kholby hears about Radmund all the time from Landon. And, he's not convinced we're just friends, even though I've told him a hundred times at least."

"Who are you trying to convince, Sis? Him or you?" He fluffed the pillow and leaned back in exhaustion from the long drive.

She sat by his side. "He asked me the same thing. I email you about this stuff. What do you think?"

"Okay. Let's see. You tell me about the deep conversations you have with Radmund. How the two of you had the magical night with your purity vows. That he knows all about your past and how supportive he is when you really need someone to talk to. And how much you love to watch him with Landon." He paused. "Right so far?" But, he did not wait for her response. "And then all of a sudden I start hearing about Kholby. 'He's sooo cute'," he imitated what might have been her high-pitched girly voice.

She smacked his thigh in rebuttal. "Stop making fun of me!" she demanded humorously.

"Oh, and he's working for Habitat. He's a gentleman and cares a lot about other people. Wants to do whatever he can to help people in need." He looked over at her. "I don't know. Sounds like you need to blend the two together for the perfect man. Oh wait, then you'd have me!" He elbowed her. "And that would just be gross!"

"Landon doesn't like him as much, but Kholby is really patient," she added.

"Do you two connect? You know, totally honest and all?"

She looked hurt, "Why would you ask me that? You know I told you all about his mission work. That's pretty special."

Marc replied, "Sure, but that's not dating material. I mean, do you know his innermost thoughts? And, does he know yours?"

"It's just that I don't know him very well yet. I'm sure I'll have lots of other deep stories to share with you once we've dated for awhile."

"Is that what you're doing – dating?"

"I think so," she replied thoughtfully.

"Well, he seems like a really nice guy. And if he makes you happy then I'm okay with it, I guess." Marc wasn't as convinced as he sounded. But he had learned a long time back that his sister was a fragile being and she needed to learn to stand on her own. "So, have you told him?"

"No. I don't want him to know."

"Oh man. That's not a secret you keep from a guy unless you're not really that serious about him. Do you think he's marriage material?" He was the voice of Big Brother now.

"I haven't really thought that far, honestly. And, I just wanted to date someone without my stupid past in either of our minds at all."

"So, you'd rather he think you'd been easy and careless as a teenager?"

"I know it sounds awful, but yes. Today's world is filled with teenagers who make bad choices like that. It's so common that nobody thinks twice about it anymore. But if you tell someone you were raped, well, that's a different story. Then the guy gets all creeped out and thinks you'll never be normal again. And, they certainly don't want to marry a girl with that baggage, especially if there's a kid from the rape. Why would I expect anyone to be able to deal with that?"

"So you are thinking about marriage." He sat up and put his arm around her in comfort.

"I don't know. I've only known him a week. But I do want to find a great guy, fall in love, and get married someday. And, it'd be great for Landon to have a father."

"Sis, would you keep a secret like that from your husband, whoever he ends up to be?"

"Of course not!" she exclaimed, shocked that he would insinuate otherwise.

"Well, seems to me that if you think this guy has any potential, then you should trust him enough to tell him the truth *now*, before you fall madly in love and risk breaking his heart … or him breaking your heart."

"What if he doesn't want to be with someone who was raped?"

He took her hand and looked her squarely in the eyes. "Exactly! Would you even consider dating a man who would walk away from you because of that? What's that say about his commitment to you, or *your* trust in him?"

"Geesh, Marc. Why do you always have to make so much sense?" she smiled hugging him more gently that time. "I'll think about it, okay?"

He yawned and stretched back out on the couch, knocking her off the edge onto the floor. "Okay," he sighed half asleep. She tucked the cover under his arms, kissed his forehead, and quietly stepped away. "Hey Sis," he whispered as she turned off the lights. "I love you."

"I love you, too," she affirmed. "I'm so glad you're back."

Fears, Faith, Frustration

The March rains stayed away long enough for the festival to end in the flourish of which the Plant City citizens are so accustomed. Rap mixed with pop rock belted out of the concert venue, filling the entire fairgrounds and surrounding blocks with a worship fit for the King. Fireworks lit up the night sky to celebrate the end of another successful year as all the planners and guests cheered to the success of the festival's theme. And, Delia proudly displayed her blue ribbon for winning the "Best Soup" category in the festival's strawberry recipes contest.

Unfortunately, on Monday, the Heavens opened and rained out the picnic dinner date Kholby and Allison had anticipated. "I think Landon is most disappointed," Allison noted as they set the table with leftover fried chicken, mashed potatoes, and the ever-popular coleslaw. "He loves the park. And he and Marc were going to put some master Lego thing together tonight, but then Marc got called in for a meeting so that just messed up Landon even more."

"I'm sure he's had rainy days before. What's the big deal? We've got the same great food, just inside." Kholby could have cared less where they were, as long as they were together. "And, I'd love to help him with the Legos!"

"I know. But he's feeling really vulnerable right now. He knows something is changing in my life. Even though he's not really great with social stuff, he has an excellent 'sixth' sense. And right now it has him on edge."

Kholby was intrigued. "So you think something is changing your life?" he began. "… For the better, I hope?" His hinting caught her off guard.

She shrugged and tried to hide the huge smile, which was hopelessly out of control by that point. "I think so," she flirted. "What about you?"

He didn't hesitate. "You bet! I got a job at Habitat. Free room and board for a few weeks. And this food is to die for! I'd say those things are major good changes in my life." His eyes twinkled as he teased her.

She set down the last plate for dinner as he spoke. For a moment she was confused by his teasing, then lightly punched his shoulder when she realized he was tormenting her. "You forgot how great Toby Mac was last night!"

"Oh, yea, and that we got in free! That was sweet." He took her hand and pulled her onto his lap in an embrace as the teasing ended. "And, of course, there's you," he finished sweetly. "Now that's an awesome change I never expected."

She put her arms around his shoulders. "It's about time you got serious," she chided eyeing him with the abyss of emotion. "You are definitely a positive change in my life. Landon will be okay when he realizes how much you mean to me." He pulled her close, into a passionate kiss. The sweetness of his touch comforted her. She knew he would never force her into anything which made it so easy to melt into his arms. Likewise, he found such innocent joy in her kiss – a reassurance of her trust in him. Together, they were lost in the moment, until a sudden rap at the door flung them both back to reality.

As tough as it was, she pulled herself free of his arms. "Gee wiz, Marc. Did you forget your key already?" she asked loudly. A glimpse of red revealed her mistake as she flung open the door. "Oh my gosh! Radmund! You're home!" She jumped forward in a "welcome home" hug – much different from the embrace she'd been in a moment earlier.

Hearing the commotion, and the name of his best friend, Landon came running from his bedroom. "Radmund! I knew you'd come back," he squealed jumping into the reunion. Both Allison and Radmund were shocked at the intensity of the boy's emotion.

"Hey Sport. How ya been?" He tousled Landon's hair, then lifted him into his arms for a huge bear hug. Still holding Landon, he turned his attention back to Allison. "Man I missed you guys!"

"He's talked about you every day," she replied, affirming the sentiment was truly reciprocated. "Do your folks know you're home yet?"

"No, just got here and had to get to the apartment to clean up and unpack first. I'll go over there in a few minutes. I also wanted to check in on you guys." It wasn't until then that he looked into the kitchen to see a stoic, dark-haired stranger sitting at a dinner table clearly set for three.

"We have dinner ready," Landon invited, taking his friend's hand and dragging him to the table. "I'll get a plate for you."

"Um, hi," he began hesitantly. "I'm Radmund."

"Yes, I know," Kholby replied in a vain effort to hide his dismay. "I'm Kholby."

Allison saw no problem; she refused to see the problem. "Kholby, this is Radmund. He's my best friend." She turned to Radmund, "Rad, this is Kholby. He's my ..." The sudden realization as to how to describe Kholby to Radmund sent her reeling.

Kholby decided to jump in full-force noticing her confusion. "I'm her boyfriend," he confirmed winking at her. "I've heard a lot about you. Mostly from Landon."

Radmund was stunned. For two weeks he'd prayed that the old adage, "Absence makes the heart grow fonder," would come true for them. He'd accepted being patient with her resistance, hoping she harbored deeper feelings for him than she would admit. Even though he knew his prayers might be in vain, he never expected to find her so quickly involved with another man. *Obviously she meant it when she said we're just friends,* he berated himself. *I was a fool to expect anything more.* Everything in him boiled without warning, and he turned to go without a word.

"Rad! You can have dinner with us, please?" Landon begged.

"Hey Sport," he turned to reply only to the little boy. "I can't tonight. But I'd love to have lunch with you tomorrow, if you're available that is."

"Okay. I'll bring my new transformer and the green top. We can have a war with them," Landon explained laying out the next day's agenda in full detail.

Allison walked him to the door, without any eye contact. When she finally looked up at him, she saw the pools swelling in his eyes as he blinked, fighting the keep them from pouring down his cheeks. "Rad," she whispered. "He's a very nice guy. I know you'll like him once you get to know him bett..." She tried to finish but he cut her off.

"I'm sure I will," was all he said with his back turned walking out the door.

***

"What's he got that I don't?!" his voice boomed later as Delia and Henry tried desperately to console their son. "We can't date because she's not ready for any kind of a relationship, but this guy strolls into town and she's immediately smitten? She's like a little girl!" His eyes flared in a mixture of red anger and pain. Sweat dripped from his palms as he wrung his hands tightly over and over.

"Honey, I know this is painful, but you're right. She's never dated before so this is all really new to her ... like a teenager." Delia explained, "Kholby is a missionary. She knows he's going to China soon. Maybe he's just a diversion, you know. Deep down he's safe because of that."

"Oh stop! Don't try to get my hopes up. She's not interested in me, and she's been telling me that for over a month now. I'm just too stupid to accept it."

"Hey, her brother is in town now. Maybe he can help," Henry added. "He came by the restaurant this morning. You haven't met him yet, but he's a great guy. Why don't you talk to him?"

Radmund contemplated the idea. "What do you think he'd do?"

"Well," Delia started. "He told us he's the new resident ER doc at Brandon, so you'll be working together soon. And he's only a year older than you. I bet you'd hit it off well."

Henry finished the idea, "And, his influence is a huge weight with her. She takes his advice as gold."

Radmund finally plopped onto the couch, still wringing his hands. "Tell me more about this Kholby guy. Is he good to her?"

"He's a very nice young man. His grandparents are good friends of the Travis'. That's how we met him, in fact. He's working here on a Habitat project, and they brought him in the Stop a few days ago to meet everyone," Henry explained.

"Great, so he's a nice guy. Not a jerk. I suppose I should be thankful, huh?"

"Yes, you should. He is a gentleman. But, he is distracting her. That's not really his fault, though. She's never dated anyone, remember. This is all very exciting to her." Delia paused, then explained. "She mentioned that it's hard to concentrate in class lately because she thinks about him. He was at the restaurant every day last week to have lunch with her and Landon."

A lightbulb glimmered in his mind. "What does Landon think of him?"

"Not sure," Henry admitted. "They play a little at lunch, but Landon doesn't really talk to him much that I can tell."

"Good," Radmund grinned, wishing the worst.

"Rad, don't go there!" Delia warned. "If you do anything to use that little boy against her, it will backfire on you like a bomb. You just keep that sweet relationship with him separate, and let Allison have her space for awhile."

"This sucks," he began. "I come home so excited to see them again. Great homecoming!"

"Sweetheart, she never led you on at all. Be patient. You know that saying. If it's really you, let her go and she'll come back committed to you forever. If she doesn't come back, it was never really you to begin with."

Rad grimaced. "Mom, that's not quite how it goes. Sucks just the same, though."

"Not if the ending is what you want," Henry reassured him. "Listen to your mom, son. She's the wisest woman I've ever known." He put his arm around her shoulders, drawing her close to kiss her head.

"You guys are right, as usual," he sighed slumping onto the couch. Then he finally broke down and cried. "I have to let her go. I have to accept her as a friend and move on. I have to." His parents wrapped their arms around him, enveloping him in both physical and spiritual support as they all prayed for comfort and wisdom.

***

A handful of strangers were sorely disappointed that Wednesday when they approached The Whistle Stop to find the following sign on the door: "Due to family circumstances, The Whistle Stop will be closed until Friday.

We are truly sorry for this inconvenience. Please come back in two days for free strawberry shortcake as our gratitude for your understanding." It didn't really matter, though, if Friday's visitors had been there during the closure or not. Everyone would get free dessert in honor of what Henry believed would be a complete success in his wife's surgery.

"Well, guys," Marc came out late that morning to address Henry, Radmund, Allison, and Landon. "Delia came through like a champ. Just what you'd expect from someone strong as she is," he grinned. "Dr. Westborough said they got all the mass. They did a blood test just to make sure there are no cells lingering. We'll know the results later this week hopefully."

"What about the reconstructive piece?" Henry asked purposefully avoiding any further information on her blood test.

"That went really well. But it will prolong her recovery. The tissue will be very tender and painful for several days, even weeks. Do not let her jump back into work. From what I know about her, I think that will be your most difficult hurdle."

"Can I go see her now?" Henry asked hopeful.

"Sure, down the hall and to the left. Room 27. She's groggy, though."

Henry quickly jumped to follow Marc's directions as Allison took Landon to the bathroom for a much overdue break – for both of them. Radmund approached Marc. "Marc," he began shaking his hand, "thanks for your help. I know we just met yesterday, but it's obvious you are a good man. Allison speaks highly of you for good reason."

Marc glanced down the hall at his sister, then back at Radmund. "You and I should get to know each other better. She talks about you all the time."

"Really?" Rad queried. "That's odd since she thinks we are 'just friends'." The indignation in his tone was undeniable.

"I know. She told me you were upset about Kholby." He glanced around the waiting room. "Where is Kholby anyway?"

"Had to work. So sorry he couldn't be here. Would have except they're on a really important part of the foundation and he really couldn't leave the project today." Radmund was obviously mimicking the excuses rendered by Allison on Kholby's behalf earlier that morning. "But don't worry. He is praying all day for all of us."

"I sense a lot of resentment," Marc affirmed.

"You think?" he retorted.

"Whatever you do, don't let Allison hear you this way. I know my sister. That's the quickest way to push her away from you forever. When our folks turned her out, she tried desperately to reach out to them. Their rejection changed her gentle heart. The worst thing she still deals with is her immediate and intense reaction when she thinks somebody blames her for something beyond her control."

They sat down for a moment. Then Marc continued. "She told me she got upset with Kholby a couple of times because she thought he resented Landon like he was intruding on them or something. Don't tell her I told you that, okay?"

"I won't. Thanks for letting me know, though." He glanced to make she wasn't returning yet, then whispered. "Marc, do you think I have a chance with her, other than friends I mean?"

"I'm not the one to ask. I'm there for her no matter what she needs … and I won't give her advice on a guy unless he's a jerk. But, I believe you are her best friend. She loves you, just not like you want." He paused, sipping much-needed coffee after the long surgery. "Kholby is not a jerk. He seems like a nice guy. I'm sorry. I know you don't want to hear that, but it's true. I think you should move on for your own sake, but let her know that your friendship is solid no matter what." A final thought crossed his mind suddenly. "And, whatever you do, don't ever sever that relationship you have with Landon. I don't think my nephew could handle losing you."

"Thanks. I'll think about what you've said. And, don't worry. Nothing would keep me from being there for Landon whenever he needs me. I couldn't love him more if he was my own."

They noticed Allison and Landon returning as they stood. "I've got to get back to ER now. They were great to let me out today to be in on your mom's surgery." He hugged his sister as she walked back into the waiting area. "You holding up okay, Sis?"

"Yep. We're fine, aren't we Landon?"

"Umm huh," he mumbled. "Uncle Marc, Momma said you helped make sure Delia is okay. Thank you."

Marc picked up his nephew in the same bear hug Radmund used. "God helped all the doctors make sure Delia is okay. So, really He's the one we should thank in all our prayers tonight, okay?"

"Okay," Landon agreed as he reached the floor again. He turned to take Radmund's hand. "Your momma is good as gold. Don't worry."

"I'm not worried, Sport," he smiled. "But it was really nice to have you and your mom here. Thanks for playing transformers with me this morning. It really helped me feel better."

***

By Friday, Delia was released to continue the extent of her recovery at home per the doctor's orders. Radmund and Allison took the helm at the restaurant, forbidding Henry to come in at all that day. Returning home with his fragile wife, Henry tried to help her from the car inside the house, but she was determined to test her limits already. "Walking as soon as possible," Henry reminded her, "does not mean jumping back into regular life full force. The doctor clearly said to take it slowly."

"I'll take it easy. I promise," she confirmed happy to be home. "No worries. I'm not even able to lift my arms." She grimaced as she struggled to sit on the couch without use of her arms for support.

"Hey, let me help you," her husband demanded running to help her down gently. "Here, this should make you feel better." He opened a box filled with cards from well-wishers all over Plant City and beyond. Together, they snuggled as he opened and read a few cards to her. After the first few, though, she began to relax and breathe deeply, barely able to keep her eyes open. "Okay," he whispered covering her with a blanket. "Pain pills kicking in I see. We'll read more later."

"Henry," she whispered back. "You are the love of my life."

"I love you too." He responded kissing her forehead just as his cell phone rang. Noting her slowed and rhythmic breathing, he quickly stepped into the kitchen to take the call. "Hello," he answered. "Oh, hi Marc. Yea? You got the results for us yet?" His heart raced at the tone in Marc's voice. Tears poured from his eyes as he hung up the phone.

***

"Delia, you'll need chemo for about six weeks. We'll do another test then to see if you need anything more like radiation or more chemo treatments. We found traces of the cancer in your blood stream. I'm really sorry." Marc explained as Delia's family gathered in her living room that Friday night for the update. Having come down with a bad sinus infection, only Kholby was absent, which Allison found strangely relieving.

She immediately grabbed Radmund's hand as they all absorbed the impact of news they'd hoped to avoid. "Hey, sweetheart," she whispered to Landon who sat by her side. "Why don't you go in the toy room and play with those trains you love for a few minutes." Landon loved it in the Edmunds toy room where he happily commenced playing with the trains.

Henry immediately began wringing his hands. "What does that mean, exactly?" His wife sat close by, silent, calm, looking off into nowhere.

"Well, we thought the mass was contained, and it was mostly. But we did find evidence of a few cancer cells, kind of floating in the blood stream. It doesn't mean it's anything radical. However, if we don't treat it with the chemo, it could get bad." He turned directly toward Delia. "Listen. We treat women with this all the time. The chemo is pretty rough, but most women come through cancer-free. I see no reason that won't be the case for you also."

Delia looked around the room, taking in all those whom she loved so dearly. Radmund's eyes were as red as his hair; Allison held tightly to his hand repeating to herself, "This is wrong!" Henry cursed under his breath, unaware that all in the room heard anyway.

"I want you all to understand something," Delia began. "I do believe that God already has this one for me. I was reading the Bible this afternoon and this is what God led me to in James, 'Anyone who meets a testing challenge head-on and manages to stick it out is mighty fortunate. For such persons loyally in love with God, the reward is life and more life'. So you see, how could God share this with me if He didn't mean it? And who am I to question the One who created the universe?"

Silence permeated the room for a few moments. Finally, Henry spoke up, "Well, there you have it." He leaned over to kiss his wife on the cheek. "This woman is the strongest, wisest, and most amazing person I've ever met. I think, perhaps, it's the rest of us in this room who need the toxins cleaned out of our blood, not her."

Later that night, as he gently helped her in bed, tears poured down his cheeks for the umpteenth time. "Sweetheart, I want to be full of faith and brave like you, but it's so hard."

"Henry," she whispered mustering all her energy. "I absolutely believe that God will heal me. I'm completely certain of this. But don't get me wrong. I'm terrified of what is coming. And, I don't know exactly what His healing plan includes for me at this point. I do know that if he heals me on this earth, then you and I will enjoy a celebration like no other. But, if He, in His infinite wisdom, chooses to heal me in Heaven, then I'm okay with that. I'll just have to wait a few years to celebrate with you in eternity instead. Either way, a celebration will happen, and that makes me very happy."

He snuggled in bed beside her, gently wrapping his arms around her fragile body. "I will be here for you every step of the way. Whatever you need."

"I know," she softly breathed as she drifted off into deep, peaceful sleep.

Storms

By Monday morning, Radmund determined he needed some type of diversion in his life. Between his mother and Allison, he felt as if his every nerve were on edge – even moreso than he'd ever experienced on the battlefields. And, he knew it was in his best interest to accept Marc's advice and move on with life.

"Okay, we're here. What's the big surprise?" Allison asked as she and Landon rushed over per Radmund's request that evening.

"I just thought you should know I've decided to get a roommate."

"What? Rad, I don't think that's a good idea," she responded deeply concerned.

He took note of the concern in her eyes, finding a bit of joy at what he perceived as an envious twitch in her response. "Hey, you could've brought Kholby. I'd like for him to meet her also."

Landon piped up. "He's not here tonight. He's still sick. Momma is sad, but I thanked Jesus for making him sick."

Allison was appalled. "Oh Landon! Please don't talk that way. You know it's mean."

Landon looked to his friend for support, but to no avail. "Sorry Sport, I agree with your mom. That's not nice to ask Jesus to make people sick. You should pray for him to feel better just like I know you do for Delia. Plus, you said it makes your mom sad." He knelt down to make eye contact with the boy. "And I know you do not like to make your mother upset."

"Okay. Sorry," he pouted, head down, lip protruding to his sternum.

"So, is she already moved in? Cuz you really need to think about this," she demanded. "And, what do your folks think about his arrangement? I can't imagine this went over well with them. Plus, your poor mom is about ready to start chemo and you put this on her? Oh Rad, how could you?!"

Radmund looked around the room. "A woman? You assumed I had a girlfriend moving in? How rude!!" He whistled and then announced, "You might want to step back. Hey, Thor! Here Thor!" A thunderous pitter-patter rose from the back room, growing louder and louder by the second until they all saw the furry, four-legged culprit. Landon jumped and sought immediate security from behind his mother's legs. Radmund picked up his new roommate and began scratching her head as the puppy nuzzled into Radmund's neck. The dog wriggled and whimpered as her new owner tried desperately to restrain her long enough for Landon to peek around.

"Oh my gosh! You got a puppy?!" Allison implored hitting him on the upper arm. "I really thought you had a girlfriend moving in! That was rude! How did you convince Mr. Yang to allow you to have a pet in the apartment?"

"Calm down, Thor," Rad comforted softly petting the dog's neck. "Well, this isn't just any dog. She's a therapist-in-training."

"A what?!"

"Therapy dog … just not yet. But she will be when she's older. Right now I have to help get her ready for the serious training. So, Mr. Yang couldn't say 'no' because he already gave Miss Goldie permission for Buddy."

"But Thor is a puppy. She's going to chew and bark and wreak havoc." Even though Allison was terribly concerned about Radmund's decision, she was delighted with the adorable Golden Retriever puppy Rad placed in her arms. The dog commenced licking all over her chin as Landon began to whimper.

"I don't like your dog. It's eating Momma," he screeched pointing intently for Radmund to help.

Allison giggled as she bent down so Landon could pet Thor. "No, it's okay. She's just being really friendly. Here, pet her. I won't let her lick you." Landon cautiously held out his hand to pet Thor's backend. Thor violently churned in Allison's arms desperate to sniff and lick the hands of her newest friend. She finally wriggled free of Allison's arms and jumped down to run amuck in the living room. Landon immediately shot behind Radmund's legs for a safer view.

He picked up Landon and reassured him. "No worries Sport. Thor is just super friendly. I'm going to teach her tricks and all kinds of cool stuff. Maybe you could come over and help me sometimes?" Landon hesitantly shook his head, still focused on the furry frenzy about the room.

"Really, Rad. What a cool idea, but are you sure you're ready for this responsibility? She's going to eat your shoes and rip up your couch – um like right now!" She pointed as the dog was gnawing on a button near the leg of the sofa.

Radmund handed Landon to Allison, then picked up a soft pillow and plunked it on the dog's head. "Thor! Stop!" Thor stopped immediately, whimpered pitifully, and then recoiled into the corner.

Allison cracked up. "Is that what they said to do?"

"Yep, got her attention but didn't hurt her a bit. Just gotta be consistent. When she's good, I praise her with treats. Mostly my job is to teach her how to be really calm, especially if something bad happens to her owner."

"Oh, well you've got a huge job ahead of you then!" She put Landon down noticing the puppy seemed to settle quietly in her corner basket for the time. "Why 'Thor'? Did they give her that name?"

"Nope, all my idea! Don't you like it?"

"You mean like the god of Thunder in Avengers? Isn't that a boy-dog's name? And, it's a little ironic for a dog who is supposed to learn how to be calm, even in the strongest of storms."

"Exactly. I loved the irony of it. Thor, the god of Thunder, will be the perfect name for a therapy dog – boy or girl. Soon she'll be spade, so gender won't matter anyway," he grinned. "Not even thunder will disrupt her from her job." He pretended to swing a super-hero cape for emphasis.

Allison looked back at the puppy and cracked up once more. "Yea, well your god of Thunder is true to her name. She's raining in the corner right now."

Radmund ran to the scene. "Thor!" Soft pillow on the head. "Thor! No! No!" More whimpering followed by human moaning. "Geesh! Third time already I have to clean up after the fur ball."

Landon chimed in, finally calmed down. "Fur ball. That's funny. I get it."

"I knew you would Sport. I knew you would." The three of them enjoyed an impromptu dinner date together that night, even though the god of Thunder stole Landon's hamburger and soiled two other corners of Radmund's living room.

"Rad, I'm so glad you're home! It was really fun being together again." She hugged him, careful not to give him the wrong impression. "Maybe we can do this again when Kholby feels better. I think you two will hit it off. He's a great guy." Until then, the night had been magical just like before. But hearing that name brought the familiar knot back into his gut.

"I'm glad you've found someone. It's your turn to enjoy life." He meant every word, even though it broke his heart.

***

By the following Friday, Radmund was fed up with Kholby and his daily lunch visits. "Allison, he's totally distracting you and we are too shorthanded right now to let that happen. Look," he pointed at three tables, "Those people waited five minutes for drinks while you're over there googly-eyed with your boyfriend. I had to call Laurabelle from the kitchen to help for a little while. Your own son never took your attention from work like this."

"How dare you discipline me!" she retorted back. "You think you're in charge 'cuz your mom and dad aren't here right now. But, they left both of us in charge."

"Yea, they did. They trust you to pay attention. To the customers, not him!" Radmund's cheeks flushed crimson in a mixture of jealousy and frustration. "And, besides, Landon clearly doesn't want Kholby around while he's eating. I heard him ask to be alone three times yesterday and at least once already today. What is going on?"

"Kholby is trying to be his friend, like you. He's not doing anything wrong. Landon just needs to learn that he's not always going to get his way."

Marc's advice suddenly came back loud and clear in Radmund's conscience. *Don't make her resent you.* "I'm sorry." He sighed in remorse. "I guess I'm just a little on edge. Mom had her first chemo yesterday and Dad said it was a rough night for both of them. Sounds like they were up nearly all night as she wrenched in agony between vomiting and … well, you know … other stuff."

"I'm so sorry. I'll take her some soup after we close today," she replied sincerely. "Marc said chemo is awful like that, but it goes away in a few days."

"Yea," he agonized. "In just enough time for her to get another round of it going all over again."

Allison wiped away a tear. "She's in my prayers every night. I truly believe God will help her and your dad through this. And, Marc would definitely tell us if there was anything really serious going on."

"I know. Look, let's just make sure we don't let her down, please." He turned his attention toward the dining room again. "Help me make sure the customers receive the excellent attention they've come to expect. I'm sure your boyfriend will understand if he doesn't get all of your attention. I mean, if he's such a great guy as you say, then he should be fine."

She grabbed a pitcher and order pad. "Okay, I'll promise to pay attention to the customers first. But I also have a request for you."

"What's that?"

"Would you back off Landon … just for a few days each week. I want him to get to know Kholby better but all he talks about is how he wants to be with you instead, especially with that dog now that he's calm around her. Please."

He was absolutely crushed. Now she was taking away the other part of her that he loved more than himself. "He's been coming over at night to help with Thor. I thought we agreed it was better than the co-op babysitting group while you're in class." He looked over as Landon picked up his lunch plate and walked away from Kholby. "What will you tell him?"

"Kholby said he'd like to spend some evenings with him while I have class. They could get to know each other better that way. And I thought you might want to spend some time with your folks to help them. Marc said she'll have other stuff affect her like depression and confusion also. Don't you think your dad would appreciate some help?"

He hated the idea. Abhorred it. But his parents would definitely need some help. "Fine. If this is what you want. Are you sure you're comfortable with Kholby taking care of him?"

"Yes, I know he'd do anything for my son. Just like you. It's just that Landon is a one-person-at-a-time kid. Once he gets to know Kholby, then he'll be okay with both of you. I think it's best for him, especially since Kholby and I are getting so close."

"Really? Just how close are you, if you don't mind my 'best-friend' inquiry," he almost demanded.

"Not *that* close!" She held up her left hand pointing to the silver ring. "I didn't make this vow lightly. It's very precious to me – my purity and the promise you and I share. Besides, Kholby wouldn't do that. He's a good man. I mean, he wants to be a missionary and all."

The mission field! Radmund forgot all about that little perk. *Someday soon,* he prayed. *Someday soon God. Don't you need that new missionary in China someday soon?* The next moment he was flooded with guilt as he recalled his own advice to a young boy about praying for God to make people sick.

***

"Hey, Rad." She called to him from the doorway to the kitchen. "The dining room is nearly cleared out. Just a few customers finishing up. I'm going to take my lunch break now unless you need help back here."

"We're good," he responded replacing the last of the clean dishes back to their piles. "Slow Saturday for some reason."

"Okay, well, Kholby is out there. But call me if you need anything. Otherwise, I'll be about 20 minutes." She'd promised to be more attentive to him and the restaurant, and she was determined to be there for Delia. Even though she didn't want to admit it the day before, Radmund had been right. She was totally distracted by her new boyfriend. She spent all her waking hours thinking of him. She'd forgotten another essay and did not study well enough at all for class that week. Her grade in the class dropped to a "B" for the first time in her entire college career. Worst of all, Landon was constantly acting up vying for her attention. She knew she had to talk with Kholby about it before it got worse.

"I love spending time together," she assured him as they nestled into the back corner table for a romantic lunch together. "And, I really love that you want to hang out with Landon while I'm in classes. But I have to concentrate here also and at home when it's time to study. I've come too far to let it go now. I hope you understand."

"Of course I do! I'm really sorry I didn't notice sooner. I've just been caught up in this whole thing also," he admitted with a sparkle. "It's just that I've never felt like this about anyone before. We both need to focus more on our jobs and on Landon. I'm not going anywhere ... well at least not now."

"What does that mean?" she asked as worry lines folded at the corners of her eyes.

"You know I'm waiting for the call to China. I told you that the first time we met."

"Yeah. I just tried to forget. What will happen to us if you go that far away? What about Landon? He's just starting to get to know you."

"It'll be fine! The call is only for three months. Then, I'll be right back here ... for you ... for good if that's what we decide we want." Her heart fluttered at the thought of his implication. "But, that's a conversation for another time."

A sudden scream erupted from the front corner of the restaurant. One of the customers stood and began yelling. "HELP! He's on the tracks! Somebody please help! The train is coming!" Immediately Allison's attention zeroed in on the empty front window. She ran to the front of the restaurant, searching frantically for her son.

"LANDON!? Where are you?" She screamed, realizing the tiny red sweatshirted body stuck outside in the tracks was whom she sought. "LANDON!"

In an instant, Radmund came sprinting from the back, straight past her, through the front doors. Kholby was on his heels. She stood, motionless, as the train's whistle sounded only a few yards off in the distance. Adrenalin flooded her into instant motion then, and she burst through the door.

"Get him off the tracks!" she screamed pushing to get to him. "Radmund! Please help!" She saw him there, desperately working with the shoe that imprisoned the little boy, putting them both directly in the path of the oncoming Amtrak. She tried to get to them, to help, screaming and pushing, but something held her back. "NO! Let me go!" she continued to scream. But she couldn't move. Her arms were restrained in spite of the onset of her adrenalin strength. Violently she finally shook free, just as the whistle blared. "NO!" she screamed once more as the train screeched to a halt just past the restaurant. Everything around her swirled in slow motion. She heard herself screaming, felt herself floating forward, yet everything slowly moved to a fog of red and black, giving way to darkness.

Help him! Please, help him! she begged in the darkness of her mind. *Please, God, don't take him from me!* "Momma," she heard the sweet little familiar voice. *Yes, Landon, Momma's here,* she cried in her thoughts. *I won't ever leave you. Come back to me please.*

"Allison." *Radmund? Oh Radmund, please don't let them take him away from me,* she begged. "Allison, we won't leave you. Come back to us." She tried desperately to reach out and touch his hand, but it was too far away. *I can't reach you. Help me. Where's Landon? Please don't let them take him,* she begged to no avail.

"Momma, I'm here," he replied. *Yes, you're there! Stay right there. I'll get you.* She desperately tried to get to him, but every step she took moved him farther away. A sudden cool sensation roused her attention.

"Allison, wake up. Come back to us," Marc pleaded gently wiping her forehead with the cool, wet towel.

Struggling to make sense of everything, she laid still allowing her eyes to focus. Kholby held her close, gently cradling her in his arms. Marc sat on the other side patting the cloth on her forehead. Then, an explosion of thoughts rushed back to her. "LANDON! Where is he?" she screamed again sitting bolt upright.

"Sshh, he's fine. Look, he's right here." Kholby soothed her as Landon gently touched his mother's hand.

She lunged toward him, gripping him in her arms until he begged for release. "Momma, I … can't … breathe," he pleaded.

"What happened?" she demanded looking around for answers. Lights were flashing in the distance, coming closer as the siren began echoing off the brick walls. "WHERE'S RADMUND?" she screamed.

"He'll be okay," Marc reassured her. "Sit down. Rad probably has a concussion, but he's okay. The ambulance is just coming to make sure."

"I want to see him right now!" she exclaimed ripping herself free from Kholby's arms. Kholby took Landon's hand, guiding him into the restaurant while Marc helped Allison around the corner to where Radmund sat holding a bloodied rag on the side of his head. "Radmund!" she lunged toward him. "I'm so sorry! What happened?"

"Sis, you need to calm down," Marc ordered.

"But I saw Landon and Radmund. They were going to get hit. I couldn't get there in time to help." She looked around at the train still steaming from the sudden stop, desperate for some resolve.

Radmund took her hand in his clean, free hand. "He said his top got kicked out the door when a customer left, not realizing the toy was right there. So, Landon went after it, but it rolled over by the tracks. Somehow he got his shoestring stuck in the trestle."

"Al, why don't you sit down?" her brother requested sternly, helping her to the curb. "Radmund yanked the string and broke it free in the nick of time, but that's how he hit his head. He had Landon in his arms as they jumped away just as the train approached."

"I just couldn't get my balance is all. Landon's okay, though, right? Where is he?"

"He's fine," Marc reassured them all. "He's back inside with Kholby now. They're playing with the trains. Actually, it's thanks to Kholby that **you** didn't get hurt, Al. He kept you from running blindly onto those tracks. You would have been hit by the train."

"That's what it was," she thought out loud remembering the restraint. "I couldn't get to them. Something … someone was forcing me back. But I kept trying to get free. He wouldn't let me go."

"He saved your life," Radmund insisted.

"And you saved Landon's life," she followed hugging him with such force that Marc quickly pulled her back before she aggravated Radmund's injury. "Radmund, I will never be able to thank you for that. Never."

The paramedics ran up with the first-aid kit. "Hey Rad, you getting some first-hand experience before you join us in a few weeks?" one EMT teased.

"Something like that," he replied. "I'm fine, really."

"Well, maybe. But it looks to me like you're going to be able to give honest answers to patients who ask if getting stitches hurts or not." The paramedic helped Radmund onto the stretcher.

"Really? Is this necessary?" he balked as the paramedic and Marc forced him to lie down.

"It's necessary," Marc replied. "Now shut up and be a good patient."

Allison forced a smile as she reached out for his hand. As they wheeled him away, she turned to her brother, "Marc, aren't you going with them?"

"No, I'm going to check Landon once more." He held up his hand before she could react. "Don't freak out. He's fine. I just want to make sure we didn't miss any scrapes that need some ointment is all." He took her arm to steady her walk. "You still need to sit down. Let's get inside and find you some water."

"I need to hold my son," she begged. "And then I want to go to the hospital to see Radmund."

"We'll do that too," he promised.

Calm After the Storm

The Tuesday after the train incident found The Whistle Stop returning to its normal charming air of calm and solitude. Radmund returned sporting a bright blue bandana around his red locks. Allison stopped wiping down the counter long enough to flash her sparkling smile and wave. "Nice contrast," she kidded him.

"Thanks. I always wanted to die my hair blue. I guess this is as close as I'll get for now." Landon jumped up to greet him. "Hey Sport! Good to see you today." He swung Landon up into his arms, giving him the usual bear hug.

"I'm glad you're back. I missed you." Landon wrapped his little arms around Radmund's neck trying to hug back as tightly as he was being hugged.

"You just saw me yesterday. Remember? You guys came over to check on me and Thor."

"I know. But *he* had to come with us. I wanted to see you by myself." Landon leaned back, safely in Radmund's arms as he held out his two favorite tops. "Wanna play?"

Rad looked around noticing that things were set to open, but no customers yet. "Sure. I'll play for a few minutes." As the battle of the tops began, he snuck in conversation. "Landon, you know Kholby saved your mom's life, right?"

"Yeah, but you saved me."

"Well, it took Kholby and me together to make sure you and your mom were safe. So you really need to thank him and be super nice to him. He's a good person. And, I think he really cares about you and your mom. Why won't you give him a chance?" Radmund's flaming-orange top spun out of control and then caved under the magnetic pressure of Landon's neon-green master blaster.

"Got 'ya again!" Landon declared victory. "I don't want anybody else. Just you."

"What about your mom? You love her, right?"

"So."

"What about Delia and Henry? Do you love them?"

"Yes."

"See, you already have more people than just me. You're really lucky to have so many people who love you. I think you just need to give Kholby a chance. He's really good to you. I've watched him, just to make sure. Maybe you should spend some time with him some of the nights while your mom is at school."

"But, we are training Thor," he protested.

"Thor is doing great! She learned how to go potty outside already, mostly thanks to you. So, I think I'll give her some nights off training lessons. I'll hold off on any new stuff unless you are there, and then we'll teach her how to sit in a few days. Deal?"

"Okay." The battle of the tops raged on for five more minutes, until just after 9:30 when the first customers entered. By 10:00 a.m. the restaurant was half full with local brunch guests. Goldie and George moseyed in, hand-in-hand as usual, right on time. *Buddy must feel a little useless*, Allison grinned to herself noticing the dog ambling in alongside the couple.

"Goldie! George! It's great to see you two this lovely morning. To what do we owe this honor?" she asked seating them at a table near the front window. "I don't have you on the schedule to play today at all. I thought you were taking a trip to one of the beaches."

"We did that already," George confirmed.

Radmund walked over to join the curious conversation. "Really? It's only ten. You must have gotten out there really early." He winked at Allison recalling their inside joke.

"Seven o'clock," Goldie confirmed. "He came to get me first-thing and surprised me with a lovely sunrise picnic on the beach. George spread out this huge blanket for us with fruits, pastries, and a special doggy treat for Buddy." George grinned at the attention as she concluded, "He's very romantic."

"A golden woman deserves a golden sunrise," he stated, eloquent as usual.

She giggled like a schoolgirl and continued the story. "Where's that storytelling chair? I want you to hear this from the official chair," she commanded. Radmund immediately fetched the rocker from the corner. As he moved it to the front-and-center storytelling position, the Travis' waltzed in through the front doors.

"Owen and Louella! Great to see you today," Allison greeted them with a hug and smile, escorting them to their usual Table 10. "The train's not here yet. Did you drive in today?"

"Yep, we want to visit Delia for a little while this afternoon. Hey, looks like a story is about to unfold," Louella mentioned motioning to Radmund as he set the rocker in place. "I think we'd like to sit closer for this one if Goldie is the storyteller. Mind if we move up front this time?"

"Not at all," Allison concurred shifting them up to Table 3, just to the right of the front door. "Now Miss Goldie, what's this story you want to tell us all?"

Goldie motioned for George to move nearby and held out her hand to take his. "As I was saying, this is one romantic gentleman. He laid out that blanket and food for our beach picnic. The sunrise was extraordinary. I understood it, which is far more beautiful than you sighted people will ever experience, I must admit. And it makes me sad for you. Perhaps you could try a sunrise with your eyes closed sometime to truly live in it yourself.

"Anyway, I digress." She grinned outward to no one in particular. "I felt that sun on my feet as it warmed the edge of the blanket and my old toes. It filled me with such special warmth, like that of the coziest hug from my grandchildren. Then George described the colors as God painted the most vivid pictures of His creation. Purple hovered over the horizon, giving way to shades of rose and burnt orange. Then a subtle yellow rose into vibrant red filling the sky as far as the eye – or mind – could see. I could feel the intensity of the warmth rising on my legs as he described it to me. Then the reds graduated into brilliant orange and pink until the golden circle rose above the horizon. I knew right when it happened. The radiance of the sun poured over me just like God's glory being spilled out on the entire earth. It was glorious every second, yet it felt like slow motion.

"I saw it in my mind. I felt it in my heart and soul. It took my breath away. Then, George took my hand and I told him about the sounds of life waking up on a beach. The turtles scurrying down the sand a few feet away. Seagulls screeching overhead, searching for their breakfast. One of them almost got one of our bagels!" She paused a moment for her audience to respond. "There was a snort in the distance. I was certain it was a dolphin, but George thought it was just a wave crashing. But, what was it my darling?" She turned to him, exposing his mistake.

"It was dolphin," he admitted. "That graceful creature jumped out of the water and smiled right at me. I'm quite certain it was harassing me for doubting the beautiful woman seated at my side."

The dining room guests remained riveted on their story, except for Landon who sat nearby contented with his Kanoodle puzzle. "So, then George said he had something I couldn't hear at all. And he handed me this clamshell. I studied the thing, held it up to my ear, and listened with all my power, but he was right. No sounds at all. 'This is a fake,' I told him. 'How did you know?' he demanded, like I'd ruined his game or something." She pulled the clamshell from her purse to show everyone. "Now he knew I couldn't see that. But he underestimated my other senses. Real clams have ridges with a little slime left on them, and a salty smell. And if you listen carefully, you can actually hear a little sucking sound like their breathing. This thing just sat there all clean and quiet."

George began beaming as Goldie continued. "'It is a fake,' he admitted to me. 'But you know how they find pearls in clamshells sometimes. Well I found something else in this one and I thought you should have it,' he told me helping me open the little thing. Oh he was so smooth when I finally got it open! I found this inside." She opened the clamshell right there in front of everyone to reveal a perfect, golden band.

"Gold for my fair Goldie," he announced. Everyone gasped as they realized the story's end.

"He said to me, 'Goldie, you are far more fair than this golden band, but I feel as if this perfect circle is about us. We've both had glorious lives and families, whom we still love dearly. We've enjoyed precious spouses with whom we will reunite someday in Heaven. But God has also brought us another full circle – to each other. And it would be my utmost delight if you would spend the rest of the circle of our lives together as my wife.'" She stopped there, as George took the ring from the box.

He looked out at the room of diners, all sitting in anticipation. "She said 'yes,'" he confirmed, placing the ring on her finger as the room erupted in applause. Landon jolted to attention and ran to his mother who consoled him quietly as she explained the noise. George looked over at Radmund to ask, "My good man. Would it be okay if we had a small ceremony here as soon as your beautiful mother is available again?"

"Of course!" he accepted whole-heartedly.

"And Allison," Goldie asked outwardly, not sure where Allison was at that moment. She handed Landon to Radmund and moved to Goldie's side, taking her hand. "Dear, would you sing for us at the ceremony?"

"Oh Miss Goldie, I'd be honored!"

The diners all received an orange juice "on-the-house" that day, courtesy of Mr. George Picardy. "A toast," he led. "To a beautiful woman who makes me feel fifty again." He paused to take in the laughter. "Well, perhaps seventy. And to all our dear friends we cherish in sharing this most precious moment with us." Glasses clinked all around.

A few minutes later, still reeling from the happiness, Allison checked in on the Travis'. "Is there anything you guys need? A Kleenex, perhaps?" she joked.

"I always carry my own, you know," Louella replied.

"I just use my sleeve," Owen countered. "Hey, we're heading over to visit with Delia and Henry for a few minutes before we leave today. Now that April has rolled around, it's about time to head back to Illinois. So, I'm afraid this is our last visit here until next January."

"Not already!" she pleaded. "You know how much I miss you when you go home."

Louella grinned at her. "We'll be celebrating our fiftieth anniversary next January. That's something for all of us to look forward to. Maybe we could have a party here? What do you think Owen?"

"Hmm, I think we should do that." He looked at Allison to explain, "Our kids will be with us right after Christmas. We're taking them on a Christmas cruise to help us celebrate the milestone. In fact, it's a huge family celebration. All three of our daughters will be celebrating milestone anniversaries themselves next year – fifteen, twenty, and thirty years!" For all his quips, Owen never missed a moment to brag on his family.

"Suddenly I feel very old," Louella joked.

Owen grinned at his wife. "There will be fifteen of us with the grandkids and all. Are you sure you can handle that many of our family at one time?"

"Of course! I will most certainly look forward to a huge celebration. And I can't wait to meet them all! I'm sure Delia will be delighted put out a huge spread."

"She's doing well?" Louella asked.

"She's hanging in there. The chemo is really rough on her, though. Henry said she's been so violently ill that it's all he can do to help her to and from the bathroom every hour or so right now. And, she lost all her beautiful hair," Allison confirmed. "It's only been two weeks since the surgery but feels like forever."

"If I know her, she's probably more troubled to be a bother to others and not here. Is that true?" Louella asked.

"You got it," Allison confirmed. "I know she's going to be so happy to see you. You two mean so much to all of us. Like family, really. Her immune system and energy are so low. That's really got her down, making it hard to start healing from the surgery also. But she thinks she'll get stronger if she keeps getting up to do stuff. Henry was complaining about her dusting the furniture yesterday. Maybe you can talk a little sense into her."

"I'll try," Louella agreed.

"Well, she'll listen to me," Owen rebutted.

Louella just glared at her husband. "I'm sure she will honey. You just keep thinking that." She stood up to face Allison. "How are you and Kholby doing?"

Allison shrugged sheepishly, "Great. He's amazing. In fact, I never thought I'd meet someone like him."

"I'm happy for you then," she concurred. "He's a good man. He certainly talks about you and Landon all the time, but he also fills our ears with chatter about China. That won't be easy for you two if he heads overseas."

"I know. We've talked about it already, actually," Allison assured Louella.

"Good. Then we might be hearing other news from you in the next few months?" Louella hinted at what Allison knew everyone else wondered about as well.

"Perhaps," Allison giggled. "I don't really know much beyond next week right now.
My classes are getting really heavy, so I spend a lot of time just trying to keep up. I made some mistakes when Kholby and I started dating. Got into some ruts at school. And, well, you heard about Landon and the train. But I'm fixing those things and I will not let my priorities get out of line again, promise!"

"We all make mistakes," Owen piped into the conversation. "We'll help keep that boy in line. If he distracts you from your education, let me know and I'll sick his grandparents on him."

Allison laughed, trying to determine if his comment was truly a joke. Deep down, though, she knew her academic struggles were in direct proportion to the time she spent with Kholby or daydreaming about him. "I promise to do my very best," she assured them as much as herself. After the accident, she had repeatedly given herself stern reprimands and vowed to make sure nothing distracted her from her son or her school work again.

"Well, we really need to get going," Owen said as he stood and pushed in the chair. He took Louella's hand as they turned to leave.

"You two are so cute together. I hope I'm as lucky as you … celebrating a fiftieth someday and still holding hands." Allison's eyes glimmered as she watched them together.

"It's not always easy," Louella stated matter-of-factly. "Loving someone for as long as we've been together takes determination, patience, and tons of forgiveness. Mostly me forgiving him, of course." She smirked at her husband.

"Yea, right," he retorted sarcastically. "Patience is definitely my virtue with her. You can tell she's a difficult woman to live with." Everyone who knew her, though, knew that no other woman alive could hold a candle to the patient and understanding nature of Louella Travis.

"Oh please," Allison joked right back. "In the dictionary there is a definition for 'nice' and another whole level higher called 'Louella-Nice'!"

"You guys are silly," Louella joined in. "I think it's time we got going, Owen." They hugged Allison, Landon, and Radmund bidding good-bye for a season. They congratulated Goldie and George and apologized for being unable to stay long enough for the ceremony.

As the Travis' returned to their car, the familiar conflicting pangs of leaving one set of loved ones to return to another overwhelmed their hearts with joy at the many people God put into their lives.

PART 3
April – July

So, what do you think? With God on our side like this, how can we lose? If God didn't hesitate to put everything on the line for us, embracing our condition and exposing himself to the worst by sending his own Son, is there anything else he wouldn't gladly and freely do for us? And who would dare tangle with God by messing with one of God's chosen? Who would dare even to point a finger? The One who died for us—who was raised to life for us!—is in the presence of God at this very moment sticking up for us. Do you think anyone is going to be able to drive a wedge between us and Christ's love for us? There is no way! Not trouble, not hard times, not hatred, not hunger, not homelessness, not bullying threats, not backstabbing, not even the worst sins listed in Scripture.
Romans 8:37-39 (MSG)

April Showers bring May-hem

As April showers merged into May, Florida's early summer heat set in. Delia's chemo treatments finally came to an end. It'd been far more difficult on her than any of them had imagined – sickness, utterly too weak to get out of bed and use the bathroom, and an incredible depression she'd never fathomed overcame her and severely threatened her steadfast faith. "I know you got this for me God," she kept whispering in her prayers as the drugs riddled her body in severe pain and temptation to throw everything she believed aside and weep in self-pity.

During her first treatment, Henry held her hand, reading Delia's favorite Scripture as the drugs entered her body. The next time he played her favorite worship music and sang along until she asked him to stop. But by the third treatment, he just sat quietly and held her hand as she cried, knowing what would befall her only hours later. As her hair fell out, he gently caressed her head reminding her that her beauty was beyond physical and nothing could ever take that away. "Besides, hair returns. The doctors said you're doing very well and will get it back in a few weeks." After only four treatments, they were thrilled to find God had once more brought them a miracle when the doctors announced there were no signs of cancerous cells left anywhere in her body. She did not need any further treatments as they first predicted.

Along with her spirit, Delia found her strength renewing each day. In fact, Henry threatened to put a bell around her neck so she would not be able to sneak around and start cleaning or cooking too soon. "Seriously, a little work here and there is good for me. It will help me get my mo-jo back sooner," she spoke compelling him to agree. He took the mixing bowl from her hands and calmly led her back to the chair.

"Your physical therapist said he is the one to help you in purposeful movements so you don't tear or strain something. You had radical surgery nearly six weeks ago. And, your body has undergone weekly hell since then. He said you need to give it at least one more week before you start lifting or moving your arms too much." Henry put his arm around her, and gently drew her to him. "I hate to see you in pain. Please don't make this harder on either of us."

She knew he was right; deep down she knew. "It's so hard to just sit around here doing nothing. I can move, you know. If I hadn't lost so much of my strength due to the chemo, I'm sure I'd be one-hundred-percent by now." She winked his way, flirting with the look she knew he could not resist. "I could do little things if someone wanted to help me with the big stuff."

"I'll do that!" He sat up excited at the idea. "I'll get the big stuff down and you can help with the ingredients and getting it all together. It's a great idea. You'll help me be a better cook and I'll be able to help you find something purposeful to do."

"Agreed!" she grinned amazed at how their thoughts so often overlapped. Then, shaking his hand in mock agreement, she leaned over kissing him with intense passion. "I love you to the moon," she whispered. "I can't imagine why God chose you for me, but I thank Him every day for it."

Henry gently brushed the new silky hair strands dangling haphazardly around her face and kissed her cheek. "Why don't we start this plan today?" He took her hand and carefully helped her up from the chair.

"What are you doing?"

"We are going to get you dressed for an outing."

"What? I'm not sure I can get into a decent shirt to go out, honey."

"No problem. I have a lovely gift for you. Bought it from the hospital last week in fact." He grinned as they walked together to the bedroom.

"Where are we going?" she asked, terribly excited to finally escape the confines of the living room for someplace other than the oncology clinic.

"The Whistle Stop," he called back from the closet.

"Really!?" she replied in sheer excitement. "Are we going to cook?"

"You bet we are, just like we planned. But I think you need this first." He swung out the t-shirt with a flourish. "See, it buttons in the back so it will be easier for you to get into for now."

She read the front and cracked up laughing, so much it hurt. "Wow! That's perfect!" Together they maneuvered her into the t-shirt, carefully wrapped a purple bandana around her head, and off they went to surprise everyone at The Whistle Stop.

***

"Mom!" Radmund exclaimed gently hugging her as she and Henry waltzed in the front door. "You look wonderful!" It was only after the hug that he stepped back to read the front of her shirt.

Yes, these are fake. The real ones tried to kill me.

"Oh Mom, I'm not even sure what to say about that." He groped for words to express his mixture of amusement and embarrassment.

Allison rounded the corner from the kitchen in time to catch the last of the welcome. "Delia! Oh my gosh! It's so great to see you out!" Immediately noticing Delia's shirt, Allison burst out into laughter. "That is priceless! Perfect!" She looked at Henry, who still held carefully to his wife's arm. "You got that for her, didn't you?"

"Of course," he admitted. "Look, it buttons in the back to make it easy for her to get into."

"Really, Henry! Must we divulge all the details of this in public?" Delia wasn't sure how she felt about her breasts and all she'd gone through being the subject of public conversation. "Let's get to the kitchen! I've got some muffins to create today."

"Mom, are you okay to do this?"

"Your father and I have a plan. So you and Allison just take care of these customers." She glanced at the chalkboard and added, "And you might want to add 'Chocolate-Covered Strawberry Muffins' to that list in about an hour."

The smell wafting from the kitchen about thirty minutes later drew Radmund in like a magnet. "I'm guessing you were successful," he said breathing in deeply. "I have so missed your experiments. Not that the stuff we already make every day isn't brilliant, but my nose does a happy dance when anything this new and tantalizing pours through the door!"

"Why thank you darling," she said accepting his drawn-out compliment. "Now that those are cooking, let's start planning a menu for George and Goldie's wedding. I am so excited for them! Oh, I hope she comes in today before I have to get back home."

"As a matter of fact, George is bringing her over around eleven to play today. Think you can make it another half hour?" Henry asked. She nodded and sat back to breathe deeply. "You okay Babe?"

"I'm wonderful. I love being here, smelling this kitchen, taking in all the colors and sounds of the restaurant. I forgot how much I missed it." She opened her eyes and looked over to her son. "How are you doing? You're not pushing yourself too hard are you? How's your head feeling?" Even though she'd been mostly holed up in the house for weeks, Henry and Radmund had kept her updated with every detail. The train story, though, nearly sent her into a full regression. It was the only day she'd ventured out for something other than a treatment, and then Henry would only allow her to go to the hospital long enough to verify that Radmund was alive and well.

"I'm good Mom. No more headaches, well except for Thor. That dog just might cause me to consider animal abuse," he grinned. They all knew he wouldn't hurt a fly, let alone a growing puppy destined to be a therapy dog someday.

"And, how's Landon?" she asked. "You haven't mentioned him much. What's going on?"

"Well, Allison wanted him spend some time with Kholby while she was in night classes. So I haven't seen him as much lately. But we've talked here and he seems to be doing okay. He understands that she wants him to get to know Kholby better. I'm trying to encourage it also so he's not so confused," he sighed.

"How are you doing with that?" she winced, shifting in the chair as Henry helped her move.

"It's getting easier every day. I've accepted that she's in love with him. I'm blessed that we've been able to keep our friendship. Sometimes I think it's even intensified because of him. Thankfully, she doesn't burden me with all the crap about their dates, though." Even as he made his case, his eyes gave away a lack of sincerity in his words.

Delia looked very concerned. "She's keeping her vow, isn't she?"

"Of course. She'd never break it. I saw her eyes the moment she realized that God saw her as pure and holy. She would never willingly give that up until the day she's married." He smirked. "But we are still each other's accountability partner just in case."

She walked in that moment, as if her ears had been ringing. "Okay Delia. There are four tables out there begging for whatever is baking in here. I told them the muffins would be ready soon. What's your E.T.A?"

Henry volunteered to check. "Timer says ten more minutes. If they can wait, tell them one muffin per table will be on-the-house as our 'Welcome Back Delia' celebration!" He walked back up behind his wife, gently folding his arms around her shoulders. "This will be the first of many celebrations you promised me. Remember?"

She slowly reached upward to grasp his hands. "Absolutely! Thank you Honey. This was the best therapy I could ever have. We really don't need to pay the professionals any more. Let's just come here and bake one thing each day." The medical therapy was required for at least two more weeks, but instinctively they both knew the baking therapy was far more successful.

***

Music rang out true and pure from the shining white piano. Delia sat back, eyes closed once more, savoring every moment of her life. When Goldie and Allison finished their performance, Delia applauded so much she wrenched back in a moment of pain. "Ouch," she laughed. "You two made me forget all about my woes. Thank you for that. You have brought such happiness to my soul today."

"And, I think your outing should be concluding just about now," Henry coaxed. "You've been out for over two hours."

"I am really tired," she admitted. "But I will be back tomorrow! Times like this make you remember to cherish every moment, and every piece of life – from the simplicity of baking muffins to the joys of Heavenly music." She half-hugged everyone on her way to the door, including Landon who was still very confused about exactly why she was not around much, and when she finally returned, she was wearing a purple bandana on her head and a white mask over her mouth and nose. "Hi Sweetheart," she comforted him. "Yes, I'm still a little sick, but don't you worry. I will be just fine in a few days. I'll look forward to you coming to visit me again soon, okay?"

"Okay." His standard reply. Turning to Radmund, Landon asked, "Do I get to see you tonight?"

"If you want to," Radmund confirmed knowing that Kholby would be busy with finishing touches on the exterior of the house until late hours that week. "Thor is ready to learn how to sit and heel. Are you up to that high-level training with her?"

Landon thought a moment then responded. "Could we take her to visit Delia one night? I think she'd like that."

Radmund clapped his hands. "That is an excellent idea! Let's see how much we can teach Thor and take her over there on Thursday."

The bell over the front door rang in another guest. Only he wasn't there to eat. "Hey Marc! Lunch break?" Radmund called out moving from Landon to cover the front counter area.

"Actually, I'm here to see Allison. It's our dad." His face was laden with worry, sunken eyes, red lines streaking from the pupils filling the whites with pinkish tint. "He's not well at all. Been battling lung cancer for a year now. They think he only has a few days left."

Radmund walked out from behind the counter to console his friend. "Here, sit down," he motioned to an empty stool. "Does Allison know?"

"She knows he's been really sick. We've talked about it a lot. I'm hoping she'll go to Tampa to see him with me on Sunday."

"Not gonna happen," she blurted out walking up behind the men. "They made it clear how they felt years ago. I'm not opening that wound again, ever."

"Sis, he's dying," Marc implored. "He knows it." Marc took his sister's hand. "He's asked to see you. He wants you to know how sorry he is for everything."

"Nice, he waited until his death bed to make up. No way!" She yanked her hand from his and stepped back. "He wants to tell me how sorry he is so I'll forgive him, and then he'll just die and break my heart all over again."

She blinked forcefully to keep the tears from streaming down her cheeks. Looking around at the crowded dining room, she said, "Let's go in the back to discuss this further, please. Rad, can you look after Landon and our customers okay?" He nodded and waved them off.

Sitting at the kitchen table, the conversation picked up. "Al, I know you love him. You can't stop loving our parents. It's not in your nature."

"What does Mom think about this?"

He paused and sighed. "She doesn't know. He asked me to keep it a secret from her."

Allison threw up her hands. "Great! She still hates me, hates Landon. And he's trying to sneak us into the hospital. That's not anything I will ever expose my son to. NO!"

"Actually, he was adamant that he see you. He's in so much pain, Al. I know he's made things right with God. I was there last week and we prayed together. It was really special. Now he needs to talk to you, and he's hoping you'll be able to forgive him." He tilted her chin upward to look in her eyes. "I don't think he can go peacefully until he's seen you … and Landon. Please Al. If not for him, for me."

"Oh, Marc. I can't see them. Especially if Mom is still so hateful. I can't do this."

Radmund walked in to retrieve a tray of lunch orders. "I'll go with you if you want. I think you should do this for yourself above all else. How will you feel if your father dies and you never gave him a chance to tell you how he feels? Especially after he begged you? You've never given yourself a chance to forgive him either, have you? Can you live with that?"

"Al, you can't harbor this resentment for the rest of your life. It will eat you up. Rad and I will be right there with you. And we'll make sure Landon is okay also. I promise."

Tears poured out, down her cheeks, spilling onto her blouse. "I'm afraid. That was the most horrible time in my life. How can I go back and face it now that I'm finally happy again?"

"Because it's what God wants to do for you and Dad, to make that healing complete." Her brother wrapped his arms around her as she trembled in emotional turmoil. "Didn't you tell me you started praying for them after the conference? Hasn't that done anything to soften your heart yet?"

It had, and she knew it. But fear was a far stronger foe than she'd even imagined. "Okay, I'll go. But I do not want Kholby to know anything other than Dad is dying. He can't know the other stuff." She looked squarely at her brother and then Radmund. "Swear to me you will not say a word to him."

"We've been through this already. You know I think it's a terrible idea to keep that from him, but I will respect your wishes," Marc promised.

Radmund raised his eyebrows, completely surprised. "Allison, you haven't told him yet?!" Marc looked sharply at Radmund, his eyes bluntly indicated to let it go for now. She needed to focus on her father and nothing else at that time. "Okay, But we need to revisit this conversation down the road," he concluded after a second's thought.

***

"I hate that I can't go with you," Kholby grimaced as they enjoyed a late-April picnic that Saturday night. "Are you sure you don't want me there?"

"No, you need a day off work. And, besides, you have plans with the mission team. You can't miss that event."

"Okay, but I'm really not sure why Radmund gets to go. I gotta say, it makes me a little jealous." He grimaced. "A lot actually. You really confide in him and I wish you'd do that more with me."

Allison winced. "I know. But I'm begging you to understand and not push me on this. You know my folks kicked me out when I got pregnant. And, Radmund helped me move past that when we went to the purity conference. He truly understands that this is purely a friend helping a friend. And, besides, he's also Marc and Landon's best friend. It makes sense that he go for their sake as well."

"I feel like you're forbidding me to go, though. And I can't help wonder why," he responded dejectedly. "I would really like to be considered a close family friend to your son and brother also."

"Kholby, we've only known each other a few weeks. You will get closer to them! I know it. They really do like you. In fact,

Marc and Radmund encouraged me to have you go with us. This is totally my choice and I'm begging you to trust me."

He kissed her forehead and they finished the last bites of dinner in silence. "Momma, can I go swing now?" Landon asked.

"Sure honey. I'll be over there in a minute to give you a huge push!" She turned to Kholby once more. "Thank you for being such a wonderful man. I am so lucky to have you in my life!"

"Well, I'm not going anywhere that I know of, anyway. Although, I can't help but wonder what will happen if I get called to China. I'm thinking I shouldn't go now."

"What? You can't give up your dream. I would never forgive myself if that happened." She tossed the paper plates in the garbage, then turned to him. "If we are meant to be, these things are simply tests that will strengthen our bond. I know that in my heart. Please don't ever consider giving up your dream for me. I would not forgive myself. And, I know you would never ask me to give up anything for you. That's not what people who love each other do." She stopped cold, suddenly realizing her word.

"Love? I like that word," he whispered taking her in his arms. "I do love you." The first kiss after a profession of love brings with it such intensity that the sun seems to explode. Neither of them could breathe for a moment as they stepped back to ponder the experience.

"I need to go give Landon a push," were the only words she could muster in response.

***

The four of them entered Tampa's LifePath Hospice House together the next day. Radmund on one side and Marc on the other, each gently holding her hands. Radmund carried Landon in his free arm. "I can't do this," she choked wrenching free of their grip and turning back. "What if Mom is here?" Gently they prodded her into the building.

"I've already told Dad you're coming. It's literally the only thing that's made him happy in a month. Please don't disappoint him now. And, don't worry about Mom. I'll handle her. Maybe he got to her by now." Their answer was soon provided, however, as they approached his room to see their mother exiting for a quick lunch. She saw the group approaching and froze in place, her face ashen white.

"What are **you** doing here?!" she demanded. "Marc, why would you betray us like this and bring her and that bastard child with you?!"

Allison cringed at her language as Radmund covered one of Landon's ears and gently tucked his head into his shoulder sheltering the other ear. Marc walked up to his mother, leaving the others down the hall. "Mom, she's here because Dad asked for her. Please give them both the peace they need, especially now."

"I can't stomach the sight of her or that kid," their mother protested. "I'm going to get lunch. Don't make your father upset. The doctors think he only has a few hours left anyway." With that, she glanced once more at Allison and Landon, then abruptly turned and stormed off the other direction.

Radmund, Allison, and Landon moved slowly to Marc's side a moment later. "Al, I'm so sorry. I just don't understand her. Deep down she knows you never did anything wrong. She just can't get past what happened. I think she feels responsible for deserting you and Landon, and she's harbored this huge guilt for so long that it's just turned into an intense anger that she can't get out of now." Marc tried to console his sister.

"I expected that," Allison began. "I actually feel sorry for her now. You know, I thank God that He's helping me learn to forgive them." She turned to Radmund. "Just like Marc said yesterday, I knew in my heart God would help me forgive them. And, seeing her now, I know that I'm finally able to do that. Maybe that's why God wanted me to come here today." She took her brother's hand. "Let's go see Dad."

They all paused outside his room. "Marc, will Landon be okay seeing this or should he stay out here with Rad?"

"Why don't we go in first and you decide," her big brother wisely advised. "He's got an IV and some oxygen, but it's not really that scary." Hand-in-hand, brother and sister entered the room. Radmund and Landon chose to go to the small waiting room across the hall and build pyramids on the Kanoodle set.

"Hey, Dad," she whispered as they approached his bed.

Groggy from pain medicine, it took him a moment to register visitors, let alone who they were. "Allison," he whispered hoarsely. "You came." A smile crossed his face and spread the distance of the room. "I prayed you would come. I have so much to tell you," but his sentence was interrupted as he tried to sit and began a violent coughing episode.

"Dad, not too much at once," Marc consoled patting his father's arm. "You need to go slowly."

Their father reached for his daughter's hand, which she grabbed. A warmth spread through her from head to toe as she realized it was the first time she'd held her father's hand in over five years. She absorbed every detail of his touch – his fingers intertwined in hers, the wrinkles covering his entire hand, the fingers yellowed from years of smoking, the gentleness of his touch as he rubbed her thumb in comfort. "Dad," she said fighting back tears. "You don't have to say anything. Marc told me you wanted me to come and that's all I need."

"No," he croaked out. "So much more," cough, cough, cough. "I have to tell you how sorry," cough. "How sorry I am. I turned my back on you when you needed your daddy the most in your whole life. I'm so sorry," he finished as sobs mixed with the coughs, wracked his entire body. "I'm so sorry."

She leaned in to hug him tightly. Marc stood back, crying. "Daddy, I know. I know. I love you so much. I think about you and Mom all the time. And I never stopped loving you. Somehow, I always knew you loved me too."

He touched her cheek, wiping away tears. "Allison, please forgive me. God has forgiven me and now I need you to do the same."

"Oh, Daddy. I do. I think God was preparing us for this meeting, actually. God found a very special way to soften my heart until I was broken in my remorse about us. I forgive you and Mom, even if she's not ready to do the same yet."

"Honey," cough, cough. "Don't give up on her. She's so hurt right now with me being so sick." Tears rolled down his cheeks as he confessed to his children. "Marc and Allison, you are my most precious gifts on this planet. And, I love your mom so much," cough. "But it's time for me to be healed. And, I can't wait to meet Jesus Christ! I'm so thankful, Marc, that you and I visited last week. Oh, how I wish I'd spent my life with God instead of just a few days." Violent coughing ensued again, lasting a few minutes as they waited. "But, I'm so thankful that He waited for me anyway. And this past week has been the greatest in my life. I don't even feel the pain anymore because He is my comfort now."

"Daddy," she sobbed. "Daddy, I love you so much. I've missed you. Would you like to meet your grandson?"

"Yes," he cried. "I'd really like that."

"I'll go get them," Marc volunteered. "You guys catch up."

A few minutes later, Marc and Landon quietly entered the hospice room. "Daddy," she said taking Landon's trembling hand. "This is Landon. Look," she pointed to his little face. "He has your eyes." Just before they entered the room, Marc had prepared his nephew for what he would see. Still, Landon clung to his mother's shoulder as she lifted him to meet his grandfather. "Landon, this is your grandpa. He's Marc's and my daddy."

Landon cautiously reached his hand outward as his grandfather stretched with all his strength to touch the fingers of the grandson he'd never met before. "Allison, he's beautiful. You were right, you know. In what you did," he said in code not knowing what Landon would understand. "I am certain this was what God wanted for you both. Thank you for letting me see him, even if it's just a few minutes."

The four of them spent the next half hour catching up on life. For just a blip in time, Allison knew God had restored the lost years, giving them all a chance to glimpse what eternity would be like someday when they would all, once more, be reunited. Landon even warmed up after several minutes to talk about his tops, and to demonstrate as he spun them together on the lunch tray so his grandfather could see the magnetic battle take place. "I really like them," Landon concluded his demonstration. "The green one usually wins. Radmund gave it to me. But sometimes the purple one wins. Uncle Marc gave me that one."

"Marc," cough. "Would you please take our picture? I know it's silly, but I really want a photo of me with my daughter and grandson." Allison lifted Landon to the side of the bed and then leaned over putting her arms around Landon and her father as he used every ounce of energy to sit upward. Marc pulled out his phone and snapped the photo.

"Allison, look at this," he noted beckoning her to view the photo. Checking the photo, she instantly noticed a radiant glow in the background that could only be attributed to Shekinah. "It's perfect," he concluded as she agreed amidst tears.

Radmund tiptoed into the room. "Hey, just wanted to let you know your mom is coming back. She's talking with the nurses right now." He took Landon's hand as they made a hasty exit. "Let's go check out the toy room again, Sport. I think I saw some of those really old-fashioned tops in the toy box. You know the kind you actually spin?" Landon had no idea but happily left the confusion and sadness of the room.

"Who was that?" her father asked.

"That's my friend, Radmund. He's so good to us, Daddy. Landon loves him, and he's my best friend," she explained.

"I wish I could be at your wedding," he grinned.

She blushed. "Oh Daddy, we're not getting married. I'm dating someone else. Radmund is my friend." She looked at Marc for help but he offered nothing, choosing to let her explain her way out.

"Darling, maybe it's because I'm at Heaven's gates. But I have a feeling about that young man." Cough, cough, cough. "Marc," he redirected his attention to her brother. "Thank you for being here for me. You're the best son in the world. Promise me you'll make sure she and Landon are always safe. And, that you will always be there to help her make good choices." Cough, cough. "And Allison," he turned to her. "I want you to keep an eye on your brother for me. Make sure he finds a good woman one of these days. Somebody who can keep up with him, but help him know when it's time to relax and settle down also."

"I promise," Marc replied first, leaning in to kiss his father's forehead. "I'll be back tomorrow. Took the day off so I could be with you. It's nice to be in charge after so many years in school!"

"I'm so proud of you, Marc. So proud of you both." Cough, Cough. He grasped both their hands, refusing to give up a second of their touch.

"I promise, too, Daddy," Allison avowed as she leaned in to kiss his cheek. "I'm so happy we got to spend this time together. I will always remember all our good times together."

"Thank you," he choked. "I love you so much. One more thing. Please make sure Landon hears some stories about his grandpa. Since I never really got to know him, you know?"

She nodded her promise that time since words were no longer an option. The three leaned together for one last family embrace. Then, she kissed his hand knowing it would be their last moments together on Earth, but her heart was filled with joy in knowing that they would one day have an eternity together to make up for lost time.

"I thought you would never get out of there. He needs his rest," their mother quipped as Marc and Allison exited the hospice room a few minutes later.

"Mom, thank you for giving us some time. You know it's what Dad wanted," Marc replied trying desperately to calm his mother.

"Well, he's all emotional now. But, if he were well, this would never have happened." She glowered at Allison.

"Mom," Allison spoke softly nodding her head. "I don't believe you hate me. But I can't figure out why you don't see that yourself. It doesn't really matter though because I love you so much. I've never stopped and I never will. And I will make sure your grandson hears great stories about my childhood with you and Daddy and Marc. Someday when you finally soften the anger in your heart toward me, know that I've already forgiven you. I have no grudge or any negative feelings toward you at all. I love you. And as he grows up, Landon will learn to love you through the great things Marc and I will tell him. I just pray that someday you will come back to us like Daddy did. Hopefully, it won't be your last hours on this earth because I'd really like to spend time with my mom again soon."

Her mother turned away, but not before both siblings noticed the puffiness in her eyes and cheeks. "I can't forgive you for what you did to us, Allison. You made a choice that ruined your life and ours. I just can't forget or forgive you. Please have the decency not to come to your father's funeral, whenever that is. I can't handle having you there." While her voice trembled with anger, her body shook as her soul burdened heavily with remorse.

"Mom, you can't ask her that," Marc began but Allison held up her hand to quiet him.

"It's okay. I wouldn't bring Landon anyway. It's too confusing. Plus, I want this precious time with Dad as my last earthly memory of him."

The next day their father passed on to be with his Heavenly Father, a smile illuminating his face as he clung tightly to his son's hand, singing *How Great Thou Art*, while staring at the picture Marc printed and held up for him to view.

Allison was clearly not herself a week later when Radmund found her in the kitchen scrubbing the counters for the fourth time. "What's up?" he asked, knowing her father's death had hit her far harder than any of them expected.

"Nothing," she lied. "Who's watching Landon?"

"Dad's out there. So is George. He's so cute. Landon actually showed him the transformer. They were disassembling and reassembling for the third time when I left."

"That's great. We went to visit Goldie yesterday. Of course, George was already there! So, we all chatted for a bit. I noticed Landon was very intrigued by him." *Or was it the other way around?* she thought in retrospect.

"Are you sure you're okay? You just polished that skillet in perfect rhythm as you ranted on there."

Allison stopped the tenacious cleaning and pulled a paper from her pocket. "Look, got this in the mail yesterday." Radmund unfolded the paper to find a grades indicator for the semester warning that she was getting a "C" in two of her classes. "If I don't get those grades up, I'll lose part of my scholarships. Can you believe it! I mean with all the junk that's happened in the last few days with my dad and all and they won't give me a break!"

"Um, Allison, this looks to me like a few late assignments and a couple poor test grades. And, it doesn't look like just the past few days to me." He gently turned her toward him. "It seems to have begun around the same time you met Kholby."

"Thanks! Rip me for not having my priorities why don't you?!

He carefully folded the paper and handed it back to her, then spoke softly. "It says you have until the end of May to get everything caught up. That's two weeks. And it looks like they're giving you a chance to make up the lower grades. That's really cool of your professors to do that."

Her cheeks flared red. "It's not my fault you know! There's so much I've had to deal with lately with the train incident and my dad and Delia's surgery. It's a little overwhelming."

"Allison," he continued to speak softly. "Who are you trying to convince?"

She fell into his arms, sobbing. "I can't believe this. I thought I had my life under control. I promised myself things would change, especially after the train incident. What happened?"

"You know what happened. You met a guy that stole your heart and you got distracted. Blame it on whatever you want, and I'm sure those things were a huge factor … don't get me wrong. But this stuff looks like it's been going on awhile."

He handed her a Kleenex as she stepped back. "I know you're right. But there's so much to catch up on now. I don't know if I can do it all that quick. It's anatomy and pharmacology. I'm so confused in both of them." She looked up at him again in remorse, "And, I haven't been reading or studying like I used to."

"I'll be happy to help. We can study after your classes and whenever there's a break here if you want. I don't mean to brag, but I did pretty well with those subjects in my classes."

She smiled and sniffled. "Thanks. I don't know if Kholby will understand, though."

"Really? That's your concern? Allison, you see the irony in this, right?" He used every ounce of strength to fight the irritation in his voice. "Look, I'll help you whenever you want, but you have to figure out if you want to concentrate on school or Kholby."

"Thanks, Rad. I appreciate your offer and I'll think about it." She kissed his cheek. "I just need to focus on work for a little while, you know, get my mind off all this stuff," she replied walking out the kitchen door.

***

"Listen, Allison," Kholby started that Wednesday as they shared lunch together. "I've been noticing how distracted you are since your dad died. I really want to help. What can I do?"

"It's not just that," she confessed. "I got bad news from school a couple days ago. My grades are still slipping, even after I promised not to let that happen again. I'm such an idiot!"

He took her hands in his, looked her straight in the eyes and ordered, "Never say that again! And as far as school goes, you need to get it together. I happen to know Radmund offered to help you catch up. You need to let him help you."

Eyes wide, she was dumbfounded. "How did you know that?"

"A little birdie might have filled me in on things. I've been so worried about you and you just won't talk to me. Plus, I learned not to pry into your life, so I was a little scared to ask you myself."

Guilt consumed her. "You were afraid to talk to me?" Lowering her head into her hands, she continued. "So Rad snitched on me, huh?"

"Nope, your brother and I had a chat. He was worried about you and asked me if I could help. I told him you were holding out on me too. We just figured it out together, then Radmund confirmed it for us."

"Oh great. You are all ganging up on me. How embarrassing."

He gently touched her chin, lifting her face to look him in the eyes. "Not at all. We all love you very much. We are all here to help you in any way we can. Now you just need to take a step and let us do that for you. You've had a horrible time these past few weeks with stuff and trying to keep things going here while Delia's out sick. Accept that life happens like that and there are people surrounding you who want to help. I mean, think about Delia. What would have happened if she'd refused to let others help her? Like you."

"You're right," she agreed. "But I can't believe you're okay with Radmund and me spending time together like that."

"I'm fine with it. Are you?"

It was such a legitimate question, to which she shuddered at the thought of an answer. Yet, here was her boyfriend, professing his love for her and totally comfortable with her spending time with the one man she knew he was still keenly envious of. "You are an amazing man, Kholby Brown. I ... um ... I don't know what I'd do without you. Thanks for understanding. I'll tell Radmund this afternoon. If you're around any this week, maybe you and Landon could play together while Rad and I study?"

"I'd love that. And, I do love you, you know."

"I know," she replied as tears pooled in her eyes. "I'm so lucky to have you in my life." Not exactly the answer he'd hoped for, but good enough considering her emotional state he thought.

***

"Hey you two! Surprise!" Kholby met her and Landon for lunch that Friday, flourishing a huge rainbow of vivid daisies and roses. "For you my lovely lady," he decreed handing her the bouquet. "And for you," he continued kneeling down to meet the little boy, "I found this awesome Beyblade stadium thing and thought of you. Maybe we could use your battle tops and play with it later? I bet it'll keep them from rolling all over the floor or out the door." He winked at Allison.

"Wow! These are gorgeous. And the stadium is perfect! He's been looking at those in a catalog we got in the mail a few days ago."

"I know. He showed me," he grinned as Landon immediately began a War of the Tops in his new arena.

"Landon, where are your manners?" Allison inquired.

Landon looked up a moment. "Thank you Kholby," he mustered out before immediately returning to the battle.

"You shouldn't have spent so much on us." She flushed a variety of colors matching the flowers as she pranced behind the counter to fetch a pitcher for a vase. "It's great to see you! I thought we weren't getting together until dinner tonight." Flowers in their place, she quickly moved back to his side, embracing him with a full, passionate kiss.

"Yea, well I have news I had to share with you and I couldn't wait. I want us to change our plans tonight and go out and celebrate!"

Allison began to feel nauseated. "What's so exciting?" she asked hesitantly, already sensing the answer.

"I got this in the mail today," he replied handing her an envelope. The return address confirmed her fears. "They want me at the Chinese school starting next week!"

She stumbled and fell back on the nearby stool. "Next week?! That's not much notice. Can't you wait a little longer?" she begged.

"I thought we discussed this. You know how much this means to me." He sat next to her, taking her hand. "Allison, this is only three months. It's a great chance for me to do God's work. It'll go by so fast, and a wise woman once told me that distance makes the heart grow fonder. Although I don't see how my heart could actually get much fonder, but I'm willing to wait for you if you will wait for me."

Her heart fluttered at the hint. "But three months? I mean, yes, I knew it was coming and I'm so happy for you. I guess I just forgot with my dad and school and all."

"I know this timing stinks," he admitted. "But you said you had the thing with your dad under control. In fact, you asked me not to talk to you about it anymore, remember? And you need the time to concentrate on those grades also."

"I know. And, I'm sorry to be so wimpy now. It's just a lot has happened and I just forgot about this China thing I guess."

"Hey, Allison," Henry called leaning out the kitchen door. "Any chance you can run a few deliveries for us today? I need to pick up Delia before she tries to drive over here herself, you know," he kidded. "Rad will keep an eye on Landon for you."

"Um, well, sure," she responded. "Kholby, I have to go. We'll talk more and celebrate at dinner tonight. Where do you want to go?"

"The guys were talking about a great Mexican place – Mi Casa. I know you love tacos. What about Landon? Would he like it there?"

"I've heard it's really good, but we've never been there. It's kind of pricey. We should go someplace cheaper. I mean you already spent so much on flowers and his new toy."

Kholby wrapped his arms around her shoulders. "Nope. I want to take you someplace fancy tonight so we'll have a special memory to tie us over. And, because I have intensive training and preparations for the trip before I go. There's all kinds of stuff they have to tell us about the do's and don'ts, the packing lists, and general things to know about travel and stuff, so I won't be able to come over this weekend." He'd purposefully held off that last bit of news.

She backed off. "What? We won't see you again 'til Monday. When are you leaving exactly?"

"I catch my plane out of Orlando on Tuesday morning." He stepped back, waiting for her reply. Instead, she said nothing. Tears welled up in her eyes. Finally she hugged him and turned to walk away, hoping he would not notice the emotion she could no longer contain.

Back in the safety of the kitchen, Radmund immediately noticed. "Allison, what happened now?" He tried not to sound as exasperated as he felt.

"He's going. His plane leaves on Tuesday." She grabbed her purse and the box of deliveries heading toward the door.

"Oh no you don't," he demanded grabbing her arm to stop her from the escape. "You need to get a grip before you get behind the wheel."

"I knew he was leaving, but it's too soon. Everything is happening at once. First Dad, then school, now this. How much more do I have to deal with?!" He took her in his arms as she soiled the shoulder of his t-shirt.

"Look at this another way. You've been so worried about catching up at school. This will make that easier. And, you'll breeze through the summer clinicals now without distractions or feeling guilty about not spending time with him."

"I suppose those are good things. And, Landon's been acting up a lot more lately. I know I need to give him more attention. He's really moody when Kholby comes around, even though you tried to help him with that." After a moment she calmed down enough for him to feel secure in her driving.

"Just be careful. You know the delivery business is new for us. Mom will kill us if we mess it up before she gets back full time to check it out herself," he quipped hoping to lighten her mood a bit more.

***

The small celebration that night was clearly overcast with heartache. "It's not that I'm looking forward to being away, believe me! It's just that I've worked for this since I was in high school. I promised God I would follow His will in my life. I didn't tell you before, but that night I also made another vow to be a man of integrity who would wait until marriage for s-e-x." He spelled the last word in case Landon would somehow take notice of the depth of their conversation. However, Landon remained fixated on the battle safely contained in the walls of his new toy.

"You made a vow also? Why didn't you tell me?" she asked alerted.

"It was kind of awkward, you know. I mean I know you told me about your promise right after we met, but it felt odd to tell you about mine since you made your vow after … well, you know after … Landon."

Pain wracked her body at the reality of what he believed were true about her past. So much so that she desperately wanted to confess. "Listen, about that …" she began. "I should tell you something."

He cut her off. "No, you don't have to tell me anything. Really, I admire you for what you've done to turn your past around to be pure in God again. And I absolutely believe you are pure. I love you for that. If we get married someday, that's exactly what I will know to be true on our wedding night."

Her heart raced at the 'm' word and she once more lost the nerve to follow through with the confession. "I am going to miss you like crazy," she said, stifling the tears. She'd determined not to ruin his joy with her sadness. Albeit however difficult that might be for her. "But I suppose it is a great opportunity for you. Just think of all the amazing ways you will help the children over there to learn about God. I admire you for that courage. Really, I do. I just wish it didn't mean us being separated."

"Allison, it's only a few weeks. Plus, you'll be busy with working in the hospital and all. It will be better if I'm not distracting you with flowers and romance," he grinned. "I want the very best for you and Landon, always and in everything you do or we do together. The very best. And I will never stand in the way of what I believe that is. That's another reason I need to go to China. If you and I are meant to be together, this will be our ultimate test and it will prove we truly are the very best for each other."

"I'm so happy you are in my life," she smiled. "And you are exactly right … about everything. But I'm still going to miss you like crazy."

The weekend dragged on for Allison, even though she was able to chat with Kholby on Skype for an hour late Sunday afternoon. He went on and on, telling her again about the school and the ways he and the other teachers had to be so careful not to mention God in their lessons. But, if the students asked, then they could answer all of their questions. "And we only get one suitcase and one carry-on bag. They said we don't have closet space for too many clothes anyway and all our other stuff will be provided when we get there. You know, like shampoo and soap and stuff. So I guess that makes packing easier."

Monday evening came incredibly fast, in direct disproportion to the lingering weekend. Radmund actually used his key to help Kholby sneak into Allison's apartment before she got home from classes. He agreed to have Landon over that night so Kholby and Allison would have some time alone. Her eyes sparkled in the dim light of the candles glowing on the table, set in romantic fashion for two. Wine goblets held sparkling cider and homemade lasagna filled the air with scents of basil, oregano, and garlic.

"Kholby! This is amazing! You went to all this trouble for us?" she asked walking in on the surprise. Landon jogged to his room to gather his battling arena, favorite tops, and transformers. Radmund knocked on the door soon after, assuring Allison that he and Landon were going to have a great time together. "Rad, this is very nice of you," she commented hugging him. He was surprised at the joy he felt for her, rather than sadness for himself.

Pulling out her chair, Kholby informed her that he would take care of the serving and cleaning that night. She was simply to eat and enjoy. And, their conversation could be about whatever she wanted, as long as it was happy. No sadness or woes. An hour later, after successfully meeting his goal, they decided to go for a walk around the pond. "This night sky is one of the reasons I love Florida," she said staring at the stars as they walked hand-in-hand. "Look at that moon. It's almost as bright as the sun tonight. Reminds me of the night we danced to Charlie Daniels."

As she looked back from stars to the earth, his eyes were there to meet hers, locked into a moment they sealed with the sweet innocence of a kiss that fueled the emotional turmoil brewing in both their hearts. Her phone vibrated bringing their amorous night to a close. "Hey," Radmund said. "I'm so sorry to bother you but I think Landon might have the flu. He's been puking for about an hour now. I thought it was just the slurpee we sucked down too fast, but now he has a fever."

"Okay, I'll be right there." She turned to Kholby. "Landon's sick. I have to go. I'm so sorry. I was hoping this night would never end. But maybe this will make it easier to avoid a long good-bye."

"Maybe," he sighed. "Let's get Landon. I'm sure he wants his momma's arms right now."

In a few minutes Landon was safely tucked in bed, puke bucket on the floor nearby. Tears streamed down his feverish little cheeks. "Momma, my tummy hurts," he cried.

"I know baby. But, that medicine will help it feel better really soon. And, I'm going to sit right here and help you feel all better. I'll tell you a story and maybe you'll be able to fall asleep in a little while."

He glanced over at Kholby standing in the doorway. "Momma said you are going to China. Is that a long way from here?"

Kholby grinned. "Yeah, it's pretty far."

"I think I might miss you a little," Landon notioned. "We can play with the stadium again when you get back."

"Thanks, Landon. I'm going to miss you a bunch! And, I'm going to miss your mom too. But I'll be back right around the time you start school! Then, maybe you can teach me more about those transformers."

"Okay," Landon agreed. "I hope my tummy feels better then."

Allison laughed. "I'm sure it will, sweetheart. In fact, I bet it will be all better by tomorrow!" She hoped it would be at least. Like most mothers, seeing her child in pain brought her ten times more agony than he would ever bear during the few hours of sickness.

The next morning Landon's fever was gone, and for that Allison's heart lifted. But at 9:00 a.m., when Kholby phoned from the airport for one last conversation, her heart broke all over again.

***

Landon and Allison were back at the Stop, resuming their normal routine by Thursday. Radmund couldn't decide if he were happier to see them or for the help he'd desperately missed when he had to cover the busiest shifts single-handedly for two days prior. "I'm so sorry you couldn't get anyone else in to help," she apologized over and over again. "I should have called a babysitter."

"No you shouldn't have. He needed his mom. Besides, if you'd come in here, Henry and I would have kicked you out!" He grinned, hugging her as she dropped the apron around her neck and tied it behind her waist to begin another day. "Were you able to catch up on some of your school stuff?"

"Yes, a little. I tried to do some things yesterday while I was home with him, but it was hard to concentrate with him whining all day. And, he wanted to cuddle on my lap. No way I'm going to refuse that!" Being autistic, cuddling was not something he chose to do very often. And when he did, it was cold and rigid, but Allison had learned to enjoy whatever he could offer. "Finally, he was so much better last night that I got quite a bit done."

"Okay, so how about a couple of hours over dinner, before you go to class tonight? Then we can figure out how to work out whatever else you still need to do over the next week, right?" He truly wanted to help her, but he also knew encouraging her focus on school would be a good deterrent from her deeper sorrow.

"Sounds great. I even got a nap yesterday. It was so cute. Landon curled up next to me on the couch and we both fell sound asleep watching *Barney*."

"I'm not surprised. Nobody stays awake during that show!" he teased. "Look at him," Radmund commented nodding in Landon's direction. "He's just playing with his toys, good as new. How do kids get over that so quickly?"

"They're resilient," she replied. "You're so good with him. In case I don't tell you enough, thank you for everything. He loves you so much!"

Radmund and Allison unlocked the front doors just as the Thursday morning regulars approached. By 11:00 a.m., the Stop was filled with guests, an overflow crowd due to the news of Delia's new line of muffins. A few minutes later, the baker herself sauntered into the restaurant, excited about another brilliant creation.

"Good morning!" Delia greeted them. Her energy was almost back to normal; she and Henry spent up to three hours each day that week working on the new treats in the kitchen. "Today's experiment … Pomegranate Molasses Muffins."

Radmund gently hugged her noticing the short hairdo made her look years younger, then said, "Mom, you look amazing! But you are going to have to stop inventing new muffin and cookie recipes every day. Or, we're going to have to get a new chalkboard for the other side of the fireplace back there."

She laughed, relieved to do so without wincing … and because God had given her so much to enjoy. "Maybe I'll just cook some of my favorites for a few days when I come back full time next week then," she announced. "Doctor said I should be fine getting back to my normal hours as long as I don't lift trays or heavy stuff for another four weeks at least."

Henry smirked. "Yeah, I don't really think the doctor said that. I think she's just using it as an excuse so we have to do all the heavy labor around here and I still have to vacuum and clean at home." He put his arm around her and kissed her cheek, then quickly stepped aside to avoid the swift arm-punch she'd regained enough movement for.

Allison loved how the two of them modeled marital bliss. Then, a moment of sadness flooded her as she thought back to Kholby, somewhere across the world settling in to a new life for a few months. *Will we be that sweet together?* she wondered. *Are we meant to be together that way?*

"Allison, did you hear me?" Radmund asked interrupting her daydreaming.

"Huh? I'm sorry, lost in thought. What'd you say?"

"Him again?" he asked. "Any news yet?"

"Yes." She was slightly excited at the short note she'd received that morning. "He sent a really quick email this morning to let me know he was settling into his apartment but didn't have his own email account. He was using a friend's and would get back to me next week sometime." She really wanted to be upbeat about the whole thing so others would not pity her. "What'd you ask me, Rad. I'm listening now."

"Table five needs service. Are you ready to start?"

"You bet!" She knew the work and special moments visiting with guests would lift her spirits.

Goldie and George got there a few minutes later, giddier than usual. "Good day my dear Allison," George greeted in his formal manner. "By chance is Miss Delia around today? She told us she might be in a bit this afternoon while you and Goldie bless all of us with your musical gifts."

"She's in the kitchen whipping up a new batch of muffins. I'll get her for you," Allison replied hugging Goldie and George and giving Buddy a friendly pat on the head. A few minutes later, Delia emerged, covered in flour as usual.

"Cordelia you are more lovely than ever! The short hairdo sets off your youthful glow," George gushed genuinely. "Goldie and I were wondering if we might set a date and menu with you for our wedding."

"Of course!" She wiped the flour from her hands onto a towel then hugged each of her friends before motioning to the table in the back corner. "The doctor said I can get back into normal routine starting Monday, so let's get this party going, shall we?" The excitement of a wedding furthered her spirits, all of which strengthened her soul, mind, and body. *Thank you God for the moments like this that remind me of how precious life is in You,* she silently prayed as the three of them gathered around the back table to plan.

***

The following Sunday was a rare occasion where The Whistle Stop actually opened, but only for a precious gathering of family and friends for the wedding of Goldie Bingham and George Picardy. Most of their children and grandchildren were present for the ceremony, which made them both radiate with joy. Seeing their family in one place showing their support for their impending nuptials was the greatest gift Bride or Groom could have ever asked for. Extra chairs had to be set up, in fact, to accommodate Goldie's enormous clan. George's family was far smaller with only one son and daughter-in-law and their three children. The Travis' sent an enormous heart-shaped floral arrangement of red roses to "stand" in their place since they were settled back at home in Illinois and unable to make the trip down there again only a month later.

Allison and Delia floated down the small aisle adorned in simple, yet elegant deep purple dresses flowing just past their ankles. Each carried a simple white rose. Radmund and Henry stood next to George, all three dressed up in such flare that the women barely recognized them at first. Finally, Landon walked in, decked out in his first suit. Allison beamed at the child as he carried the pillow, being ever so careful to not drop either ring for which he was charged to guard. She was certain he smiled down the entire aisle, even though it was only a few feet from the front door to the piano where the pastor and wedding party stood in anticipation of the bride's arrival.

Finally, Goldie and Buddy entered the front door. Delia and Allison had helped her select a satin dress shimmering in golden threads with paisleys and roses subtly woven into the background texture. Buddy, likewise, strutted as if he fully understood the magnitude of his responsibility; he, too, was decked out sporting a gold bow-tie much to the congregation's delight. As the two strolled down the aisle, Allison noticed tears rolling down George's cheeks and melting into the enormous dimples protruding from his timeless grin. Behind him, she found Radmund's gaze focused directly on her which caught her heart up into a flutter, causing her a moment of utter confusion.

After the vows and rings were exchanged, Allison sang *My Funny Valentine* – a song George and Goldie humorously selected as "their song" to commemorate their February meeting. "Ladies and Gentleman, I'd like to present to you for the first time ever … Mr. and Mrs. George Picardy." The pastor announced the delighted couple as *Trumpet Voluntary* rang out from the overhead speakers. The crowd erupted in applause and cheers as family and friends surrounded the bride and groom with hugs and well-wishes. Food, dancing, and a gala to last a lifetime commenced. The doors of The Whistle Stop could barely contain the joy spread around the room and among of all those gathered. Shekinah flowed richly through all their lives that day celebrating a union God gifted to a man and woman for the second time in their lives.

Fireworks

By the end of May, Delia was back in full-swing at the restaurant. Henry worried occasionally for her, but the doctors reassured them that all her tests confirmed her to be cancer-free and ready to resume a normal routine. Every night, they thanked God for this miracle. Every morning, they embraced another day together with God as their Guide. One steaming hot day, the first week of June, Henry and Delia sponsored a "Breast-Cancer Awareness" walk ending at the Stop. It was one of the many enormous celebrations they'd promised each other weeks earlier. Over a hundred people showed up for the event. Delia chose to wear her favorite t-shirt to the event – the one Henry had given her.

With her husband's encouragement, she decided it was time to take the storyteller chair herself. Though she preferred the less-public arena in the kitchen, her story was a joyous one that she knew needed to be shared with all who would listen. "Ladies and Gentleman," she began moving the rocker to the front of the restaurant near where Landon and Allison sat quietly reading a story. Radmund stood stoically behind the counter while Henry remained steadfast at his wife's side. "I have a story to tell you. You know I don't really like this public speaking stuff, but I know this is something God would want me to share with you. And, as many of you can relate to this story, I'd like to encourage you to consider telling your own story someday. Maybe even today," she began.

"In late November last year, the doctor found a malignant lump in my breast. My grandmother died from breast cancer and my mother had the same thing when she was only 52. I was terrified! In fact, I was downright angry. I yelled at God and …" her voice rose, then softened as she realized her tone. "I might have even uttered a curse word or two. You see, I felt that God had blessed me with a charmed life. Henry," she reached for his hand, "is one of the two most amazing gifts God bestowed upon me. My son, Radmund, being the other," she motioned his way.

"When we started this restaurant, I was so afraid it wouldn't work. But, again, God blessed us with success," she paused as Henry interjected.

"And He gave this woman an incredible talent for creative cooking which certainly helped this place gain notoriety!" Between his overflowing joy at her health and the pride swelling inside, he couldn't help but brag about her.

She patted his hand and continued her story. "Well, he might be a bit biased, but I do agree that any success I've had as a baker comes from God. I'm not sure how that works since baking seems such a strange thing for God to gift someone with, but I think it's because I want everything I do in my life to glorify Him. When I'm in there creating something," she pointed to the kitchen, "I'm just singing and praising God the whole time. It's like a really special worship time for me.

"So, when the doctor told me I had cancer, well I thought God had abandoned me. I couldn't figure out why and I was really upset. For a few weeks, I stopped singing. My work was a diversion, but all I ended up doing was cooking to forget my troubles. That made me even angrier. I questioned whether God had ever actually been in my life at all. Maybe all along my life had actually just been filled with good luck, I actually thought to myself. Then one night, about a week after my diagnosis, God spoke to me through His word in Psalm 32. It says, 'I am your hiding place, I will protect you from trouble and surround you with songs of deliverance … I will instruct you and teach you in the way you should go … I will counsel you and watch over you. Rejoice in Me.' I knew that was God's way of reassuring me that it would all turn out okay. And, He was okay with my anger! That thought really stirred in my heart.

"A few weeks later I found out I would need to have a double mastectomy, even though there was only one lump. With my genetics, it was safer that way. So, now here I am like all those Hollywood celebs – sporting a very expensive boob job!" The crowd laughed with her. "Once I turned all my worries over to God, I felt a peace that is just unexplainable. Oh sure, there were many times when I started to question things, but God always reminded me of that passage and I felt so much stronger.

"So, if any of you are still going through this, I want to let you know that you can be at peace if you let God take care of this for you. Afterall, He's already got this one covered for you really. And, if you aren't sure or are just super scared or really angry, Henry and

I would be happy to visit with you and pray for you. In fact, if anyone else wants to share their story, we'll get you the muffin du jour on-the-house and turn over the storyteller chair to you right now if you want."

The Whistle Stop bustled with emotion and stories for the entire afternoon that day as woman after woman shared tears, success stories, stories of lost loved ones, and God's abiding mercy. Through all of it, one thing emerged – resting in God's glory was the only way any of the families endured through the process, regardless of the final outcome for their loved ones.

***

"I got it!" she beamed banging on Radmund's apartment door the evening of the first Friday in June. Landon stood dutifully nearby, a bucket of his favorite tops and transformers in hand. Radmund barely had the door open as she lunged into his arms, hugging him intensely before shoving her transcript in his face. "I got all my grades up so I won't lose any of my money! Thank you so much! I couldn't have caught up without you tutoring me for those couple of weeks at the end of the semester! Now I can start my clinicals next week!"

"Wow! First, I'm not surprised," he acknowledged. "And second, I think you underestimate yourself. Once you buckled down, you caught up on that stuff in warp speed."

"I know, just needed to avoid the distractions," she agreed.

"Speaking of distractions, have you heard from Kholby lately? How's he doing?"

"He's good," she smiled at his name. "We skyped a couple of days ago. He's really enjoying the school. Said he got to tell a few kids about Jesus when they asked, but he has to be so careful. He told me that one of the little boys said he wanted to be like Kholby when he grows up – a 'Jesus' man. Kholby was so honored."

Radmund grinned. Hearing her updates in the last few weeks, he had to admit that he was pretty happy for her and Kholby. She beamed each time his name was mentioned, especially at the news of how much his work was bringing Jesus to the Chinese children. While Radmund knew his heart would always have a special place reserved just for her, he wanted her happiness above anything else. If that was with Kholby, then he'd determined to pray for her dreams to come true and for God to help him find a different woman to share his dreams. His first few prayers were wracked with tears, even though he knew it was the right thing to do.

"I brought dinner and dessert to celebrate if you have time," she announced pointing to a red wagon loaded with leftover pot roast and a variety of Delia's muffins.

"Time for you and Landon? Any day!" he declared motioning for them to come in. "How are you Sport? I see you brought my favorite toys," he grinned.

"I have a new one. Momma got it for me," he offered holding up the Bumblebee Rescue Bot. "I got a bee sting today and she said this would make it feel better."

"Did it work?" Radmund asked as Landon showed him the red welt on his arm.

"It's okay. I cried."

"I would cry too," he commiserated. "Bee stings hurt!"

Allison's smile beamed across her face as she watched the two engage in conversation about such simple things, yet with such love and conviction at the same time. "Hey, this food is getting cold and I'm starving! Let's eat," she finally commanded.

"So, first week on the new job over for you. Are you feeling settled in yet? I know Marc talks about you all the time. Says you're the best EMT they've ever had." Since Radmund started his job a few days back, they'd had precious little time to catch up.

"He's only been there a few weeks longer than me, so that hardly counts as historical evidence," he grinned. "Besides, he's biased. He's your brother and one of my two best friends." He winked at Landon.

"Well, we really miss you at the Stop, but your mom is amazing as usual. And Brielle is working out great! She's the hardest worker I've ever seen … next to you, of course."

"I miss it there, but it is great to finally work in my field. And, when I get to help save someone's life or just help them feel better, it's like no feeling in the world. It makes me wonder how much more intense it must be for the docs like Marc. They're the real heroes."

"Momma helped me when the bee stung me. I wanted to call you but she said you were busy helping sick people." Landon interjected wanting some of the attention. "I told her I was sick, but she said I wasn't."

"Well, how about if I look at it after dinner just to make sure it's still okay?" Radmund offered genuine sympathy. "But, I'm sure your mom did a great job of making it all better."

Dinner conversation moved back and forth from the bee sting to working at the hospital, finally moving back to Kholby. She excused Landon to go play in the living room for a moment of private conversation. As she and Radmund cleaned up, Allison confessed. "And, he thinks he might be home sometime the end of August. Rad, he keeps hinting at the future for us. I know I need to tell him about my past, but I just can't do it over skype." Once in awhile, the guilt was so overwhelming that she'd begin to type a confession to him, but quickly erase it before hitting the "send" button.

"You should have told him before he left. I thought you were going to do that the night I kept Landon for you."

"I planned to, but it just didn't work out like I wanted. Then Landon got sick and I forgot."

Radmund swallowed hard and admitted, "Kholby is a really good person. And, I believe he loves you and Landon very much. If you truly want a future with him, you have to be honest. But, typing something like that isn't the way, true. Promise me you will tell him as soon as he gets home, before anything else."

She glanced over at her son, happily buzzing his newest transformer around the living room. "Thank you, Rad. I know that's been really hard for you to accept, so it means a lot to hear you support us like this." She paused a moment, then finished, "I promise to tell him as soon as he gets home." Her heart thumped at the notion, but she knew it was absolutely right. "In fact, I think it will be easier now thanks to my prayer journal. I started one the day after our night at the Silver Ring conference."

"I remember you mentioned that before. It's helping you then?" he queried.

"You know how I started writing about praying for God to help me forgive my parents and He did?" He nodded as they tossed the last bits of trash in the kitchen garbage. "Well, I knew they weren't the only ones. Even though I've come a long way since the rape, thanks to God's mercy, I knew He was telling me to keep praying for Neil as well. That night you and I prayed together at the conference was just the beginning for me."

"That's the first time I've ever heard you mention his name," Radmund said in shock.

"I couldn't even *think* his name for a long time. My prayer journal helped me with that too. I started writing the prayers I knew I should say for him, and before long I was able to actually speak them. I know, now, that God is helping me to forgive him. I thought I had before, but then I'd catch myself pretending to have a conversation with him where I'd yell at him and curse and stuff. You know those imagined confrontations where you always win and the bad guy goes away feeling like a jerk riddled with guilt?" Again, he simply nodded his understanding as she continued. "Well, I knew that wasn't really forgiveness if I could still feel that much anger. But the other day I went back over all the prayers and the ways I felt God helped me, and I prayed them all again. And I think I'm finally getting over it. I really think I can truly forgive him now."

Radmund felt tears welling in his eyes as he blinked them back. "Allison, I've been praying for you since the day you told me about him, way before the conference. I knew the only way you could ever really get past it was to truly forgive him in your heart. I'm so happy your prayers and mine are finally being answered. God's timing is really interesting. Maybe this is just what you needed so you'll be able to tell Kholby when he gets back."

***

June passed by as the heat intensified. Allison settled into working a day a week at the hospital, thoroughly enjoying the incredible rewards with her job when she helped make it a little easier for someone to breathe peacefully. Whichever days she wasn't scheduled at the clinic, she dutifully helped at The Whistle Stop, still cherishing the work and interactions with the people there as well. However, after only three weeks working in the clinic, she began anticipating the fall semester when her clinical schedule would bump up to four full days each week.

Frequently Radmund or Marc would conveniently show up at just the right time to join Landon and Allison in the park for dinner. Most nights, though, they'd all end up at the pool due to the Florida humidity. With her night classes ended, her only other summer requirement was an online research course that sped by due to her extraordinary skills in writing. She and Kholby skyped or emailed at least three times a week. His updates on the school and students lifted her heart. *He's an amazing man,* she'd tell herself frequently. She'd frequently write a short poem to send him describing her perspective on a Bible verse and how it might apply to his work. Then, she'd spend a few lines telling him about a patient or something wonderful Landon had done that day. "I miss you so much," she'd usually sign off while his closing always included "I love you and miss you too."

***

The Fourth of July brought more fireworks than Allison ever expected. "What time did you say the fireworks begin?" she asked as they all met up at Delia and Henry's house for dinner that Saturday after work.

"I don't remember," Delia replied. "Probably dark, around nine, I think."

"I don't like fireworks," Landon interjected. "They are loud."

Radmund pulled the little boy onto his lap. "But, they're so pretty and they are super far away. Will you be okay if I have you sit on my lap the whole time? I'll make sure you're safe."

"And you can wear your earplugs," his mother reminded him. He nodded in hesitant agreement. "Oh, here's the schedule," she added a moment later glancing through the day's paper. "Says they're having a flyover of old military airplanes at six, a concert at seven, and fireworks at nine-thirty. All at the Stadium, of course."

"Too bad Marc has to work," Henry commented. "Plant City hasn't had fireworks in a few years, so they promise to be a great show this time."

"Hopefully he won't be too busy tonight," Delia added. "I hate to watch the news the day after the fourth, all the burns and injuries because people don't take the proper caution when lighting their own fireworks."

Suddenly, Allison gasped out loud, and threw down the paper as if the fireworks' article had literally burned her. "What's wrong?" Henry asked noticing her face was white as a ghost and the usual glimmer in her eyes went starkly dark.

All she could do was point to a photo glaring at her from the rubble of paper. Radmund read the caption and immediately understood. Showing it to Delia, he pleaded, "Mom, can you take Landon in the train room to play for a few minutes?" Beginning to understand, Delia ushered Landon out quickly.

Henry and Radmund helped Allison to the couch, each of them sitting on one side as she sat in the middle. "It's him," was all she could choke out. "It's him."

Henry, who still hadn't seen the article, looked at Radmund for help. "This is the guy who raped her," Radmund explained after skimming the article before showing his father. "He's been found guilty of two other rapes in Tampa. Says he even beat one of the girls pretty bad." Allison sat hunched over, sobbing as she struggled to make sense of the situation. Radmund put his arm around her, rubbing her shoulder for support. "He's going to jail now for a very long time."

"I should have reported him when he did that to me. I knew I should have reported it. Marc tried to tell me but I was too ashamed. It's my fault those other girls got hurt." She choked out the words, riddled with guilt at what she truly believed was her fault.

Henry lifted her face to look into her sullen eyes. "Listen to me. None of this was your fault. Nothing. And you must never blame yourself again. He chose to hurt you and those other women. You did the very best you could at the time. Besides, there's no way to know how that would have turned out if you'd pressed charges anyway. So I want you to stop blaming yourself right now. Do you hear me?" His fatherly discipline sounded slightly stern, but she knew it was filled with genuine support and love. A nod confirmed she understood, but in her heart the guilt boiled.

Radmund took his turn. "What can I do to help you?"

"I don't know," was all she could reply. "You know it's really interesting how God's timing is. I mean it was just a few days ago when we were talking about me forgiving Neil, and now this!? I thought it was so I would have the nerve to tell Kholby. Not this! Is this some sick joke that God is playing on my mind, just to make sure I'm really sincere?"

"God never plays tricks on people. Everything He does is perfect, including His timing. How would you have handled this news a few weeks or months ago?" Radmund asked.

She contemplated the idea for a few seconds then replied, "I know. And I thought being able to forgive him would give me peace. But now I just feel so guilty all over again. I don't think I really have forgiven him afterall. I hate him!"

Henry reassured her once more. "Allison, you didn't do anything wrong. You know that. God understands your anger and pain. He would not help you begin to heal only to set you up for failure. Of this I am certain."

"I have to tell those other girls how sorry I am," she mumbled. "I have to tell them."

Radmund's eyes glowered in concern. "You don't have any idea who those women were. Their names won't be made public." He paused a moment as a horrific idea crossed his mind. "But I think there might be someone you should talk to, if you think you can. It might help you bring closure to this whole thing. Maybe that's why God's timing worked out this way."

She knew who he meant, and her heart raced erratically at the thought. So much so that she could not even process the idea. "It's almost six. Landon will really enjoy the planes. We should go now so we don't miss the air show."

"You're right," Radmund agreed, reading her turmoil clearly. "Let's get Mom and Landon and head over there before the crowd picks up too much and parking is a mess."

Radmund noticed a significant void in her attention the entire evening; he'd kept Landon closer than promised because he feared her attention was everywhere but with them most of the night. When the B-1 Bomber flew over, rocketing the entire area in thunderous sounds and vibrations, she sat by, stoic, as if deaf and blind. Even when Landon reached for her comfort, she remained motionless with vacant eyes. And when the fireworks exploded filling the sky with vibrant colors of gold, red, blue, green, and purple, Radmund saw only meaningless reflections of the pyrotechnics in her pupils.

When they finally returned home, he gently walked her and Landon to their door. Then, Allison mechanically guided her son into bed. The *Barney Song*, however, was initiated by Radmund as Allison stood by humming out of habit. "Momma, are you okay?" Landon finally asked.

"Hmm?" she replied. "Sure."

Radmund filled in. "You mom is just a little distracted right now Sport. She really had fun with you tonight. You were so brave with the fireworks and all those loud airplanes! We were very proud of you!"

"I want to build an airplane. They have them in the toy store." He took his mother's hand as she remained a vacant presence in the room. "Momma, can I build an airplane?"

"Sure," she replied completely unaware of his question.

Again, Radmund came to the rescue. "Hey, Landon, how about you and I get one of those kits soon and build it together? I've always wanted to put one together."

"Okay," he replied letting go of his mother's hand. "I'm going to sleep now. You can leave." Radmund grinned at the literal honesty of his young friend. Then he helped Allison out of the room.

"No! I won't do it!" she shuddered, without warning, as they moved to the privacy of her patio.

Radmund jumped in fear at her sudden outburst. "What?"

"I won't go see him. I know that's what you meant. I can't do it. I won't!"

He felt horrible for even hinting the possibility earlier. "I'm sorry Allison. I shouldn't have mentioned anything. Of course you don't have to go see him."

"Really? I don't?" she begged more than questioned.

He held her close, noticing she was shaking uncontrollably. "I will never let him or anyone hurt you again, I promise. You're safe here." Slowly she looked up into his piercing blue eyes, knowing that he would, indeed, never let anyone hurt her or Landon. The intensity of his protective nature combined with her emotional instability overwhelmed her and she suddenly reached up to his face, pulling him into a full and passionate kiss. Astonished, he kissed her back at first, then quickly pulled away.

"Allison, we can't do this now. It's not right." His heart ached as he recalled the only other time she'd kissed him, much in the same manner for all the wrong reasons.

"Why not?" she demanded. "I know you have feelings for me."

"You're confused and really scared right now. I won't take advantage of you like that. Besides, you really miss Kholby and I won't be your 'stand-in' guy. I've worked too hard to accept us just as friends. I can't let myself feel anything more. Not now."

Allison slumped onto a patio chair and began sobbing. "I'm so sorry. You're right. I'm so confused."

Radmund sat next to her, holding her hand. "It's going to be alright. I can sleep on your couch tonight if you want."

"No, that's not necessary. I'll be fine. I'm just a wuss is all. Really, I'll be okay." She could not look at him for fear the urge to kiss him again would be too powerful. *Why is this happening?* she thought desperately. *It must be like he said because I miss Kholby so much and I'm so stinkin' upset about Neil. It must be that,* she concluded.

"Allison?" he questioned for the third time. "Are you sure you're okay?"

"Hmm? Oh yea. Just caught up in thought is all. This whole thing is just so shocking. I hardly ever think about him now, and I certainly never thought I'd read about him being convicted for the same crime he committed against me." She looked only half-way up, noticing the moonlight casting a beautiful glow on Radmund's light blue t-shirt. The urge swept her again, causing her to quickly look away. "I wish it'd been because of me that he went to jail," she admitted.

"I thought so," he agreed. "That would be sweet revenge, wouldn't it?"

"Yes it would. But, at least he's in jail now and he won't hurt anyone. Do you think I really can forgive him if I still want that kind of revenge against him?" The thought had troubled her all night.

"Yes, I do. God didn't promise you'd forget what happened. And, that memory could cause you setbacks sometimes. But, God knows your heart. And, He knows you are still working through this."

They walked to the door, hand-in-hand. "Rad, I'm so sorry about what I did out there. I didn't mean to lead you on." But even as she apologized, she desperately wanted to repeat the offense.

Somehow he sensed her underlying motives and stepped back, releasing her hand. "I know. This has been a weird night. It's okay, really. Let's just pretend it didn't happen, okay?"

"Sure," she replied. But as he walked down the hall and out of sight, she knew the kiss would linger into her dreams.

Forgiveness

For two weeks Allison struggled with the turmoil brewing in her heart. She denied everything that pounded fiercely on her mind, praying fervently that God would give her wisdom to understand His will. But silence seemed to prevail. Her prayer journal remained empty in the column marked "Answers." She and Radmund passed at work and occasionally caught up with each other at the park or the pool, but their evenings together stopped. Landon started pouting and acting out more. Even in their conversations, Kholby sensed a distance between her and the world. She stopped writing poems for him, and their conversations dwindled to only a few minutes a couple times each week. When he asked about it, she'd reply curtly, apologize, and then come up with something Landon needed as her excuse to go.

"Miss Goldie," Allison softly spoke after they finished the Friday Fifties set. "Do you have a moment?"

"Of course, dear. I have all the time in the world for you. I hear concern in your voice. What's troubling you?" Goldie took Allison's arm as they shuffled from the piano to the privacy of the back corner table.

"I'm really confused about something," she began as the elderly woman sat intently. "The man who raped me is in jail now, and I feel like God wants me to do something that I just can't do. And Radmund isn't helping matters either."

Goldie listened carefully, more to what was left unsaid than spoken. "Sweetheart, what is it you are not telling me? I can't help you unless you are completely honest."

Allison should not have been surprised by Goldie's insight. "Well, I feel like maybe the only way I can really forgive this guy and get peace is to face him, to tell him I forgive him. But I'm terrified to see him again. Do you really think God wants me to have to face him again after all these years?"

"I think that God always has the very best plan for our lives. And, if He wants you to go see this man, then I am certain God will give you all the courage and wisdom you need to get through it just fine."

"But how do I know for sure if that's really what God wants me to do? I mean, what if it's just me thinking that and I go and it's awful? Then I'll be a mess all over again."

"I believe that God would help you through it, regardless. Of course, that is if your intentions are not planked by revenge. I assume you've been in prayer and devotion on this?"

Allison pondered the question a moment, then replied. "Yes, so many times in the last two weeks I can't even count. And, I keep a prayer journal about it, but I haven't really felt any answers."

"Honey, God doesn't promise we will always know, without a doubt, His answers. Sometimes we have to take a leap of faith and do what we believe is His will. If your purpose is pure and truly to forgive this man, then God will bless you in this visit. I'm certain of this."

"Miss Goldie, thank you so much for your advice. I know you're right. Would you please pray for me?"

"Allison, you don't even have to ask. George and I pray for you and Landon every night already. It will be my pleasure to lift this to God as well. Please let me know if you decide to go so I can be on my knees at the exact time you visit."

"Thank you so much. I'll let you know what I decide. I wish I could ask Radmund to go with me."

"Why don't you? I'm certain he would be happy to accompany you. In fact, I can't believe he'd let you go without him."

"No, we haven't really spent much time together in the last couple of weeks. I mean, he's done a few night shifts this week so we haven't seen each other here like we used to. I see him at the hospital some when I'm working there, but he's in and out with the ambulance so much that we just cross paths and that's about it. And, I saw him flirting with one of the nurses the other day, so he's kind of distracted."

Goldie leaned forward to pat Buddy's head. "And? I can hear that you aren't smiling. That's very unfortunate. What else is burdening your heart my dear?"

Allison sat in thought a moment. "That's just it. I don't really know what it is," she finally admitted.

"Oh, I don't mean to pry," Goldie empathized. But before she could continue a sudden pain shot through her entire left side, causing her to convulse forward so violently that Buddy jumped to attention in loud barks, which he never did. Allison grabbed the elderly woman to keep her from falling out of the chair.

"Help me!" Allison screamed. "Somebody call 9-1-1!" She carefully cradled Goldie's head in her arms, comforting her. "Miss Goldie, it's okay. The ambulance is coming. You just breathe easy and we'll get you some help."

"Call … George …," Goldie pleaded.

Delia came running over with a cool rag at that moment. "What's wrong?" she asked gently placing the rag on Goldie's forehead.

"I don't know. We were talking and she jumped really hard and then slumped into my lap like this. Buddy freaked out."

"I know. We heard him all the way back in the kitchen." Delia leaned to address Goldie. "Hey, Miss Goldie. I called the ambulance. You just hang in there, okay?"

"Darling, I'm … an … old … woman," she labored between words, then began to relax as Allison coaxed her into a more rhythmic breathing. "If something happens to me … God will be there waiting with open arms. … But, if it's not my time … then I'll just end up with a huge hospital bill … and more time with all my sweethearts."

Moments later the ambulance sirens blared outside the Stop as Radmund rushed inside with medical supplies and his partner pushed in the gurney. "What's going on?" he asked Allison.

"She had a violent convulsion and then slumped into my arms. Her breathing was pretty erratic for a few minutes, but she's calming down now. She seems coherent. Her pulse was over a hundred fifty for a couple of minutes. But it's in the nineties now."

"Nice recap," he complimented. "Sounds like you know your stuff!"

"Just take care of her, will you? You're the expert, right?" she begged as he began checking Goldie's vitals.

An hour later, Goldie was resting peacefully in one of the cubicles at Brandon Regional. George sat at her side, gently patting her hand, as Buddy whimpered on the floor nearby. "Please let me see him," she requested. "He's so pitiful when he whimpers like that. It drives me crazy."

George smiled, relieved his bride was well enough to joke. "Anything you wish, my dear," he complied encouraging Buddy to jump up to the side of the bed so he could see his mistress. "See, Buddy, she's fine. I told you." Buddy licked her hand, showing his utter devotion and affection.

"I'll be out of here in a few hours, Buddy. Now you stop whimpering, okay?" she commanded. A bark signified his understanding, followed by the dog's retreat to the floor where he lay quietly following her orders. Every few minutes, though, he would poke his head over the side of the bed for reassurance as she patted him and cooed softly to him once more.

Marc pulled the curtain aside a few minutes later, clipboard in hand. "Well, Miss Goldie, it looks like you're going to be around for a little while longer. You have a mild case of angina, but nothing really to worry about. We're giving you some medicine to help control it so you don't have those sharp pains or other symptoms again. Also, I'd like you to start taking one aspirin a day. That will keep your blood from clotting, which can sometimes happen when you have angina at your age."

"Hey!" she complained. "Are you calling me old?"

"Miss Goldie, you are an amazing woman. Your age only enhances how lovely and physically fit you truly are." Marc's bedside manner was one of the constant compliments patients noted on his follow-up surveys.

"Amen to that," George jumped in. "The most beautiful woman I've ever seen!"

"Stop it you two!" she joked loudly as Buddy jumped up and began whimpering again. "See what you've done! You went and got the dog upset again."

"George, you are welcome to help her get dressed now. She'll be released to go home in a little while. I'm going to call Allison so she can tell the others what's going on. I know they're all worried sick." With that reassurance, Marc left the couple to the privacy of a curtained-off room.

George gently took her hand and kissed her forehead. "My darling, I'm so glad you are well," he noted as tears streamed down his cheeks.

"George Picardy, why are you crying?" she demanded as he helped her out of the bed.

"Sweetheart, your hearing is incredible. But, mine are tears of joy, for truly you and I are meant to enjoy life together a little longer. Two months just isn't long enough."

***

Radmund, Allison, and Landon enjoyed a picnic dinner together in the park that night – something they hadn't done in over two weeks. "I want to go see her for just a few minutes later," Allison commented as they polished off the deli sandwiches and potato salad. "She and I were chatting about me visiting Neil when she had the attack."

"Really? What did she say?" he replied.

"Words of wisdom, as usual," Allison agonized. "And, I know what I have to do. I just need to tell her thanks."

"You're going to see him, aren't you?" Radmund glanced at Landon happily swinging nearby.

She nodded. "I have to. You know that. I think you've known it for awhile, but you knew I had to figure it out. You're so wise like that." Sitting side-by-side, she fought back the urges that had been creeping into her dreams since the night they'd kissed. *I must really miss Kholby,* she thought reprimanding herself. *Rad's my friend. Just my friend.*

"What about Landon?" he asked breaking the awkward silence.

"No, he can't go with me. I was hoping you would keep him for me, if you don't mind that is. I have to go this Sunday since Neil gets moved from Hillsborough to the Zephyrhills Correctional Institution next week to start serving his sentence."

"I think somebody should go with you, Allison. Please don't go alone."

She'd already thought through the entire visit, actually. "I've already asked Marc to go. I don't mean to hurt you, but he was there for me the whole time and I really want him with me. He's my brother."

Radmund nodded his acceptance of the plan. "That makes perfect sense. And, I'll be happy to keep Landon. We'll go to the dinosaur museum again. You know he loves that place!"

"Thanks," she responded with a friendly nudge. "You are always here for us. Thank you." Her heart fluttered once more, causing her to stand creating a greater space between them.

"Allison, what is this going on between us? What are you avoiding?" he asked as he stood, but carefully guarded the space she'd set up between them.

She grimaced at being so transparent. "I don't know. You said the other night that it's just because I miss Kholby so much. I'm sure that's it. I would never hurt you." She folded her arms, invisibly pushing him away as she stepped back further to emphasize her point.

"It's getting late. Why don't I get Landon home and ready for bed while you go visit with Goldie and George?" He offered, knowing he had to avoid any further conversation about their relationship – for both of their sakes.

***

Before retrieving Landon from Sunday school, Marc and Allison, Goldie and George, Delia and Henry, and Radmund gathered around for prayer. They begged God to have mercy on Allison, to give her wisdom and courage. Then they forced themselves to pray for Neil, that he would open his heart to forgiveness and find salvation. When all was said and done, brother and sister drove off for the Hillsborough County Jail in Tampa – an extremely long 30-minute drive as far as Allison was concerned.

"Allison and Marc Pershing," she answered at the reception window for the facility as they both slid their driver's licenses under the partition for verification. "We're here to see Neil Fredericks."

"Wait here," the officer stated as he slipped away to finalize the visiting status and send for the prisoner. A few minutes later he returned with ID badges for both guests, and strict orders, "You are limited to forty minutes per visit. Do not remove any clothing. Do not speak in code or write anything down for the prisoner. An armed officer will be in the room at all times. If you have any concerns, get up immediately and he will assist you out the door. Go to Booth 10 and Mr. Fredericks will meet you there in a few minutes."

"Yes Sir," they both replied intrepidly. Then another officer led them down a corridor that seemed to go on forever, ending in a large rectangular room with several plastic blue chairs lined up along one very long counter separated by vertical partitions about every three feet. Plexiglass sheets were nestled between each partition, separating the guest from the prisoner in each booth. Allison trembled in fear as she sat down at Booth 10. Marc stood behind her, gently rubbing her shoulders. It was only a moment and then he was there, facing her again after nearly six long years.

"Yeah, whad'ya want?" he demanded, clearly not recognizing her. "If you're selling something, I don't think I'm in the position to buy right now." He grinned balefully at her. She shuddered. Marc placed his hands securely on her shoulders afraid she might jump right out of the chair.

After a few seconds just staring intently at him, she choked down her fears and began. "I'm Allison. You took me to prom."

He leaned back in his chair on his side of the plexiglass, narrowing his eyes toward her in an attempt to gain recognition. Then the vile grin returned, dulled yellow teeth glaring through his pursed lips. That time, Marc felt her entire body convulse. "It's okay. You can do this Sis," he coaxed gently. "Just breathe. God will give you the right words."

"Oh yeah," he seethed. "Prom. Blue dress." His grin turned pure evil as he leaned forward, almost touching his nose to the clear divider. She jumped back. "You were feisty! It was amazing, wasn't it?"

That time it was she who held Marc back. He fiercely lunged to the glass, startling Neil so much that he fell backward off his chair. "No Marc, please don't get us kicked out of here," she begged as her attacker regained his composure and seat.

"Everything alright here?" the police guard demanded coming to check out the commotion.

"Yes, Officer. We're fine. Thank you," she replied calmly. In fact, a calm immediately engulfed her so that she sat in amazement for a moment wondering if she were having an out-of-body experience. *I can do this,* she realized. *I'm not afraid anymore!* She looked him squarely in the eyes, riveting his gaze so that he could not force himself to look away. "You raped me. It was horrible. And, I hated you for a very long time. I'm sorry I didn't press charges against you back then. Maybe it would have prevented you from hurting those other women. But I don't hate you anymore. I feel sorry for you. God had great plans for you and you ruined all of it. Now you will suffer a very lonely life for a very long time." Not once did she blink or shift her glare.

"Those girls are liars, and so are you. I never did anything you all didn't want and you know it. My appeal will prove I'm innocent." Even his best efforts to defend himself could not hide the quaver in his voice. Her presence had him bewildered and on edge.

"Even if you tell yourself that a million times, it will never be true. The only way you will ever be innocent of these sins is to beg God's forgiveness. The law will not pardon you and you know it. But, God will. All you have to do is confess your sins to Him and ask for forgiveness. At least then you will know freedom in your heart and, one day, in eternity."

"Oh, so you're one of those Jesus Freaks now, huh? It figures. Well, I don't need forgiveness. Didn't do anything wrong."

"We all need God's grace. Right now, I think you need His overpowering conviction, though. But someday, if you do give your life to Christ, I want you to know that I've already forgiven you for what you did to me."

"You forgive me?" He forced himself to look away, shattering the gaze that had held him compelled for so many minutes. "Why do you forgive me?"

"Because it's what God wants. But, I've had to pray a lot to have God help me. And, I think coming here today was God's way of sealing the deal for me. I know now, looking at you, that I can honestly have mercy on you. I no longer hate you. I forgive you. It's up to you to repent and ask God's forgiveness for yourself now." Even though he could no longer look her in the eyes, her gaze remained steadfast on him in such a way that he felt the intensity of an unexplained heat searing into his chest.

"Is that why you came here? To see me in jail and rub in some long-term revenge for what happened? For what you think I did to you?" His anger returned, fueled by sudden conviction.

"At first, yes. But now, I no longer think about you that way. In fact, I will not think about you again after today. And, I have Jesus Christ to thank for that healing power. But, you will probably think about me and the other girls a lot in the next few years." She stood up, knowing she'd said all there was to say. God's glorious presence swept over her with an overwhelming freedom for the first time in six years. "Thanks for seeing me. I'll be praying for you."

"Yea! Well don't waste your breath. I don't need your stupid prayers," he yelled after her as she and Marc solemnly walked away, neither looking back at Booth 10.

Once outside the station, she allowed herself to deeply breathe in the fresh air once more. "I can't believe it! We did it! I feel like I can fly," she jumped joyously waving her arms in pretend flight. "Thank you God!" she sang out to the Heavens. Marc stood nearby, flooded with solace as he watched his sister return to the full glory God intended for her life. He thought he even saw a radiant glow about her as she sang out in praise to God, "Praise God we don't have to hide scars. They just strengthen our wounds, and they soften our hearts. They remind us of where we have been, but not who we are. So praise God, praise God we don't have to hide scars!"

Part 4
August – September

I pray that you may have the power to comprehend, with all the saints, what is the breadth and length and height and depth, and to know the love of Christ that surpasses knowledge, so that you may be filled with all the fullness of God. Now to him who by the power at work within us is able to accomplish abundantly far more than all we can ask or imagine, to him be glory in the church and in Christ Jesus to all generations, forever and ever. Amen.

Ephesians 3:18-21 (NRSV)

Confusion

August brought the scorching temperatures and humidity that causes most Floridians to hide inside the protection of central air conditioning. Allison and Landon's attempts to have a relaxing night at the park had completely halted. With the burden of her past miraculously lifted from her heart, her life sprung back into a normal pace she'd forgotten those six years earlier. Chats online with Kholby intensified as they shared hopes and dreams, memories, and recaps of events from the week ... all except the one event she'd recently overcome. That story never breached her keyboard.

She felt free again to spend time with Radmund ... just as friends. Since he'd moved permanently to the day shift, they'd easily reconvened a habit of spending most nights together at one or the other's apartment for dinner and a movie, games, or an attempt to cool off in the pool. Marc joined them whenever his schedule allowed. On Thursday, the second week of August, Landon announced, "I want to go swimming." Generally, he had to be coaxed to do more than sit on the first step.

"Excellent idea!" his mother agreed, stunned at his sudden courage. "You're doing so well with your lessons. Wanna try jumping from the side this time?"

Landon looked concerned. "No. I still want my float. And Uncle Marc to stay by me when I try to swim."

"Honey, you're doing so well. I saw you swim across the pool at the Y the other day. I know you can do it."

"Then, let's get going!" Landon announced impatiently, instinctively understanding that his sudden onset of nerves might not last long.

"Wow! He's really maturing lately. And, he even speaks with more emotion," Marc noted.

"I know. It's so great!" Allison agreed. "I think it's because whenever he's around Radmund, the two of them just don't shut up!" She grinned at her friend knowing words would never be enough to express the gratitude she felt for the way he treated her son.

Radmund chimed in. "Hey now, we talk about important stuff."

"Oh yeah. Whether the *Mythbusters* episode is really possible or not. Whether the green or the purple top will win the battle. What are best super powers? If you were a transformer, what would you do? If you put a super-charged jet pack on the back of a locomotive, would it do a wheelie when it took off? Yep, you two have some terribly intellectual conversations," she teased.

"We're curious," he suggested in support of their experimental endeavors.

She tousled his red locks. "I know. I'm kidding. Truth is, you're awesome," she commended. "Landon never thought about things like that until he met you. I'd try to read him books or watch something educational with him, but his attention lasted about two minutes on a good day. But, with you, he's like a robot fixated on figuring out all kinds of things."

Landon bounced into the room, bright blue swim trunks hanging haphazardly from his skinny hips, backwards with the tag hanging out. "Hey, let's go give those another try, shall we?" she offered scuttling her son back to his room. "Why don't you two boys," she noted glancing at Marc and Radmund, "get your own trunks on so we can get to the pool before it closes!"

In a few minutes, all four were happily splashing in semi-cool water. Sitting all day in record heat, the pool water was a not-very-refreshing 95 degrees. But, it was better than the stifling heat. "Look at him," Allison whispered as she floated toward Radmund. "He's doing it!" She beamed as Marc waded nearby while Landon courageously doggy-paddled from one side to the other of the shallow end.

"Way to go, Sport!" Radmund congratulated as he swam up to give Landon a high-five. Landon's subtle grin, another personality trait emerging through maturity, showed slight curvature on both sides finally. "You swam the whole nine yards all by yourself!"

"Is that how long this pool is?" Landon asked while pushing his wet, chocolate-brown locks out of his eyes.

Allison arrived in time to enjoy Radmund's explanation. "That's another idiom. It means you did the whole thing all by yourself."

"Why does it say 'nine yards' then? Is that how big the pool is?" Landon looked across the pool wondering. He turned at the wall and began swimming back to the other side, counting off imaginary yards with each stroke to test his hypothesis. At the other side, he announced triumphantly, "It's twenty yards. You have to say I swam the whole twenty yards."

Still on the other side of the pool, the three adults cheered the little boy's victory. Without reservation, he returned to them in another moment, verifying his imaginary count along the way. "That was so brave of you!" Allison gushed hugging her son as he swam into her arms. "I am so proud of you!"

Landon looked at Radmund. "Well?" he urged.

"Okay, you swam the whole twenty yards," Radmund agreed proudly.

Marc added his own encouragement. "I bet you'll be ready for the deep end and diving lessons by next summer."

"Hey, don't push it!" Allison implored. "I know I have my lifeguard certification, but the last thing I want to do is use it for my own child."

Radmund waded toward them holding out his arms for Landon. "Come on Sport," he cajoled. "Try jumping over to me." Without any reservations, Landon leapt from his mother's arms safely into Radmund's. "See! You've got the idea. Now, how about over to your Uncle Marc?" On cue, Landon jumped straight into his uncle's arms giggling with delight at the new game which continued for at least another five minutes, until all three adults were exhausted.

"See what you've done," Marc teased Radmund. "We'll never get this kid out of the pool now. And, I've got the early shift. So, if you two will excuse me, I'm going to head back to my place and get some shut eye."

"Later Marc," Allison turned and waved just as Landon surprised her with a leap into her arms, knocking them both over into the depths of the three-foot water. Sputtering, she struggled to get them both back to the surface. "You okay, Landon?" she choked between spurts of water as he clung, terrified, to her neck while she desperately tried to steady them both.

"Here, let me help," Radmund offered trying to pry Landon's hands free. Frightened, Landon immediately jumped and clung tightly to Radmund's neck, knocking him backward in the process.

Allison reached forward reflexively to grab them both before they went under again. For a moment, they balanced in the water, she holding him, him holding her, child cradled between – their eyes fixed on each other reflecting something far deeper than the water.

Radmund was the first to look away and back to Landon, who trembled in his arms. "Hey, it's okay. Part of swimming is learning how to go under. You're okay."

"I don't like it," Landon whined. "It got in my nose."

Allison kissed her son's cheek. "You are so brave! When we fell, you just helped me get back to the surface, like you were a lifeguard or something."

Landon looked totally confused. "I did?"

Radmund jumped into the charade. "Oh yeah. I saw it with my own eyes. You were super brave to help your mom like that!" Landon cautiously released his grip. "See, you're a natural in the water," Radmund encouraged as the little boy slowly swam back to the side.

An hour later, with Landon nestled in dry pajamas, the three of them gathered in his room for the nighttime ritual. Allison led them in the Thursday song, *Angels Watching Over Me*. It wasn't one of Landon's favorites because the tune was a little complicated, but Allison loved the words. Every Thursday, she'd sing them out with full emotion in the richness of the prayer they lyricized.

"Allison, thank you for letting me be a part of his life," Radmund announced out-of-the-blue a few minutes later as he prepared to leave. "I can't imagine my life without him," he finished.

His sudden confession startled and confused her. "Rad, I think it's the other way around. I can't imagine our lives without you. You will always be a part of our lives. I promise."

"Hey, don't make promises like that. You might not be able to keep that one, you know."

"What?! Are you kidding me? I would never, ever let anything come between you and Landon."

"Okay, well, if you and Kholby should get married someday, then what? Do you think he's going to be fine with me playing the 'father' figure while he struggles each day to earn Landon's affection?"

Allison stepped back in shock. "Where is this coming from? Landon is blessed to have you, Marc, Kholby, and your dad in his life. He's got plenty of men to support him."

"I'm sorry. Didn't mean to upset you. It's just that I really love him like my own … and, well, I'd understand if Kholby wants that role when he gets back. And, it was obvious from before that my presence is in the way of them developing a stronger relationship."

She took his hand in hers and gently touched his cheek. "I don't know what will happen when Kholby returns, but I know that nothing will ever come between you and Landon. I will make sure of that. I love you both too much to let anyone hurt either of you."

"Hey, I'm sorry. I'm just feeling a little confused right now is all." He desperately wanted her to know – to know how the last few weeks had meant so much to him, how important she was to him, but how determined he was to move on.

"I know, me too. I mean, I love it when Kholby emails or we get to Skype. I know he loves me and Landon. And, I can't wait until he gets back!" She paused, breathed deeply, then finished. "But, I don't understand what's happening with you and me. You're my very best friend and I love you so much. But it's different with Kholby … isn't it?"

He forced back all emotion to speak stoically for her sake. "I can't have this discussion with you, Allison. You said we are just friends. I even agree that you and Kholby are really good for each other. We've been through all of this before."

She hugged him and then stepped away. "I'm so confused. Miss Goldie and I talk about you guys a lot. She thinks I'm avoiding my true feelings."

He opened the door to go. "I think it's not fair for me to have this conversation with you when your boyfriend is a thousand miles away. You are just missing him is all. And, I don't want to mislead you that there's anything more between you and I than friendship. In fact, there's a nurse I'm thinking of asking out."

"I figured so," she admitted feeling slightly upset. "I saw you flirting with her a couple of times."

"Good, then you understand. See, I really don't want to be anything more than your friend. Please don't mistake my attention or affections toward Landon for anything more between you and me." With that, he walked out and closed the door quickly before she could respond. By the time he got to his apartment, his heart was broken at the lie he'd felt forced to tell her. *It's in her best interest, and mine*, he consoled himself.

***

"Marc," she asked the following Monday as they worked the clinic floor during the same shift.

"Hmm?" he responded glancing up from a chart.

Radmund's words had plagued her the entire weekend. She couldn't figure out why, but a cocktail of anger and helplessness began surging in her stomach at the thought of him dating someone else. "Is Radmund dating one of the nurses?"

Marc laughed as he put the chart on the counter. "I don't know. But there are a lot of them that think he's the 'catch of the week' ... next to me of course."

"Funny," she responded pretending to be amused. "It's just that he told me he was going to ask out one of the nurses. I saw him flirting with her, but I think he's also upset with me. He said we were just friends and that I was confused if I thought it was anything more. I don't know why he'd think that because he knows how I feel about Kholby anyway. So, I just hope he's happy and that whoever she is realizes what a great guy he is. That's all."

Marc motioned to a private room where the two of them sat down to finish the conversation. "Al, you've made it clear to him for a long time that you only want to be friends. Then, Kholby leaves and you two start spending every free minute together."

"What? You're around all the time too, so it's not just the two of us you know."

"Really? You're like an old married couple, but he knows it will all change when Kholby returns. So, he's trying to protect all three of you from heartache." Marc looked directly at his sister. "Radmund is an exceptional man. So is Kholby. You have to figure out who you really want to be with in life. Who do you believe God wants for you? And, then let the other one go."

"I can't do that. I think it's Kholby, but I can't imagine not having Radmund in my life. In Landon's life. What's wrong with just being friends?"

"Nothing, if that's really all you plan for it. But, that means you need to treat him like a friend and nothing more. And, what happens if you and Kholby get married and move to a mission field somewhere far away? You know that's what he feels called to do. Are you committed to love him so much that you can move far away from everyone here?"

Allison's face wrinkled in despair. "I never really thought about moving away. I just figured he'd work somewhere around here and everything else would be the same."

"Oh Sis. Really? You think he's going to be okay with the time you and Rad spend together? Is he going to be okay with the way Landon treats him compared to Radmund? Do you seriously think he's going to be happy *merging* into your life here?"

"I don't see why it has to be that way. Kholby knows we're just friends. You guys just underestimate how much he really understands about my life. We've talked about it, you know. He understands."

Marc stood to close the door, then sat back down. "Really? If you're so sure he understands, why won't you trust him enough to tell him you were raped?"

A glower raged in her eyes. "Why do you people keep bringing that up? I told you and Radmund that I'm going to tell Kholby when he gets back. Besides, it shouldn't matter! I've worked for years to get over that and now you guys keep reminding me of it. Just stop!" She gasped in a deep breath. "You know, he's so awesome that he loves me even though he thinks I had a careless encounter as a teenager."

"That's not what I was asking you. I'm asking if you love him enough to trust him after you tell him the truth." Marc gently took his sister in his arms as she began shaking.

"Dr. Pershing to room eighteen. Dr. Pershing to room eighteen." The announcement boomed overhead, bringing a sudden halt to their conversation.

She stood to go, no intention of answering his last question. "Sounds like it's time for you to go save a life," she whispered.

"Think about what I said. I just want the very best for you, whatever and whomever that might be. You and Landon deserve it." He kissed her forehead and headed down the hall to Room 18.

By the following Saturday, Allison's moping became so pitiful that Delia asked her to work in the kitchen so she would not disturb the customers. "What is wrong with you?" she finally asked after the lunch crowd dispersed. "Something wrong with you and Kholby?"

"Sort of," Allison admitted. "Radmund's been preoccupied with some nurse, so he hasn't spent time with Landon this week. That means I have a whiny kid to deal with lately. And, I haven't heard from Kholby in a week. Last time we talked I told him I wasn't sure what would happen to us when he got back. He took it really hard and we haven't talked since then. But, he thought I wasn't sure about us. I just meant that I had to tell him something really important that might change the way he feels about me. But he hung up before I could explain and now I can't get ahold of him."

"So you're finally going to tell him about what happened?" Delia began sifting flour and baking soda together as they talked.

Allison nodded, then handed her the butter and sugar. "I have to. I should never have kept it a secret. Plus, I promised Radmund I'd do it." After passing the fresh raspberries, Allison continued. "Did you know he was going out with that nurse?"

Delia looked at Allison, not sure how to respond. "Yes, he brought her to dinner last night. She's very nice. He seems happy. How are you with this?"

"I'm happy for him. Landon misses him, though. But I guess this is for the best. Besides, it will help Landon and me be more prepared to spend time with Kholby when he gets home."

Together, they began spooning out the dough for white chocolate raspberry cookies. "Landon will adjust, especially with school starting soon, and I'm sure Radmund will make time for him no matter how it goes with Nichole."

Nichole, she thought as her stomach churned a bit. *So that's her name. I should try to meet her next week.*

"Hey Allison, someone here to see you," Henry interjected peeking in through the kitchen doors as a huge grin spread across his face.

Allison looked confused, then quickly brushed the flour from her hands. "Me? Who?" But Henry retreated quickly to avoid giving away the surprise. Delia needed no visual to confirm her suspicions as she could hear Allison's squeal of delight throughout the restaurant. "Kholby! You're back!" As soon as she had exited the kitchen doors, his vivid green eyes and dark brown hair took her breath away. Running past tables filled with customers, she leaped into his arms, tears pouring down her cheeks. "This is why you didn't respond! You were coming home! I thought you didn't want to talk to me anymore."

"No way," he replied breathlessly. "Nothing could keep me away from you." A kiss they'd both dreamed of for three months propelled them together with such momentum that all time and space stopped around them. Customers *ooed* and *awed* at the joyous reunion. Even to those totally unaware of the details, it was obviously a moment both had anticipated for a long time. Several moments later, still gazing into each other's eyes, he finally broke free to look to the front window. "Hey, Landon," he addressed the little boy who'd been sitting dumbfounded by his mother's reaction. "I've missed you so much!" Kholby walked over cautiously to hug Landon.

"Hi Kholby," Landon said as he stood up. "I missed you a little bit. Momma missed you more."

She laughed nervously at being so exposed. "Of course I did," she accepted. "I can't believe you're back already. I didn't think you'd get back for another two weeks at least." The three of them sat together near the front window. Landon selected his favorite transformer to accompany him to the conversation.

"Well, our last skype had me a little nervous, so I thought I'd take the early flight out. The others are almost done anyway. I was going to tell you, but I wanted it to be a surprise."

"This is the best surprise in the world!" she beamed helpless to control her excitement. "And just in time! Landon starts school next Wednesday. Will you be staying around here again? Maybe you could go with me to his first day drop off?"

"I'm not sure I can be here then. I'm not really staying at my grandparents' trailer this time. I kind of need to get settled in my new job, that is." He grinned slyly at her, waiting for her reply.

"What new job? Tell me! What's going on?"

"Habitat offered me a permanent position at one of their main offices in Miami! One of the reps went with us to China to help with construction on part of the school. He liked my work and offered me the job on the way home. I start the third week of September!"

Something in her churned. "But, I thought you wanted to teach English and be a missionary? Now you want to work in construction?"

"I want to be close to you guys. And, maybe, we could … well … I'll get to that later," he paused with an enormous grin. "Anyway, they said I can teach English as part of the job since we work mostly with the Cuban immigrants. They have a lot of needs there. It's a way to do both – help Habitat and be a missionary!"

He continued for several minutes about all the wonderful things he'd seen and learned in China, about the possibilities of the new job, and how happy he was to see her and Landon again. But in her mind, confusion began to swirl viciously in a circle around the thought he alluded to but didn't finish, about what she knew she'd need to tell him before he could finish that thought, and something about Miami. None of it, however, could she focus on long enough to find clarity.

Radmund showed up at the Stop around closing, but snuck into the kitchen before Allison noticed his presence. "Hey Mom," he whispered sneaking up behind her as she put the day's baked goods in boxes to deliver to the food pantry. "Can we talk for a few minutes?"

"Of course!" she replied. "Want a cookie? Today's special is white-chocolate raspberry … spectacular if I say so myself. Allison helped me come up with this idea."

"No thanks. But she's who I want to talk to you about." The two sat down at the back table. "I'm just avoiding the truth with Allison. I need to tell her the truth before Kholby gets back, just so she knows how I really feel. I lied to her a few days ago and told her I didn't want to be anything more than friends. She really thinks I'm all past my feelings for her now. I even told her I was dating Nichole. I guess I thought it would help both of us if I moved on as well."

"Honey," his mother began, but could not get his attention long enough to continue.

"But, I really think she's started to have feelings for me, more than just friends I mean. She's confused since she misses Kholby. Maybe if we talk about it, she'll realize how she really feels for me and that he was just a passing thing. What do you think?"

"Kholby got home this morning. He reserved the whole place tonight as a romantic dinner for just the two of them, after we close. We're babysitting Landon. She doesn't know about that part yet." She took her son's trembling hand in her own. "I'm so sorry sweetheart. But, if you'd seen her reaction when he got here, I think you'd realize how much she cares for him. I honestly don't know why she didn't fall for you in a heartbeat, but I'm a bit biased. And, those things are for God to determine, anyway."

"He's back? It's too early," Radmund choked on the words. "I really thought I could do this, but I can't." He buried his head in his hands. "Mom, why would God let me love her so much if He intends for her to be with someone else?"

"God doesn't control our emotions. You know that. I told you this before. Give her space and time to figure this all out. I'm sure that God's got it all under control. Whatever the answer is, you must have complete faith that it's all in His hands, not yours."

"I'm sick of giving her space and time. Sick to death of it!" He finally looked up, eyes sunken and stoic. "Mind if I join you guys for dinner then? I haven't seen Landon in a couple days. Really miss the little squirt." He forced a smile as she nodded and hugged him.

Proposals and Confessions

The Whistle Stop had been magically transformed soon after Allison left for the day, thinking she and Kholby would enjoy a lovely dinner at her place. Instead, he'd snuck back to put a plan into action that he'd spent the entire 15-hour flight home organizing. Tables were adorned in delicate white satin tablecloths, with all colors of roses displayed in varied fashion. Table 10 boasted deep burgundy buds bursting from a black ebony vase. "Beautiful" was scripted in ivory paint along the front of the vase. Table 11 had a dozen yellow roses lying around the perimeter with the word "Friend" written in the middle. Another table held two simple lavender roses, crisscrossed in the center with "Love at first sight" written around the edge of the tablecloth. The front table held a simple white vase with a bright pink rose. "Sweet and Gentle" had been carefully scripted around the vase. Two white roses, in full bloom, stood in contrast to the deep green foliage extending from the metallic purple vase. That table's note included a drawing of two simple silver rings, intertwined together with the word "Purity" nestled in the middle. Two other flowers, long-stemmed red and white roses ascended from a candy-cane striped vase in the middle a table set for two, with two lit candles flickering rhythmically as they reflected on the plates and around the crystal vase. A note had been carefully rolled into a scroll, secured with one red and one white ribbon, and tucked away for later.

"Don't open your eyes yet," he commanded as he held his hands over her eyes and attempted to maneuver her into the restaurant without the two of them tripping over each other's feet. When they finally stood in the middle of the room, he slowly removed his hands. "Surprise," he whispered kissing her cheek.

She gasped, unable to breathe or speak. Slowly she turned full-circle, taking in the array lovingly spread out for her. Gently touching the lavender flowers at the table closest to where she stood, she finally spoke, "Love at first sight," she looked back at him as she lifted one of the flowers to her nose. "Two flowers. I get it," she whispered. "You and me. Love at first sight." Then, one by one, she visited each table, breathing deeply to take in the fragrance of each flower and word. When she reached the table of white roses, though, her heart fluttered. "This is amazing! You did this for me?"

"Well, sort of. I did it for us, really," he answered taking her hand in his as they stood facing each other in the midst of the room. "What can I say? I'm a closet romantic." The candles paled in comparison to the radiance of his smile.

Her face flushed in emotion. "How did you get this together so quickly? You said you just got back this morning."

"Let's just say Henry and I had a few email chats in the last few days."

"He knew you were coming! I should have known. He didn't seem surprised this morning at all." She looked around once more, realizing that as powerful as the human eye is, nothing would make it possible for her to truly savor the magnificence of that setting. "I have to get a picture of this," she uttered fidgeting to get her phone from her purse.

"While you do that, I'll get our dinner. I believe it's in the oven waiting for us," he informed her. After two trips, he successfully placed two dinner plates loaded with filet mignon, scalloped potatoes, and asparagus at the table. As she completed the photo session, he uncorked a bottle of merlot and poured. "I believe this is a very good year," he announced. Together they swirled and sipped the wine, giggling at the ruse that either of them knew anything about determining a good wine from juice.

"Alright, I believe that you decorated this whole place. But there is no way you cooked this food. This has Delia written all over it," she hypothesized. "Don't mean to hurt your feelings, but I've had your hamburgers and they're nothing like this."

"You're right, my dear. Henry set that up for me also. But, he was worried about her letting the surprise slip, so he didn't tell her until I got here this morning! I was a little concerned that she'd have enough time, but I should have known she could do anything."

"That's why she sent me home early! I thought it was just to give me time to get ready for our date. She's a sly woman, that Delia!"

As they nibbled the steak and sipped the wine, both sat quietly to allow the moment to linger in the room mingling with the aroma of roses and sheer joy. She was certain it'd been over an hour since breath or heartbeat had taken place. He stared at her, watching the flicker of the candles reflect off her auburn hair and sparkle in her eyes. Finally he took her hand in his, across the table, handing her the scrolled note. "You know each of these roses tells something about you and me, but this vase is the most significant," he motioned to the one between them with the white and red roses. "I love you with all my heart, way more than a red rose will ever symbolize. While I was in China, I thought often about you. Well, actually, I had to try really hard to get you off my mind so I could do my work." He grinned at her. "But, one thing kept coming to me over and over again. I kept seeing how life could be with the three of us as a family. So, I wrote this note for you one night and started planning this whole thing."

He took the scroll and carefully untied the red and white ribbon. As he read it aloud to her, something she'd buried in her subconscious rushed to her heart and began pounding on her chest.

My Dear Allison,

These roses symbolize the many things I see in you. When we met, I knew it was love at first sight, for me at least. And, within one date, we were friends. Your beauty is far more than in appearance; it is in your soul. Everything about you is sweet and gentle – the way you are with Landon, with everyone around you, with me. And, as far as I'm concerned, you are pure to me in every way. Finally, the red rose means, of course, how much I love you. But the red and white roses together mean something more. They represent unity. The kind of unity that comes when a man and woman love each other so much that they become united as one in marriage. That's what I want more than anything with you.

Will you marry me?
Kholby

As he handed her the note, he reached for a small, unopened black box. "So? Will you marry me?" he repeated.

A lump grew in her throat, far larger than what she could swallow. She glanced back at the white roses, sighed deeply, then responded. "I can't answer that right now," she cried. "I have to tell you something first. And, then, we'll see if you still want me to answer or not."

He set the ring box down – still closed – and sat upright. Heart pounding at the implication in her voice, he finally mustered the will to ask, "What's wrong?"

"You know how I didn't want to talk about Landon's father?"

"It's okay," he sighed in relief realizing that her confession would not be about Radmund as he'd feared. "I told you I'm okay with not knowing. See, the white roses? That's why I put those there to show that I believe you are pure because of what you told me about that conference and God's forgiveness. Please, if that's all, just forget about it. I don't want to know."

"You need to know. And, I should have told you a long time ago, but I thought it'd be easier for you if you just thought I'd had some careless night with a guy. You know, society doesn't really think of that as such a big deal these days. So, you cave to peer pressure and the guy uses you for sex. Then, you get pregnant and he dumps you. Generally the girl is the one people feel sorry for in fact. It's almost like some girls are more honorable for getting over that mistake and rising above it as a single parent and all. At least that's why I thought would be easier to let you think that way about me. But, that's not what happened. It was prom and my first … and only … date. I didn't cave to peer pressure." She paused a second to catch her breath and courage to continue.

He took her hand and interrupted before she could begin again. "Allison, please don't do this. Really, I'm fine with not knowing." In his gut, he instinctively knew he did not want to hear anything else.

"Well, I'm not fine with it. It's a lie to let you believe that about me. Plus, it's not who I am. I am truly pure in God's eyes. He doesn't find fault in a woman who was … raped." The last word was barely audible but it resounded like a gong in his head. He flinched back in shock, letting her hand fall to the table.

"What? You were raped and you let me think you just had sex with some guy … for whatever reason? But, he raped you and you didn't tell me?!" Tears poured out the corners of his eyes as he looked away. "Why?"

"I told you. I thought it'd be easier for you to get over careless sex than rape. Guys don't really know how to deal with that. I was afraid." She tried to take his hand in hers, but he jerked back reflexively. "Please, don't be mad. I was so afraid. But, I've come so far now. I found out a few weeks ago that he'd been arrested for attacking two other women. And, I've been praying for God to help me since the silver ring conference. I know I've forgiven him. I even told him that when I visited him in prison. I'm over it, really. That's why I could finally tell you."

His eyes steamed through the tears, but each of his words rose in anger and volume. "You saw him again!? In prison? A few weeks ago? By yourself?" He paused, "Oh, wait, of course not. Radmund went with you, didn't he?"

"No, Marc went with me. He's always been there for me. He helped me through the whole thing." She spoke softly hoping to calm him with her tone.

"Does Radmund know all of this?" he demanded, already sure of her response.

She hesitated, knowing the answer would not help. "Yes."

"Right. Best friend. Did he know that you didn't tell me?"

"Yes. He kept telling me I should tell you the truth. So did Marc. It's my fault. I was so afraid you wouldn't ..."

"Understand? You were afraid I couldn't handle it? You didn't trust me enough to tell me the truth? But, you trusted Radmund." He sat back, wiped his eyes, and sighed as pieces of her life began to make sense all of a sudden. "Is that why you wouldn't let me go with you to see your dad?"

"My parents kicked me out of the house when I refused to have an abortion. They didn't understand how I could choose to keep the baby. But, I knew God had something planned. They never talked to me again until that week when my dad asked to see Landon and me. Mom still hates me, though. She told me to stay away from Dad's funeral."

"You didn't want me to know, so I couldn't even comfort you in that horrible time. But, he was there, wasn't he? Radmund. He went with you. 'To help with Landon,' I think you said as your excuse." The tone in his voice continued to escalate.

"Please try to understand. I haven't dated anyone at all since it happened. I was only sixteen. And when my parents kicked me out, well, I thought my life was ruined. If it wasn't for Marc's help, I'd have killed myself."

He glared at her. "You thought about suicide? And, you didn't think you should tell me that one either?"

"I'm so sorry. I should have trusted you. But I really liked you and I just didn't know what to do. Like I said, I was too afraid to date anyone after it happened. So, you started dating a twenty-one year old woman with the naivety of a teenager. I'm not trying to make excuses. I know it was wrong and I don't blame you for hating me. I just hope you'll try to understand and forgive me for hurting you so badly. I'm so sorry." Sobbing uncontrollably, she got up and ran to the kitchen to hide her sorrow and shame.

Several minutes later the kitchen door slowly opened as he walked in and turned on the light. Eyes puffy, but dry, he held out the single red rose. "Would you tell me what happened?" he said gently. "I promise not to run away."

"Really? You still want to talk to me?" She wanted to hug him right there, but the truth had to come out first. "I'll tell you everything. Promise." For the next few minutes, in the solemnity of the kitchen, while the romance in the dining room awaited their return, she extolled the entire story including the conversation with her father in his last days. She explained her visit with Neil in the prison and the road God led her on to finally be able to forgive him, but that he was resentful and rude in return. Finally, she said, "That's everything. I'm sorry I didn't trust you enough to tell you earlier. I've ruined your beautiful, romantic proposal."

He took her hand and led her back to the romance in the dining room. "Remember what this red one means?" he asked still holding the red rose from the vase. "That hasn't changed for me at all, Allison. I still love you, and I still want to marry you. But, I have to ask you something first."

"Anything. I promise to answer honestly from now on."

"I know you and Radmund are friends. But I can't help but wonder if there's more that you aren't even admitting to yourself."

"Oh no, not you too!" she huffed.

"Me too? Who else says that?"

"A few people actually. But they're wrong. Even Radmund said we're just friends. He said he's happy for you and me."

"Allison, I want you to think very carefully about this before you answer. Can you honestly say that you love *me* more than you love Radmund, friend or not?" he asked compassionately.

She cringed at the question, squinting at him. "Why would you ask me that? I just told you we're only friends."

He gently touched her cheek. "You haven't actually ever said you love me. You hinted at it a couple of times but kind of like you were avoiding saying it for real. And even when we skyped or emailed, you never wrote 'I love you.' See, I didn't really think anything about it at all until just now. But, now, I have to ask you if you've noticed that. And, I want you to think very carefully about it. Do you love me?"

He handed her the red rose, but all she could do was stand silent. *Why can't I answer him,* she wondered struck at the reality of the situation. *Of course I'm in love with him, aren't I?* "Kholby, I … I …," she started to answer holding her breath as she spoke. Finally, breathing out fully, she replied, "I know I care so much for you, but I can't say it like that. I don't understand."

"I do," he replied as the reality stung through his words. "Tell you what. I need to go to Miami to get things set up, find a house, and stuff for the job. I'll be gone about a week, but I'll try really hard to be back by your birthday. I'm leaving this here with you." He took her hand and placed the black box in her palm, wrapping her fingers around the still unseen ring. "Think about it for awhile. Before I left for China I said I wanted the very best for you and Landon. I meant that with all my heart. I would never want to be the one who stood in the way if something … someone … else was actually God's plan for you. I'll be praying for you and me and whatever God wants for us."

"Kholby," she started. "I'm really happy you're home. This was the most romantic night of my life. Thank you."

"You're welcome. I'd do anything for you. Even walk away if that's what you want. But, if you decide it's me you want to be with, then I'll be thrilled to place that ring on your finger whenever you are ready to say 'yes'."

They quietly gathered all the roses into one large vase he'd brought along, assuming they'd gather the flowers with more flourish. After cleaning up the remaining items, he took her home and walked her to the apartment door. In all that time, only a few words of casual conversation were uttered between them. Her mind on his question. His mind on her answer. "Kholby," she stammered. "I'll really miss you this week."

"I'll think about you all the time. But I'm not going to call or email. And, I won't answer if you contact me. I want you to really think about our future without any interference from me at all." He leaned in close to her at that point. "But I'll leave you with this to ponder." And with that, he kissed her with such passion she thought she'd melt into his arms. Everything in her wanted to yell "Yes!" when they finally parted. But both instinctively understanding the temptation, he turned to leave quickly as she walked through the doorway and closed the door without looking back.

First Day of School

"I'm proud of you my dear," Goldie said after Allison replayed the whole scene for her the next afternoon. "I thought you seemed a bit reserved in church this morning. Usually you sing out with such beautiful harmony. But today I thought you weren't even there at one point."

"What should I do?" she replied.

"Sweetie, I'm not going to answer that question. You need to think about it and decide on your own, just like he asked you to do. But my advice is that you carefully examine your heart before you give him an answer. Marriage is not something to be taken lightly. George and I are truly blessed to have a second chance at something so precious in life. Whenever you get married, make sure you know without any doubt that you are completely and utterly committed to that man for life."

"I agree. That's why this is so hard. I thought he was the one. I still do. But when he asked me to tell him I loved him, it just wouldn't come out. Maybe I was just scared. I mean, I think I'm in love with him. Please don't say anything. I don't want Marc or Radmund to hear this from anyone else. Last night, when Rad dropped off Landon, I was like a zombie or something. I know he's suspicious but he was great. Just made sure we were okay and didn't ask anything."

"I won't say a word, except to George of course. We do not keep secrets. Besides, he's a prayer warrior so I know he'll join me as we ask God to give you wisdom."

"Thank you. I just don't know how to figure this out. How can something be so confusing when I thought I had it all sorted to begin with?"

"Matters of the heart are rarely clear-cut," the elderly woman advised.

"Radmund wants to go with me to drop off Landon on Wednesday for his first day of Kindergarten. And I know Landon wants him to go also. Do you think I should do that or stay away from him for a few more days?"

Goldie sat back in thought, contemplating all possibilities before answering. "I know Landon will be much happier if Radmund is there. So, I think you should keep your plans for your son's sake. Perhaps you could ask Marc to go also."

"I did, but he has to work. I asked Kholby to go, but he went to Miami … and won't be back by then. So, I hate for Landon to start school without a father figure there." The term lingered on her mind a few minutes after she said it.

As if reading her mind, Goldie asked, "Allison, I know you are concerned for your child, but don't let that interfere with what God has given you in your heart and soul. Landon will be fine. He's too young to understand right now."

"I know. I think that was part of why I couldn't answer him last night. But, don't get me wrong, I know Kholby would be a great dad to Landon. It's just going to take some time, especially if we have to move to Miami."

"That could be the only way to make this work," Goldie offered. "I'm sure Landon will miss his friends here, but he's a wonderful little boy. His disability might make it hard to socialize in normal ways, but it doesn't keep him from learning to love the people who love him so much."

"You're right," Allison said kissing Goldie on the cheek. "Thank you so much for chatting. I've got to get him now. He and Rad and Thor went to the park to play Frisbee. It's a new skill they're learning together, I'm afraid. I just hope neither of them ends up with a black eye!" Even though Goldie couldn't see it, she clearly heard the smile spreading across Allison's face.

"God, please give her the clarity of Your plans for her life," Goldie silently prayed as they parted.

***

Landon caught the Frisbee just as his mother arrived to see the feat. "Wow! That's awesome," she encouraged him. "You're doing great!"

"I know. I have quick hands. That means I'm good at catching the Frisbee," he explained using his newest colloquialism in his usual monotone style. "But Thor is really good. She jumps and catches it every time. Rad thinks Thor should be a trick dog instead of therapy."

Allison sat down the picnic basket she'd filled before going over to the park. "Toss it to me, sweetie," she asked as Landon flung it her direction. Masterfully, she grabbed it even though it wobbled toward her, and flicked it firmly through the air to Radmund in one full motion.

"Wow! Where'd you learn to do that?" he asked catching it just inches from the ground.

"Marc, of course. We used to play in the backyard all the time. So, let me see this trick dog of yours," she chided. Radmund happily obliged, tossing the Frisbee to Thor who leaped into the air at least equal to her height, caught the Frisbee cleanly in her mouth, and trotted to return it to her master. "Amazing!" she confirmed. "She's growing so fast. How's that working for you in the apartment?"

Radmund grinned. "Hmm, well her latest thing is sleeping at the foot of the bed with me, which I did not encourage. I try to kick her off but she just whines so pitifully."

"Let me guess, now she's sleeping next to you?" She laughed knowing the answer. Landon walked over to pet the culprit as the adults continued chatting a few more minutes. "Would you like to have a picnic together tonight? I've brought some fresh lemonade, bologna sandwiches, and chips. And, it's a gorgeous night, especially for the last of August." She glanced at Landon as he and Thor began their own game of Frisbee Fetch.

"Sounds great!" He jogged to her side, offering to carry the basket for her. She watched him traipse to the picnic table wondering what, if anything, she should tell him of the previous night's events.

The four of them happily munched on sandwiches and chips a few minutes later. "I can't believe you feed her bologna," she teased watching Thor devour an entire sandwich. In three bites, she finished and looked up begging for more. "See, now look what you've done," she laughed.

"It's fine. Teaches her to be more human like. That's what they want for therapy dogs, so they can really relate to their owners. But, you haven't seen the best yet. She's so smart she's mastered all the tricks already!"

"Can I show her?" Landon begged. "Momma, I can make Thor do tricks."

"I'd love to see this," she lilted. Happy to oblige, Landon took a handful of Thor's favorite treats something Radmund never left home without when the dog accompanied – and walked to the edge of the pavilion. One by one, Thor responded to tricks of heeling, sitting, rolling over, and staying. Each time Landon offered a treat, just like a professional trainer as far as his mother was concerned. "That's so good!" she exclaimed. "Landon, I think you could be a dog trainer when you get older."

"I am older. I could do it now, couldn't I Rad? You said so," he obviously repeated from earlier conversation.

Radmund winced at the look Allison shot his direction. "What have you been putting into his head?" she demanded eyeing him suspiciously.

"Nothing. … Okay, he asked me if I'd ask you to get him a dog. I mean, look at how confident Landon is around Thor. That's part of the purpose. Thor's training is better because of Landon and Landon is learning a lot about communication because of her. The dog goes to school during the day, so you don't have to worry about it in your apartment. It's perfect when you think about it."

"Now is probably not the best time for us to think about getting a dog," she noted holding back on the underlying reasons. Changing the subject, she asked, "Hey, how's it going with Nichole? I heard you two had dinner with your folks last week. That's quick, meeting the parents already, you know."

He shuffled on the bench, then turned to watch Landon and Thor. "Well, turns out she's not really interested in me."

Allison stifled her laugh. "What? Not interested in you? She's a fool."

"She likes your brother. Apparently she knows he and I are friends, so she used me to meet him."

"Ouch. I hope you warned Marc. If not, I will."

"Marc's a big boy. And, Nichole is actually a very wise woman." He paused a second thinking whether to add the last comment or not. Finally, he added, "She also thinks I'm distracted by someone else and was just using her to divert my attention. So I guess we used each other."

Allison gasped a moment, trying to determine how to continue from there. "Oh, I'm sorry," was all she found fit to offer.

"It's okay. I'm working on it, you know. So, hey, how'd it go with Kholby last night? I'm really happy for you two that he's back. Really, I am." He wasn't sure if it was himself or her he was trying to convince. "And, it was great to spend time with Landon last night and today."

"Yeah, I heard all about your train wars last night. It took me a half hour to get him to bed after you dropped him off. Why'd you leave so quickly?"

"Allison, I saw the flowers on your table. And Dad told me about the romantic plans he helped Kholby set up. It sounded very special. You seemed like you had a lot on your mind and if you wanted to tell me, you would have started yammering away as soon as I got there."

"I don't yammer!" she replied faking insult. "But thanks for understanding. You're so good at that." Landon trotted to the swings with Thor at his heels. "Looks like one of us needs to give him a push, unless you've taught the dog that trick too."

After helping Landon get airborne, Radmund sat in a swing two down, next to Allison. "Rad," she spoke softly so her son would not overhear. "I told Kholby the truth about everything last night. That's why I was like a zombie when you dropped off Landon." She slowly dragged her feet in the dirt debating what else to tell him. Finally, she stopped and whispered, "He had all those roses and it was so romantic. He asked me to marry him, and I ruined it because I'd been lying to him for so long."

Radmund stopped his own swing abruptly, struggling to keep his heart in his chest. "How'd he handle it?" he finally mustered through baited breath.

"He was pretty upset at first. I don't blame him really. But, then, he was so great. And we talked all about it and he just listened while I told him everything, even about my dad and visiting Neil in prison." She snuck a peek at Landon who continued to swing effortlessly, oblivious to anyone except an attentive dog. "He got a job in Miami and decided to go there this week to set up stuff … You know, find a place to live and all … and get away for a little while."

"So, is it over between you two?" he asked, trying to repress the hopeful tone in his voice.

"No, that's what's so amazing about him. After we talked, he said he still wants to marry me. But, we agreed to wait until he gets back before I give him an answer." She stopped there, knowing to relinquish the true motives for her introspection could not possibly help either of them at that point.

"I'm glad you told him everything. And, I'm not surprised he handled it with such grace. He's a good person. You two will be very happy together." He turned to glance at Landon and then back to her. "What about Landon moving to Miami? It's going to be hard for him to make that change after school starts." *And for me*, he thought as his heart broke.

"Rad, please. You've gone and married me off already. I don't even graduate until December, remember." She was fairly annoyed for some reason. "Geesh! It's like you can't wait for us to leave or something."

"Cant' wait? Are you kidding me?" She shushed him, pointing to the little boy swinging only a few feet away. "My heart is breaking at the idea of you guys moving away. I love Landon with all my heart and it's killing me to think I might not see him very much. Or that he would have someone else in his life ... a real dad."

"But you will always be super important to him," she reassured him. "So ... he's the *only* one you'll miss?" she asked enticingly.

"Of course I'll miss you too. But we can email and stuff like friends do. Heck, maybe I'll even start a facebook page." He forced a smile to return, but it turned more like a grimace. "I need to go now. I've got an early shift and Thor has her first round of trials tomorrow. We need sleep." He scooted out of the swing to say a quick good-bye to Landon before calling Thor and turning toward his apartment. She sat by silently, sorting through all he'd just said ... and what he'd left unsaid.

***

Even though they both worked at the clinic that Monday, there was no sign of Radmund anywhere. "Marc, isn't Rad working today?" she finally asked as she and Marc had lunch together.

"I think I saw him earlier, but it's been crazy here today. Had two accidents and three heat strokes. Then there were the usual chest pains, broken bones, and hypochondriacs. Yep, just another normal day in ER." He truly loved his job, no matter how sarcastic he sounded at times. Helping people had been gifted to him at birth, and he knew it was not something to be taken lightly. "Did you two have a fight or something?"

"Something," she replied. As he paid for their food, she decided to change the subject. "I wish you didn't feel you had to buy my lunch all the time. I'm a big girl now, you know."

"And you are in school, not making any money while you're here. I promised Dad I'd take care of you no matter what. Besides, I think buying you lunch obligates you to make dinner for me, right?"

"Any time and you know it." She looked at him with a mischievous glimmer in her eyes as they gathered utensils and sugar packets for their coffees. "Do you know Nichole? She knows you."

"Hmm? Nichole? What are you talking about?"

"The nurse that Rad dated a few times. Seems she likes you and only went out with him hoping he'd introduce her to you."

"Oh, that's rude. I do know who you mean now." The two of them sat at a corner table, per Allison's request. "She's really cute, though. I suppose it wouldn't hurt for me to ask her out, being that she finds me so irresistible."

Allison playfully punched his shoulder. "Wow. Conceit is not becoming to you Dr. Pershing." Her joy was set aside quickly, though, as she began shuffling her salad around on the plate, not eating anything.

"What's up Sis? You're very distracted today. I thought you'd be all giddy and stuff since Kholby got back."

"I am, but I'm not."

"Okay, perhaps you should visit the psych ward upstairs?" he kidded.

"Funny. But you'll understand after I tell you what happened." He scarfed down a huge pile of spaghetti while she nibbled on her salad and replayed the events of Saturday night over for him.

"Sounds like you've got a lot to think about this week, Sis. I understand why you're so distant now." Marc wiped his mouth. "What does your heart tell you to do?"

"I keep thinking it's obvious, but when I picture myself saying 'yes,' I just feel nauseated. Why would that happen?"

"Does this have to do with Radmund?"

Allison stirred in her seat. That thought had, of course, crossed her mind a hundred times in only three days hence. "Probably. But I honestly don't know why. We're friends. That's what we both wanted. He even agreed. Now, though, I can't figure out any other reason why it'd be so hard for me to admit I love Kholby. Listen, I didn't really tell him the whole story, just about how I confessed everything and that Kholby still wants to get married. So don't you go telling him anything, understand?" she commanded.

"Is that why you're looking for Radmund? To convince yourself of something?"

"No. I just wanted to know if he's coming to Landon's school with me on Wednesday or not."

"Of course I'm planning to go with you guys," Radmund answered approaching the table where Allison and Marc sat unaware of his presence. The three remained fixed in their spots for a very long, awkward moment of silence. Allison prayed he had not overheard anything before her last comment.

Finally Marc broke the silence. "Well, you two can hang out here and ponder whatever it is going on between you, but I have patients to check on. Al, I'll see you later for dinner."

"Thanks for lunch, Marc," she replied waving as he walked off and Radmund sat down with his own lunch tray. "Radmund, it'd mean a lot to me if you go with us on Wednesday. But I understand if it's weird for you."

He honestly wanted to be joyous and support her decision, so it surprised him as the hurt spontaneously rose high in his voice, surging out with such a sharp tongue. "I'm going for Landon, not you. Please don't misread my intentions. I figure I only have a few months left to be in his life anyway."

She recoiled at his tone. "Okay ... Well maybe we could meet at the school around eight to help him get situated and meet everybody?"

"Sure. It's going to be so hard when you move. I wanted to be at all of Landon's school stuff, not just his first day. I just can't bear it if he thinks I let him down."

"Thanks. I know this is hard, but I promise you can visit and Landon can visit you anytime." Before the tears could escape, she stood to go, gathering her things on the tray for disposal. "I need to get to my rounds now." Escaping quickly down the hall she finally paused to regain her composure. *How can I hurt him like this?* she berated herself. *How will Landon handle this? Why is this so hard?*

***

"Each day we'll start off by talking about the date and weather," his teacher explained as parents stood nearby watching their children wiggle in the small chairs. "What is today's date?" she asked hopefully.

A petite blonde in the front row immediately shot her hand in the air and clucked proudly, "It's September one."

Landon sat perfectly still, unlike most of his classmates. He hesitantly raised his hand. Mrs. Hemingsworth nodded his direction looking at his nametag. "Yes, um, Landon. Do you have something to add?"

"My mom's birthday is in two days." Allison and Radmund stared, amazed at the confidence of a little boy who'd shied away from any social interactions with strangers only a few months earlier.

She giggled, whispering to Radmund, "I think he's been holding out on us a little."

He replied softly, "It does appear he's not as shy as he'd like us to believe. Or perhaps it has something to do with that little blonde in front of him." His face beamed in pride as if speaking of his own flesh and blood. His heart ached knowing that would never be true, however.

"Parents, it's time for you to leave now. Your children will be just fine, I promise." Mrs. H – the shortened version of her name she used for the sake of her young charges – had to encourage parents three more times before they all cleared the room and class could begin.

"Well, I need to get to work now," Radmund murmured as they approached their cars. "That was really cool to be there with you guys today. Thank you for inviting me. You doin' okay with him starting school and all? I mean, I've always heard a mom's roughest day is when her baby starts school." She started to hug him, but stopped short, awkwardly shaking his hand instead.

"I'm fine, really. But thank you for worrying. A few months ago I'd have been a nervous wreck about whether he'd be okay or not. Now, seeing him in there like that, though, I know he's going to do great things. And, a lot of that is due to your influence Rad." She took out her keys, then turned back to him as he opened his own car door. "Would you have dinner with us tonight? Marc will be there also, and I know Landon would love to have you there to hear all about his big day."

***

"I made paper boxes instead of writing my letters," Landon explained at dinner. "I know how to write 'A' already. She told me to write them anyway. It was boring so I just hid under the table."

Allison had so hoped for a different scenario at the end of his first school day. Yet, this was no surprise. While the autism disabled his ability to perceive social norms, it also strengthened his will. She knew that would be a hurdle throughout school. "Landon, school is a place with lots of rules. Just like your bedtime rules. You have to follow them like all the other kids."

Marc contributed his own ideas. "Did you tell Mrs. H that you already know how to write the letter 'A'? I bet she'd let you do another letter instead."

"That's true," Radmund interjected. "Maybe tomorrow you could ask your teacher to help you learn to write the little 'b' and 'd' we worked on a few days ago. Those are tricky letters."

Landon looked around irritated, then offered his own conclusion. "You didn't let me finish my story. She said she liked the boxes and told me I could write my letters on some special paper and then make the boxes with the paper after she saw it."

Allison's original concerns began to subside. "Well, she sounds like a really nice lady."

"So what else did you do today?" Marc asked.

"We played some games, but I just wanted to watch. Mrs. H said it was okay. She didn't make me play. So, I gave her five boxes before we left. She smiled really big at me and said she'd use them for the stuff on her desk. I saw her put them there too. I'm going to look if they're still there tomorrow."

"You're very lucky to have such a nice teacher," Radmund conceded. "I have a feeling she'll help you learn a lot this year."

The four of them crammed into Landon's little bedroom for the nighttime ritual. "I want a new song tonight," Landon announced out of the blue. "We learned it today in music. I'll teach you." Not waiting for their reply, he began singing *Five Little Monkeys*. "Now you sing the next verse," he directed after the first two verses, just as his music teacher had done earlier. Availing to his wishes, they all sang out in chorus through to the end, agreeing to put all the monkeys back in bed.

"What a day he had!" Marc laughed as they plunked down on the chairs in her living room. "Man, that teacher is in for it with that little guy."

Radmund smiled and added, "How cool was it to let him make the boxes like that? Sounds like a pretty understanding teacher to me."

Allison rounded out the conversation. "She knows about his condition. He's already got an IEP, so I'm sure she'll do whatever she can to help him. The principal told me Mrs. H was the best teacher for kids with special needs in the school. I think Landon already understands that in his own special way." All the other ills of the week vanished for a few minutes while the three of them celebrated the child God had created in such unique manner.

Birthday Surprise

The entire restaurant was decorated in brightly-colored streamers and helium balloons two days later as Allison entered to a rousing chorus of "Happy Birthday to You." Goldie pounded with exuberance on the piano as Delia, Henry, George, Radmund, and Marc attempted some sort of harmonies.

"Wow! This is wonderful!" she exclaimed hugging each one in turn. "Thank you so much." However, her excitement became subdued when she turned to face an empty front window. "I miss him being here," she quavered, then quickly recovered. "But he gave me 22 kisses this morning, one for each year. It was so cute! And, this surprise makes my morning complete! My whole day actually. Thank you guys!"

"Well, this is just the beginning," Delia announced raising a huge birthday cake from behind the counter. "Decorated it myself. Just another of my many talents," she teased.

"Delia, it's gorgeous! Purple and orange. My favorite colors." Allison saw the knowing look in Delia's eyes.

"And what's your favorite flavor?" Marc asked, knowing the answer hadn't changed since she'd had red-velvet cake for the first time on her fifth birthday.

"It's red velvet too?" she implored. "Awesome! Birthday cake for breakfast, lunch, and dinner. Now that's my idea of a great day!"

"And, there's presents," Henry added pointing to the back table covered with decorative bags and wrapped boxes.

"You guys should not have gotten me any gifts. This is great just having you here to share with like this. Really! And, the cake is all I need. Well, maybe some ice cream." Her eyes glistened as she focused on the glass lid of the ice-cream freezer and noticed a gallon of cookie-dough that hadn't been there the day before.

Goldie and George moved in to hug the birthday girl. "We have an aerobics class at ten today. I'm sorry we can't stay longer. But I'll be back later to play more songs and sing with you so we can celebrate a little more," Goldie explained as she handed Allison a gift from the two of them.

"Save me some cake," George begged. "I get an extra-large piece since I'm doing exercise first, right?"

"George, that class is to keep us healthy and limber in our old age, not to give you an excuse to indulge in sweets," his wife ribbed. "Go ahead and open it," she motioned as Allison read the card, then opened the bag.

"Miss Goldie, this is lovely!" she exclaimed as they all admired the hand-knit blanket. "You said you were making this for the shelter when I stopped by the other day. You lied to me!"

"My dear, I'm a blind old woman. I forgot it was even out until you asked about it. What was I to do but lie … for a good cause of course."

"Of course," Allison agreed hugging Goldie. "Thank you so much." She turned to hug George as well. "And thank you. She told me you helped her hold the yarn and make sure the colors were in the correct pattern. I'm assuming that part was true, right?"

"Absolutely," Goldie confirmed. "I couldn't have made that without his help." She leaned in to whisper, "He even learned to knit while we worked on it together. Put in a few rows himself!"

"Goldie, that was supposed to be our secret," he replied feigning embarrassment. "And now, we must be off my dear before you offer up our little secret about the ballroom dance classes." He smirked and snapped his fingers. "Now look what I've done." He shrugged as if offering surrender. "Alas, my darling wife has inspired me to attempt things I never dreamed of before. What can I say?"

"This one now," Delia announced offering a large box soon after the Picardys exited.

Allison ripped the paper and pried open the cardboard flaps. "No way! This is perfect! Oh, but you should never have spent that much money! How'd you know I wanted one?"

They motioned at Marc who raised his hand in guilt. "Guilty," he admitted. "You kept telling me how much you loved Delia's fresh breads, but couldn't find time to make your own. So we all went in on a bread maker for you. Now you can make those fresh loaves every day if you want."

"And you guys can come over anytime you want, especially you Delia. Take a break and let me cook some for you!" She was so excited that she failed to see the one remaining bag Radmund held up for her to open last. "Rad, I thought you went in on the bread machine. You shouldn't have gotten me anything else."

"Actually, I got this for you awhile back, but saved it until now. Marc helped also."

The floral gift bag held one simple box inside, closed with a shiny silver hook-and-loop clasp. "Rad, the box is so pretty. I can't imagine what's inside could be any prettier."

"You'll just keep imagining until you open it," Henry teased impatiently.

She carefully unhooked the clasp to peer inside, then gasped at the purple, white, and red beads adorning a matching necklace, bracelet, and earrings. "Rad, this is extraordinary! I've never seen beads like these before. They look hand-made." She gently removed the necklace and motioned for him to help her get it around her neck. "Where did you find something like this?"

"That's actually the really cool part," he began. "A few months ago, Louella showed Mom some jewelry she'd had made from the flowers they saved from her mother's funeral. Mom really liked the idea so she got the name and address of this place in Chatham, Illinois – just a little down the road from where the Travis' live. She told me about it when you didn't go to your dad's funeral, so I asked Marc to get some of the flowers off your dad's casket bouquet for me.

"Some of your favorites, Sis. Roses and irises. You know, I showed you the pictures."

"After he brought them back, I sent them off to the florist and they made the beads out of the dried flowers. It's kind of a keepsake for you since you didn't get to go … and, well you know."

Delia handed Allison a box of tissues from behind the counter, but it took three Kleenex and several seconds before she could respond. "You did all that for me?" she finally choked out.

Marc put his arms around her. "Hey, remember me? I got the flowers," he kidded pretending to take some of the credit even though they all knew who the true mastermind was. "I even had them make a tie-tac and bookmark for me when Rad told me about the idea. Pretty cool, huh?"

"I just can't believe it," she cried. "This is the most precious gift anyone has ever given me!"

"There's one more thing in there," Rad pointed out as his heart pounded with joy at her radiance. "See the little envelope at the bottom?"

She pushed tissue aside to retrieve the little package. "It's to Landon," she smiled. "Should I open it or wait for him?"

"You can peek inside if you want, but don't give it to him until he's old enough to understand," Radmund explained. "It's a bookmark for him, just like the one Marc got. See," he pointed out as she held it up, "the silver shepherd's hook goes over the page and the beads hang outside. We thought he'd like it someday when he's old enough."

"Wow," she sighed. "You guys, this is unreal! I don't know what to say."

"Well, I do!" Henry jumped in. "I say let's cut this cake. I'm starving and we have a restaurant to open in ten minutes!" Together, the five of them shoveled in cake and ice-cream until their stomachs rumbled in revolt.

Before Radmund left for work, she stopped him to thank him once more. "Rad, this jewelry is really the most amazing gift anyone ever gave me. I love it so much. And, I love that you thought of me like that." She fingered the beads on the bracelet. "Every time I wear this, I will remember how special you are in my life."

"You're welcome," he replied. "I just couldn't stand the thought of you missing your dad's funeral and all. It seemed like the perfect way for you to remember him in a really good way. So think about *him* when you wear it, not me. That's what it's for."

"I will," she agreed, kissing him on the cheek. He touched her cheek in response, then quickly left for work.

***

The empty front window of The Whistle Stop caused Allison to grimace each time she served any of the nearby tables. Even though it had been a huge strain on all of them to watch out for him all those years, she'd grown to love having Landon around all the time. Now, the reality of his life moving forward was almost more than she could bear.

"Delia, I miss him so much!" she admitted as they chatted in the kitchen. "I love that he's doing so well, don't get me wrong. Yesterday he got to lead the class in saying the Pledge of Allegiance! His teacher had to coax him a little, but he did it and that's what counts." She glowed recalling the story his teacher shared Thursday afternoon when she'd picked him up. "Sometimes I allow myself to think he could actually grow out of the autism."

"Allison, we've always known Landon was on the high-functioning end of the spectrum. He's so smart that it helps him compensate for the other weaknesses." Delia put a full tray of muffin balls in the oven. "He's going to be fine. It won't be easy all the time, but it never is for any of us. I believe God has something incredible in mind for that boy."

"I've always known that in my heart as well," Allison agreed as they began cleaning the baking supplies. She paused in retrospect for a moment, fingering the necklace for the thousandth time, then continued. "Delia, do you think I could be a missionary's wife? And that Landon could survive that life if we have to move around a lot?"

Delia wiped her hands on her apron. "I think that if you truly believe Kholby is who God set apart for you then God will also give you and Landon everything you need to be invaluable to His work in the missions and in your family."

"How do I know if I truly believe that or not?"

"When Henry asked me to marry him, there wasn't a single doubt in my mind. God had actually already prepared me for life with that man through my dreams. Whenever we were together, I could envision the amazing things we'd do as partners in life. I just knew, without any doubts, that he was the man for me." The timer went off signaling a different batch of muffins was finished. As Delia retrieved the hot pads, she continued. "Don't get me wrong. I don't know if God makes it that clear to everyone. Or if He even has only one special person for us in life. I mean, look at Goldie and George. But, I think if you listen to your heart … and frankly, your gut … then you will have a pretty good idea if it's right or not."

"Thanks, Delia. You've been such a treasure to Landon and me all these years. And, now especially, with Radmund and all, you still give me such great advice without any bias. I love you and Henry so much!" Delia sat down the hot tray of muffins and grabbed her young friend in a hearty embrace.

"Allison, Henry and I have always wanted the very best for you. You're part of our family, you know. We will miss you both so much, but people do visit here all the time. I'm pretty sure the train even runs from Miami up here once or twice a week!"

255

"And, it's only about four hours to drive, so we could even make it in a weekend if we want to," she agreed consoling herself as well as Delia. As the women walked into the dining room to refill drinks and take new orders, Allison glanced once more at the empty front window. "He's growing so fast that it seems like he doesn't need me very much anymore."

"He'll always need you," Delia confirmed. "A mother's job is never finished, even when her children are adults. There will always be those times he calls you for advice, or stops by to have you do his laundry. Or, if you're lucky, he'll invite you over for dinner, and then propose that you cook it!"

"Delia, does Rad still do that to you?" Allison chuckled somewhat in disbelief.

"Not anymore," she grinned slyly, then cracked up as she finished. "I've stopped answering the phone when I see his number. So, now the boy just comes to my house instead. Henry and I are thinking of changing the locks."

I am so lucky, Allison thought forcing her mind to move past a lonely heart as the two women, still giddy, began taking new orders. *This is the best birthday ever!*

***

"Excuse me, but I understand there's a beautiful young woman working here who has a birthday today," the voice beckoned from the front doors just after closing later that day. Allison jumped in excitement and recognition.

"Kholby! You're back!" She ran to him, lunging into his open arms. "Just like you promised. Back by my birthday. I've missed you so much." Glancing to see if there were any lurking spies, and noting none, she leaned close kissing him.

"Uhh ummm," Henry sounded, pretending to clear his throat. "Am I interrupting?"

Allison and Kholby quickly separated, wiping their lips as they both grinned in embarrassment. "Sorry, Henry. I thought you guys were all gone," Allison offered sheepishly.

"Nope. I planned to leave here by three today, but that's obviously not going to happen since it's almost four. Hey, aren't you supposed to get Landon by now?" Henry was still trying to catch up on her new schedule.

"Really? Can we go get him?" Kholby replied in excitement. "I've missed him so much."

"Actually, Radmund picked him up. They're going to watch Thor in her finals today. At least that's their story. I think it was a ploy for Landon to get me a card, though." She smirked at Henry, then returned her attention to Kholby. "But now, I want to hear all about the job. How'd it go?" She took his hand leading him to a nearby table, anxious to catch up on the week.

"Well, don't mind me then," Henry quipped. "Guess I'm a third wheel."

Kholby laughed. "Sorry Henry. Hey, thanks again for helping me with everything last week. I really appreciate you keeping it a surprise and all."

"What can I say? I'm a sucker for romance," he grinned. "I'm locking the doors. You two can stay as long as you like, though."

Goose bumps instantly covered her arms as she thought back to a week earlier as they sat alone in that very room, with the question still lingering in the air. "Kholby, why don't we go to the park instead for a little while? I don't think Rad and Landon will be home for at least an hour yet."

"Sounds great," he agreed.

Filling the basket with lemonade and snacks, she and Kholby set out for the park. They laid out a plaid blanket in the middle of a grove of trees on a little hilltop at the outer edge of the park. "This is a little more private anyway," he confirmed nestling contentedly on the blanket with her by his side.

"I thought about you all week," she assured him as they toasted with wine goblets filled with fresh lemonade. "It drove me crazy, actually."

His eyes sparkled. "Really? Me too. I mean thinking about you. Not me thinking about me. Oh, you know what I mean," he laughed as he finished rambling.

Not ready to discuss their future yet, she jumped in before he could resume. "So, tell me about the job. Did you find a house? What'd you think of it all?"

"Okay. Well, job is amazing. I can't wait to start!" And he continued to extol all the virtues of the position – how he'd oversee construction sites for needy people, the English class he'd start teaching one night a week, and the church he visited. "It's an amazing place. Huge! They even have a Spanish service on Sunday nights. And I found an awesome apartment for now. Real estate is a little expensive so we might have to wait a year or so to get enough for a down payment on a real house."

She shuddered nervously at his pronoun – *we*. "It all sounds like everything you've dreamed of, Kholby. I'm so happy for you!"

"Well, while I was there I wasn't just imagining living alone, you know. I even visited the elementary school near the apartment complex. But ... well, you'd look at it too of course, if ... So tell me about Landon's first week at school." He didn't know how to proceed to the question, so he abruptly switched gears.

After reviewing Landon's first three days, she paused to gulp some lemonade. "It's so hot out here again," she stated averting his eyes.

He took her hand. "I can't wait any longer, Allison. I have to know. Do you still have my little gift?"

She reached into the bottom of her purse, retrieved the black velvet box, and handed it to him. "I never looked at it, though. I wanted you to open it the first time I see it." She had to force all her weight to her legs just to remain seated for fear she'd float away right then and there.

On the other side of the park, two wanna-be Frisbee players and one excited dog emerged on the pathway leading to and from the apartments, hoping to sneak in a game before the little boy's mom called him inside for dinner. Landon's first shot ricocheted off Rad's legs – a perfect shot he should have caught if not for being distracted by the couple on the other side of the park, snuggled on a blanket as he unveiled a sparkling diamond that took her breath away.

"We need to go now!" Rad said sharply causing Landon to whimper in dismay.

"We just got here. I want to play more."

"Sorry Sport, time to go. I think I'll take you to visit Henry and Delia, actually. Maybe we can play in their yard a little while." He quickly ushered Landon back down the path, guiding him so that he would not look back in the direction of the happy couple as they embraced in what was obviously a celebration.

Two hours later, Allison was surprised to see Delia with Landon at her door. "Delia, where's Rad? He called to tell me they'd be late, so I thought they were still together."

"They were for awhile," she answered. "But Rad had some important things to take care of in Tampa. He left for a few days." Her tone clearly did not match the unassuming words she carefully crafted.

"Momma, I made you a picture for your birthday," Landon offered handing her a paper with 'Momma' carefully scrawled on one side and a colorful scene on the other. "And I made you something," he continued handing her a carefully constructed paper box. "It's for your jewelry. Rad said you would really like it."

Allison stared at Delia still wondering about Radmund's sudden absence, confused but unable to ask the questions lurking in the back of her mind. She turned her attention to the gifts instead. "Thank you honey! I do love it. It's perfect for the gift Rad gave me today," she agreed showing him the jewelry she had proudly worn all day. "And this picture is spectacular! I love it also. Tell me, who are these people?"

"That's us," he explained. "We drew it in class today. Mrs. H told us to make a picture of our family." Allison stared in disbelief at the picture, haphazardly sketched but still clear enough to determine a woman with long reddish-brown hair, a little boy with curly brown hair, and a man with bright red hair.

"I'm going to put this picture on the refrigerator! It's perfect! Now, go wash up for dinner, okay?" She ushered him away quickly.

"Okay," he obediently responded jogging off to the bathroom.

"Delia, is everything okay with Radmund?" Allison asked as soon as Landon was out of range.

"Sure, I think so. How about with you? Are you okay?" she asked expecting to hear the news that had devastated her son a couple hours earlier.

Allison had previously determined that Rad would be the very first person to hear of her news. She couldn't imagine sharing it with anyone else before him, so she feigned ignorance. "I'm fine. Why? It's my birthday, you know. And, I have leftover cake!" She pointed to the box on her dining room table.

"I figured Kholby would be here," Delia admitted. "Henry said he showed up at the restaurant today just as you all were leaving."

"He was here. We had a really nice time in the park earlier. He could only stay for a little while though. Wanted to make sure and get here for my birthday. But, then he had to get back to the trailer to start packing up his things for Miami. He actually starts his new job on Tuesday so he wanted to make sure and get his stuff moved down there this weekend."

"Well, that was really quick! So, is that all?" Delia prodded, hoping for additional information.

"Yep, I think so. Why? Do you know something I don't know again? I heard you were in on that little surprise dinner last week." Allison replied coyly, causing Delia's curiosity to skyrocket.

"Nope, nothing I know of." She started to leave but turned back, unable to take it any longer. "Actually, yes I do know something. He saw you with Kholby in the park today. That's why he left town. Said he had to get away for a little while."

"Oh, I'm sorry to hear that," Allison lowered her head, worried. "How long will he be gone? I really wanted to talk to him before anyone else."

"I expect he won't be back before Monday since it's a holiday. At least that's how long he warned us we have to keep that dog." She opened the door to leave. "Maybe you could call him?"

"No, that wouldn't be right. I'll just wait until he gets back." As Delia walked into the hallway, Allison stopped her. "Delia, thanks again for my birthday party and cake today. It was so incredibly special for me. I love you all so much!"

"You're very welcome," she started. "Like I said, we'll always be here for you and Landon … and Kholby."

Allison's heart pounded furiously that night as she tossed and turned, trying to sleep. *How do I tell him?* she wondered restlessly rehearsing the conversation over and over in her mind.

Decisions

Saturday and Sunday seemed rather surreal to Allison. People floated around her, giving her a questionable look of expectation. Sneaking glances at her left hand, they moved on with the question still lingering at the absence of an expected jewel. *They don't get to know until I tell Radmund,* she kept telling herself, although the wait was killing her. So much so, that she called her brother Sunday night to come over. "Do not tell anyone else! I mean it," she commanded him.

"You can trust me. But, I can't say I'm surprised," he grinned at her. "And, I don't think he'll be terribly surprised either, frankly."

"Yea, well I think it's better if Rad hears this from me, so I don't want anyone else to know and go blabbing it to him before he gets back."

That Labor Day morning and afternoon, Allison and Landon made three separate visits to the park tossing the Frisbee around – his new favorite pastime – and a perfect way to spend the holiday she thought. *It's so much better than sitting around playing with those tops and transformers,* she said to herself as he spent more time running to get the disc than actually catching it. *I wonder how he'll take the news,* she pondered at one point. She continued chatting with herself for a few more minutes until Landon finally walked up, breathing heavily. "Momma, I'm tired. When's Uncle Marc coming?"

"He should be here anytime now, actually. Let's go get on our swimsuits. I know he wanted to see how well you're doing swimming all by yourself. Then, we'll go to the pizza place for dinner to celebrate, okay?"

"Okay. Are we celebrating Labor Day?" Landon asked knowing they never went out to eat unless it was a very special occasion.

"Not really. Marc and I just wanted to celebrate your first week of school and how well you are doing. Is that okay with you?" There was more to celebrate, of course, but nothing he'd understand yet.

"Okay," he replied simply. *I need to teach him another way to respond,* she laughed to herself.

The three of them decided to meander through the park on their way home from the pizza place. "I need to walk off some of that food," Allison joked holding her gut. "Why did you let me eat so much?"

Marc denied any responsibility. "Me? You were like an animal. I was afraid you'd eat my fingers if I hovered too long over a piece of pizza."

Just then she grabbed his arm, stopping him mid-step. "Marc, he's back. Look. Over on the swings." She motioned to the rhythmic movements of the swing clearly indicating a therapeutic motion instead of fun. "I have to go tell him now or I'll lose my nerve."

"Okay, I'll put the leftovers in your fridge and then take Landon back to the pool. Call me if you need anything," he concluded. She hugged her brother, then her son as they headed off to violate the rule about waiting an hour after you eat before you go swimming.

"Hey," she muttered slowly ambling toward him. "Heard you were out of town this weekend. Did you get everything sorted out?"

He looked up at her, eyes as red as his hair. "Not really. I don't think it'll be okay for awhile actually."

"Oh, sorry to hear that." She finally got up enough nerve to sit next to him. "I need to talk to you about something."

He looked over at her, then back at his feet scuffling in the dirt. "Yeah, I thought you might. I saw you with Kholby in the park on Friday. I wasn't spying, promise. Landon and I just came out for a quick Frisbee game and there you were, dimples shining as bright as the diamond he was flashing in front of your face."

"I'd like to explain, if you don't mind."

"No need. I get it. Besides, it's not like you didn't warn me. I'm happy for you, really. Just not so much happy for myself right now is all. I'll be fine though." He got up to leave when she grabbed his arm and jerked him back into the swing.

"Would you shut up for a minute and listen, please?" she demanded, much to his surprise. He sat back and resumed staring at his feet as she began again. "Life is like these swings, you know.

We think we have to work really hard to swing high, like working so hard to get the really awesome things in life. And sometimes we just get too tired to pump our legs and start to slow down, like when things in life seem to weigh you down too much and you forget to let God help you reach the heights He wants to give you. We try to take control and push our way there instead.

"But sometimes you just have to jump off the swing, like taking a leap of faith. That's when everything becomes clear – when you stop swinging and start looking at life while you're standing still, when you take time to stand still in God's glory. I learned that when you do that, it's amazing what He can show you that you couldn't see before you jumped. See, I was in the middle of all that swinging when you and I first met. And I started swinging really fast and furious because I thought that Kholby was one of those amazing highs in my life – a blessing from God that I had to work for. And, then there was your mom's cancer, my dad, and Neil, and I just didn't have the strength to keep pushing for God's reassurance in my life. I forgot that God doesn't make us work for His blessings; He gives them freely when we stand secure in His glorious Light. I first learned that when I finally faced my dad and Neil.

"Then when Kholby came back, I forced myself to take a huge leap of faith. I jumped right off the swing believing that God had put Kholby there to catch me. Kind of like when Landon jumps and trusts you to catch him. But something happened that I didn't expect. After I jumped, I stood still long enough to see God's plan more clearly, I realized something precious."

He looked over at her, bewildered at the strange analogy. "I'm confused. What exactly are you trying to say?"

"You know Kholby was gracious enough to give me time to really think about his proposal. He said he wanted what was the very best for Landon and me, even if that wasn't him. He's an amazing man and yes, I did think I was in love with him. But I realized that I didn't love him the way a marriage needs. Actually, I think he realized it before I did. He was my diversion for the intense feelings I have for you – the ones that scared me to death – the ones that kept me pumping harder and harder on the swing. I was terrified of what I'd find if I jumped too soon.

"You saw him give me the ring, but you didn't hear our conversation. I looked at the ring and wanted so badly to say 'yes' to him. When I looked at him though – when I finally stopped swinging – God showed me you instead. And, Kholby was smart enough to realize that, even though it hurt him so much. I thought I wanted to marry him, and in a way, he even helped me jump off the swing. Then he made me take a hard look around first. And, when I did, the only person I saw standing there to catch me was you.

"You have always been completely committed to Landon and me, and moreso, you have always made sure God was the center of our relationship. I never had anyone show me what true love looked like before you. And that confused me. Heck, it terrified me to have someone other than my own brother be so loyal and kind. Then, God showed me that kind of love looks like a man who spends time loving my son as much as me, being with me at the lowest points to the best, knowing what I need before I know myself, and letting me be there for him when he's at the lowest or highest points of his own life.

"The whole week I kept thinking about my answer for Kholby, God just kept showing me you. It just took me awhile to figure that out." She paused a moment to exit her swing and stand in front of his. Taking his hands in hers, she finished. "I love you Rad, like I've never loved anyone in my whole life. I can only explain it as a God-given love, because nothing on this earth could possibly define how complete I am with you unless it were blessed by God. As my sweet friend Goldie puts it, 'You make my soul dance.' Please forgive me for being blind for so long."

Tears poured from his eyes as he looked up into her resplendent face. It was the first time he'd seen her eyes completely free of any confusion or stress. She was finally standing in the radiance of Shekinah, and they both knew it. "I'll forgive you," he started, "under one condition."

"Anything," she agreed.

He stood from the swing and pulled her close, "Would you have dinner with me tomorrow night?"

"You mean like a date?" she flirted.

"Not *like* a date … **a** date," he replied without any hesitation.

Their eyes locked a second before their lips met in full passion and joy. She kissed him as if it were the first kiss of her life; for him it was the moment his dream came true. "By the way," she whispered as they parted, "I meant it that time!"

Author's Notes

The characters in this story are fictional. However, most of these people were inspired by someone I have the pleasure of knowing in real life. Ultimately, God helped me weave many stories into this one lovely, fictional tale of a blessed community of people who are graced by God's Glory – *Shekinah*. I'd like to introduce you to a few of the people who inspired the characters in this novel.

Alyssa (Allison) is a beautiful woman who radiates God's peace in her life. We believe she is incapable of anything other than joy in her heart. The day she met Eddie (Kholby), her life was transformed as their friendship grew and blossomed. Eddie, however, was committed to a life of mission work overseas, mostly in China. Knowing this was his calling, he found the strength to put aside his feelings for Alyssa and commit fully to God's plan. A few months after he left for China, Alyssa was reunited with a childhood friend, JD (Radmund). Their romance blossomed from an intense friendship to a love and marriage sanctioned by God.

Charlie (Landon) is a young autistic boy I had the pleasure to know for a short time in one of my classes. His intellect and literal views of the world fascinated me. He is an endearing young man with a flair for life. The day he gave me my first paper box as a gift is a day I will cherish above most of my teaching memories. "I wanted you to have this," he said handing it to me. "It's very special. I made it for you." Each day he would teach me about a new battle top or transformer he was fixated on for that time. He went out of his way to memorize new jokes, hoping to learn how to be funny since he realized it would never just come naturally to him. In spite of his condition, he definitely taught me far more than I ever taught him. Charlie is also the originator of the insightful quote at the front of this book.

Marti and Jerry (Delia and Henry) are the current owners of the real Whistle Stop in Plant City, Florida. They are as friendly as their portrayal in this story. Their restaurant is depicted to best of my recall, including signs, displays, and some menu items. However, many of the recipes included in this story are my original ideas – hopeful creations to see on the Whistle Stop chalkboard someday.

Marti did, indeed, battle cancer midway through her life. Her journey of faith, endurance, and recovery are celebrated on the walls of the restaurant. It was her story that first inspired me to use this beautiful location as the setting for the story. While they do have a very handsome son, he is not the impetus for Radmund. You can learn more about The Whistle Stop by checking them out at: https://www.facebook.com/WhistleStopFL.

Miss Mary (Goldie) was indeed an elderly blind piano player who graced The Whistle Stop for months with her talents. A beautiful white baby grand piano still sits in the back of the main dining room, longing for another guest to fill the venue with Heavenly melodies. George is totally made up, but I wish he were real because I'd really like to sit and chat with him awhile.

Owen and Louella (Owen and Louella Travis) are actually my own parents; they are much the same as portrayed in this story. They do migrate to Florida every January with many of their senior-citizen friends – about 100 of them to be exact! My parents introduced me to The Whistle Stop one year as I visited them over Spring Break with my own daughter, Sydni. We were immediately enthralled with the establishment, its rich history, the stories that flowed from the walls and people, the trains, and the incredible smells wafting from the kitchen. Like their counterparts in this novel, my parents are a joy to be around – filled with life, laughter, love, and utter devotion to each other and God. And, they celebrated their 50th anniversary in January 2014. It is an honor to include them in this story.

All sites in this story actually existed at the time of this writing. I've attempted to be realistic in anything noted about the locations, but some things were embellished for the sake of the plot or setting. One particular business I'd like to highlight, though, is the *Beads & More* flower and gift shop in Chatham, Illinois. When my grandmother passed away, we kept many flowers from the arrangements. This shop freeze-dried the flowers and used them to create beads for necklaces, bracelets, earrings, and bookmarks for several of our family members. These keepsakes are timeless and priceless! You can learn more about this florist at: http://beads-n-more.homestead.com/contact.html.

Author Bio

God embedded me with a passion for writing and education many years ago. In addition, He has blessed me with two education degrees focusing on written expression and communication arts and several other teaching certifications. I began writing by publishing numerous curriculum units, working as a freelance writer of Sunday School curriculum and youth drama productions, and helping to develop a homeschool setting for highly gifted eighth-grade students. But, I am truly blessed to have been a public-school teacher at the same time as these other adventures. I currently work full-time as a sixth-grade Communication Arts teacher.

In my life and career thus far, I've been blessed to work with children of all types of learning needs, from exceptionally advanced to exceptionally challenged. In addition, God gifted me with family and friends who bring a variety of unique gifts to this world. All of these amazing people are the inspiration for fictional characters in my stories. This is why you will find characters in all my books that embody the joys and hardships with life's struggles such as: Alzheimer's, fetal alcohol syndrome, Down Syndrome, blindness, autism, breast cancer, intergenerational relationships, unwanted pregnancy, foster care, and many more. But above all, my stories take these struggles and show how amazing God is in the face of adversity, how He will triumph over all things if we trust in Him, and how His abiding grace is for anyone who believes – no questions asked.

Soli deo Gloria,

Janice

Janice and her family live in St. Charles, Missouri.
You may email her at: jkdavis64@yahoo.com.
You are also welcome to visit Janice's Facebook page by going to fb.me/SoliDeoGloriabyDavis.

78923064R00148

Made in the USA
Columbia, SC
22 October 2017